THE DAILY DOSE

THE DAILY DOSE

A Quick Shot of What the World's Best Thinkers Thought
(and What We Can Learn from Them)

M. D. RIDENOUR

To my family, who taught me the meaning of unconditional love;
and to my friends, who taught me how to laugh at myself.

"Life is really simple, but we insist on making it complicated."
— Confucius

INTRODUCTION

Like many of you, I like to read, and I do manage to read quite a bit: In addition to various newsletters and research reports, I subscribe to three magazines, take two daily newspapers, and usually have two books going at once. And, of course, there is a seemingly endless stream of internet articles that grab my attention. But what I really like are daily readers, like this one. I like little snippets of trivia; I like gleaning insights from history; I like the simple food-for-thought aspect of philosophical inquiry. Learning something new every day is important to me, but the truth is I especially like daily readers because they encourage me to set aside some quiet time each and every day: to relax, to think, to contemplate. In a way, it's like having a standing appointment with an old friend. In my case, that appointment is for morning coffee, and I never miss it.

The idea for putting together my own daily reader came about a few years ago, when I began to study philosophy, in general, and Stoicism in particular. I found myself enthralled by Seneca's *Moral Letters to Lucilius*. I've also read Marcus Aurelius, and some Epictetus, but for me, reading Seneca's *Letters* was like sitting at my grandfather's knee, listening to him talk and picking up the bits of wisdom that he would weave into his stories. I found it very comforting. I also found myself wondering:

What is the point of accumulating knowledge, experience, and wisdom if you don't share it or pass it on?

This is the question that prompted me to begin this journey. I'm a parent, and although my kids are grown, I still feel the need to impart what little I know, in the hope that it might be useful to them at some point in their lives. It simply cannot be helped, but I also wanted to do something that might help them to know me, not just as their father, but as a person. I did not want them to ever have to wonder what I thought or felt about the various things that we all think about but don't necessarily talk about all that much. I wanted

1

them to know not only what I have found to be true, but what people much smarter and wiser than I have shared with the world.

And so I enlisted a little help — which is how we ended up with *The Daily Dose*, a daily reader that sneaks a peek at What the World's Best Thinkers Thought (and What We Can Learn from Them).

The expert thinkers I've assembled here have plenty to say, usually about things they know very well and often about the things they know best. That being said, I wasn't particularly interested in yet another book full of famous people and their most familiar quotes. This isn't Bartlett's. No, I wanted to go just a little bit off the beaten path. The same goes for the mini-biographies: what interested me was sharing some of the lesser-known details about the lives of these remarkable people, not rehashing the same old stories that everyone already knows by heart. In other words, I wanted to make sure that we could all learn something new, or ponder something new, each and every day. That was my goal, and I can tell you that it made for a very interesting intellectual pursuit. Hopefully, you will find reading it equally enjoyable.

A few words on the way things are organized . . .

Each day begins with a word that is related to the human condition. It might be Compassion, or Adversity; Denial, or Forgiveness; Love, Purpose, or Consequences. Each of these words is a building block: an emotional or intellectual starting point that is then reflected in or connected to a quote from one of history's greatest thinkers. The quotes are in turn followed by a paragraph or two that expounds on a general thought or idea that is inherent to the word and the quote. These "blurbs" are generally observational in nature, and it is my hope that they prompt the reader to think, and encourages him or her to *do*. Each day then ends with a mini-biography of the Thinker — and if you are paying attention, you may notice that a subtle thread often runs through each of the day's components, from the word to the quote to the blurb to the mini-biography. Or does it?

Happy hunting, and thank you for reading The Daily Dose.

ADMIRATION

"I cannot help thinking that there is something to admire in everyone,
even if you do not approve of them."

— E. M. Forster
English Novelist, Essayist
1/1/1879 – 6/7/1970

There is always some measure of humanity, no matter how small, no matter how well-hidden, in each and every one of us. And within that humanity, we can be certain that there is *something* — an unflappability, a sense of humor, a love of animals, *some kind of animating principle* — that is worthy of our appreciation. It's there; we've simply got to find it.

———————◇———————

E. M. Forster was a novelist, short story writer, librettist, essayist, and literary critic. He was nominated for the Nobel Prize in Literature in sixteen different years.

Forster is best known for a trio of novels: *A Room with a View*, *Howard's End*, and *A Passage to India*. He typically wrote about the hypocrisy inherent in British society, and the attendant snobbery and condescension therein.

A pacifist, Forster managed to avoid conscription into the British Army during World War I by signing on as Chief Searcher with the Red Cross. In this role, he spent three years in Alexandria, Egypt, interviewing wounded soldiers in order to get information about their fellow soldiers who had gone missing in action.

After the war, Forster spent time working as a private secretary to a Maharajah in India. His experiences there would lead to *A Passage to India*, which explores the complexities of cross-cultural friendships amid the backdrop of the growing movement for Indian independence from British rule. It was the last of Forster's novels to be published while he was still alive.

REVERENCE

"All people have a natural desire to be needed, to have
their importance to others tangibly confirmed."

— Daisaku Ikeda
Japanese Buddhist Philosopher, Author
Born 1/2/1928

Where there is kindness, there is deference — a certain devotion to the idea that all lives are worthy of respect, and even reverence. Sometimes, it is as simple as saying "thank you": a small token of gratitude that is both an acknowledgment of a kindness freely given and an appreciation of another's contribution to our happiness. There are many little kindnesses that often go unnoticed, or unappreciated, which is a shame, because that moment of acknowledgment is itself a gift shared by both the giver and the receiver.

———————————◇———————————

Daisaku Ikeda is a philosopher, educator, author, and poet, and a staunch advocate for nuclear disarmament. He is committed to the idea that every person has innate dignity and possesses great potential.

The fifth of eight children born to a family of seaweed farmers, Ikeda was a teenager during World War II. The horror and devastation he witnessed instilled a life-long passion to work for peace. According to Ikeda, we all have the same issues and fight the same battles over and over again, and we should be talking about them instead of going to war over them. In 1993, he founded the Ikeda Center for Peace, Learning, and Dialogue, which promotes worldwide peace and understanding through dialogue.

January 3rd

HUMILITY

"The higher we are placed, the more humbly we should walk."

— Cicero

Roman Politician, Orator

1/3/106 BC – 12/7/43 BC

It is easy to forget all of those who have contributed to your success, especially when you have worked so hard yourself. It may be lonely at the top, but it has a nice view, and if you'd like to stay there, you'd be wise to remember that those who helped you will continue to have influence, and favor, in places you may not even be aware of.

Treat everyone as your equal — not only will they help you to reach the top, they'll help you to stay there.

———————◇———————

Although famous for his public speaking ability, Marcus Tullius Cicero was also a philosopher and lawyer. He served as the Roman consul in 63 BC, which is the equivalent of prime minister or president.

In 48 BC, as Rome turned to oligarchy in the form of Gaius Julius Caesar, Cicero remained a tenacious advocate for a return to republicanism. When Caesar was assassinated and control of Rome fell to Octavian, Lepidus, and Mark Antony (a political alliance known as the Second Triumvirate), Cicero initiated a series of vicious verbal attacks on Mark Antony; predictably, this earned him a designation as an enemy of the state. He was executed in 43 BC, and as a final indignation, Mark Antony had Cicero's severed head and hands displayed on the Rostra, an elevated platform from which speakers would stand to address the gathered crowd.

CONFIDENTIALLY...

"We rarely confide in those who are better than we are."

— Albert Camus
Algerian-French Philosopher, Author
11/7/1913 – 1/4/1960

Can you keep a secret? Does it matter if the secret is your own, or someone else's?

Secrets are power and, like gossip, some use them as social currency. Are you discreet? Trustworthy? A good way to judge is to ask yourself: Do people tell me their secrets, or am I always the last to know? On the other hand, if you are told others' secrets, it might be a pretty good gauge of the type of company you keep.

———————◇———————

Albert Camus will always be tied to the philosophy of Absurdism, which is essentially a commentary on our tendency, as humans, to seek meaning in a life in which we are fundamentally ill-equipped to do so.

Camus was a study in contrast and hypocrisy. Although his behavior and body of work proved otherwise, he consistently denied that he was a philosopher, of any sort. He was also a proponent of Moralism, and believed that governments should be guided by morality, yet he is known to have engaged in multiple affairs during his two marriages.

Early on, Camus decided to work in "cycles"— he would write a novel, then an essay, and finally a play. During his lifetime, he completed two cycles, and was working on a third when he died, at forty-six. His best known work is probably *The Stranger*, about a man who kills someone simply to watch him die.

In 1957, Camus became the second-youngest person ever to receive the Nobel Prize in Literature. He was forty-four; Rudyard Kipling won at the age of forty-two.

POETRY

"Poetry is not a matter of feelings, it is a matter of language.
It is language which creates feelings."

— Umberto Eco
Italian Novelist, Philosopher
1/5/1932 – 2/19/2016

The thing about poetry is that it cuts right to the heart of the matter, using the fewest possible words to elicit the most circumspect of emotions. Too often, in our day-to-day lives, we do the opposite — we use far too many words to say far too little of consequence. Take a step back from the incessant babble and listen carefully; listen with purpose. Can you determine who is trying to communicate something really important, and who is just spewing words?

———◇———

Meet Umberto Eco, the best-selling Italian novelist, professor, and semiotician behind the medieval historical mystery, *The Name of the Rose*. He is also known for *Foucault's Pendulum* and *The Island of the Day Before*. An avid book collector, he amassed over thirty thousand volumes for his personal library.

Signore Eco knew a thing or two about deciphering the hidden meanings in our words and actions. A semiotician is a person who studies signs, gestures, language, semantics, and symbols, and Eco wrote two books on the subject: *A Theory of Semiotics* and *Semiotics and the Philosophy of Language*. As a professor at the University of Bologna, Eco was very much like a real-life Professor Robert Langdon, the fictional "symbologist" of the Dan Brown novels.

ADVICE

"Most people who ask for advice from others have
already resolved to act as it pleases them."

— Khalil Gibran
Lebanese Writer, Painter, Poet
1/6/1883 – 4/10/1931

The funny thing about advice is that we tend to shop around until we find someone who agrees with us. This is because we often ask for advice when what we really want is affirmation. The goal is not necessarily to find someone who will help us to make the right decision, but rather to find someone who will confirm that the choice we have already made is not entirely unreasonable.

———————◇———————

Author of *The Prophet*, one of the all-time best-selling books of poetry, Khalil Gibran considered himself to be a painter, first and foremost. He was educated in Lebanon, America, and France, and spent much of his adult life in New York and Paris. Although he was read and quoted by famous musicians such as Elvis Presley, John Lennon, David Bowie, and Johnny Cash, he is perhaps best known in pop culture for his saying, "If you love somebody, let them go, for if they return, they were always yours. If they don't, they never were."

Gibran died a relatively young man, at age forty-eight, reportedly due to cirrhosis of the liver, attributed to excessive drinking. He willed all future royalties to his hometown of Bsharri, Lebanon, to be used for "good causes."

FATE

"Fate leads him who follows it, and drags him who resist."

— Plutarch
Greek Biographer, Essayist
46 AD – 120 AD

Does it ever seem like, no matter what you do to avoid it, you still end up in that place you were trying to avoid, doing that thing you didn't want to do? For those who believe in fate, or destiny, the answer is easy enough, but what of those who do not subscribe to the idea of predestination? How can they reconcile the way things tend to end up despite our best intentions? Perhaps it isn't providential, but intentional; perhaps it really *is* our actions, whether conscious or subconscious, which ultimately lead us to our fate.

———————◇———————

Considered one of the most influential writers and philosophers of all the ancients, the Greek Plutarchos took the name Lucius Mestrius Plutarchus upon becoming a Roman citizen.

Plutarch served as a priest and interpreter for the Oracle at Delphi, which was about twenty miles from his hometown of Chaeronea. He filled various other roles as well, in particular as judge and mayor. He also took on the occasional duty as ambassador.

Today, Plutarch is best known for his studies on morality and ethics, and for his comparative biographies of prominent Greek and Roman citizens (*Parallel Lives*). His writing style served as a template for future historians and essayists through the Middle Ages and beyond.

PREDESTINATION

"I have noticed even people who claim everything is predestined, and that we can do nothing to change it, look before they cross the road."

— Stephen Hawking
English Theoretical Physicist, Cosmologist
1/8/1942 – 3/14/2018

Some say we cannot escape our destiny; no matter where we go, there it is. Better to accept things as they really are and deal with them on our own terms than to waste time and energy trying to circumvent the inevitable. But what if our destiny is what we make of it? Isn't that the very essence of free will?

———————◇———————

It could be argued that Stephen Hawking was a son and heir to Albert Einstein in terms of both genius and pride of place in popular culture. *A Brief History of Time*, his highly readable treatise on the mysteries of the universe, brought him international fame and worldwide recognition, but it was his sense of humor and stoic acceptance of his body's betrayal that really endeared him to us. Perhaps the best thing he taught us was not about space and time, but to accept our limitations and focus on what we can do instead of what we cannot.

Hawking was born on this day in 1942, which coincidentally also marks the three-hundredth anniversary of Galileo's death.

GENEROSITY

"The best loved by God are those that are rich, yet have the humility of the poor, and those that are poor and have the magnanimity of the rich."

— Saadi
Persian Poet
c. 1213 – 12/9/1291

What is it about the generous that so endears them to our hearts? When we witness an act of generosity, it doesn't have to be directed at ourselves for us to be heartened by it; simply seeing or hearing of it and knowing the difference one person must have made in the life of another is almost like being a recipient of the gift ourselves. And while it is certainly virtuous to give when we have plenty, it is particularly poignant when those who have little to spare share it willingly, unconditionally, with others.

———————◇———————

Musharrif al-Dīn ibn Muşlih al-Dīn, known as Saadi, was an Iranian poet, philosopher, and literary figure of the medieval period. Known for writing about virtues and morals, he also wrote humorous anecdotes and aphorisms about the absurdity of life. A fragment of a poem from his "Gulistan" (The Rose Garden) is engraved on the entrance to the Hall of Nations of the United Nations building in New York:

Of one Essence is the human race,
thus has Creation put the Base;
One Limb impacted is sufficient,
For all Others to feel the Mace.

HAPPINESS

"Happiness is a choice that requires effort at times."

— Aeschylus
Greek Dramatist
525 BC – 455 BC

Sometimes it is difficult to put on a happy face. To smile when we want to pout or to pretend we are cheerful when all we want to do is mope takes determination; and sometimes, it takes all the perseverance we can muster.

Is it worth it? Not always. But here's the thing: Just trying to be happy attracts happiness. It may not always be yours; it may be the happiness of those around you that becomes manifest in those moments you spend together. And guess what happens when you are around people who are happy?

It isn't always easy, but make the effort anyway. You aren't the only one who will be glad that you did.

———◇———

Aeschylus was an early Greek playwright who is widely known as the Father of Tragedy. He is probably best known for *Prometheus Bound,* in which the Titan is punished by Zeus for giving fire to mankind. As part of his eternal punishment, Prometheus is chained to a mountain, and every day an eagle is sent by Zeus to eat his liver. In what seems like a line taken straight out of a Greek tragedy — or Life imitating Art — Aeschylus purportedly died when an eagle flying overhead dropped a tortoise and shattered his skull.

DEEDS

"Act as if what you do makes a difference. It does."

— William James
American Psychologist, Philosopher
1/11/1842 – 8/26/1910

A few years ago, I started taking our dog for a daily walk. Occasionally we'd see or hear other dogs, but we rarely saw them out and about with their owners. We really enjoyed our walks, and I always smiled and waved to everyone I saw. Slowly, over the course of a couple of years, I began to notice that more and more people were out walking the neighborhood, and many had a dog in tow! We met quite a few people, often stopping to chat for a few moments while the dogs said hello. More than once, I was told that they had seen us walking and eventually they decided to get a dog or to take the one they had out for a walk. One day it struck me: What kind of influences were in play now, within our neighborhood, and more importantly within the lives of these people, now that they were getting out, getting exercise, and getting to know their neighbors?

Make no mistake: Your actions can (and often do) have a profound effect on others in ways that you can only imagine.

———————◇———————

A doctor and psychoanalyst, William James maintained that we have the power within ourselves to alter our psychological makeup. Like Aeschylus, James believed that being happy is a choice, and that we are capable of being happy irrespective of our circumstances. He was also a pragmatist, who believed that the chief function of thought is to guide our actions, and that the value of doing a thing is proportional to the practicality of its purpose.

James spent over thirty years teaching psychology and philosophy at Harvard. His students included Theodore Roosevelt, George Santayana, and Gertrude Stein.

January 12th

FRUSTRATION

"All that is necessary to break the spell of inertia and frustration is this: Act as if it were impossible to fail. That is the talisman, the formula, the command of right about face which turns us from failure to success."

— Dorothea Brande
American Writer, Editor
1/12/1892 – 12/17/1948

Have you ever resigned yourself to the fact that there was no getting out of it — you were going to have to buckle down and face something very unpleasant, impractical, or impossible? You took a big step that day. Taking action and seeing a thing through to the end is a big deal; a very big deal. Way to go!

Facing down the difficult, the challenging, and especially the frustrating bits that come along in our lives isn't always the easiest thing to do, but it's something you should always, always, *always* take pride in doing.

———————◇———————

Deep in the heart of the Great Depression, amid a flurry of self-help bromides designed to provide temporary distraction from the ongoing deprivation facing millions, came *Wake Up and Live!*, a best-selling book from Dorothea Brande. Her theory encapsulated a simple, yet effective pop psychology mantra: Once you conquer your fear of failure, there is nothing you cannot do.

January 13th

VISION

"Where there is no vision, there is no hope."

— George Washington Carver
American Botanist, Inventor
1/1864 – 1/5/1943

If we can dream it, we can envision a way to make it happen, but absent faith and optimism, we can never take those first steps that will turn our dream into reality. All things, no matter how grandiose or mundane, begin with a vision. Only when you see how you wish things to be can you hope to make it happen.

———————◇———————

George Washington Carver's name is often associated with peanut butter, and although he did not invent it, he did discover over three hundred other uses for the peanut, as well as hundreds of uses for pecans, sweet potatoes, and soybeans. He was a strong advocate for rotating crops, which not only helped restore nutrients to the soil but also improved the diets of those who worked the land. Born a slave, Carver nevertheless became one of the most prominent chemists of his or any other generation, his scientific genius leading to a great many inventions, from dyes and cosmetics to paints and plastics.

After receiving his Master's degree, Carver accepted a job offer from Booker T. Washington to serve as the Director of the Agriculture Department at Tuskegee University. He became well-known for his expertise in plant research, and provided advice to Mahatma Gandhi on agricultural and nutritional matters.

Carver was the first African-American to have a national park named after him. The George Washington Carver National Monument is in Diamond, Missouri.

MISERY

"I have always held firmly to the thought that each one of us
can do a little to bring some portion of misery to an end."

— Albert Schweitzer
French-German Theologian, Humanitarian
1/14/1875 – 9/4/1965

What does it cost us to be nice to someone else? If we are aware of
another's suffering and we do nothing, the price can be quite dear to us both.
As individuals, we may not be able to change the world singlehandedly, but
sometimes an opportunity presents itself so that we can change one person's
world for an hour, for a day, or for a lifetime.

Never believe that a grand gesture is the only way to help; it all adds up.
Sometimes a simple kindness can be the spark that lights a fire in someone
else's darkness.

———————◇———————

Nobel Laureate Albert Schweitzer was a writer, musician, philosopher,
and physician who is perhaps best known for his missionary work in Africa.
Determined to alleviate the suffering of others, he established a hospital in
Gabon, where he spent over fifty years providing medical care to those who
desperately needed it.

Schweitzer strongly believed in the sanctity of all living things, and he
spoke out against nuclear tests and the dangers of nuclear fallout late in his life.

January 15th

EVIL

"There is some good in the worst of us and some evil in the best of us.
When we discover this, we are less prone to hate our enemies."

— Martin Luther King, Jr.
American Minister, Activist
1/15/1929 – 4/4/1968

The more we recognize our similarities, the less likely we are to despise our differences. Whether you examine the facts superficially, or take a deeper look, it is clear that we are all very much the same. On the surface, from a strictly biological standpoint, each of us has the same basic parts: two arms, two legs, a head, a heart. Metaphysically, we all experience joy and pain, love and hate, good days and bad days. And no matter where we are born, no matter what our race, or color, or creed, we all have a soul and we all have doubts about the meaning of life and our purpose in it. Once we acknowledge this grand and mutual struggle, it becomes difficult to perceive even our most strenuous adversaries as merely one-dimensional beings who deserve our harshest judgements.

Dr. Martin Luther King, Jr. was a Baptist minister and activist who, like Gandhi, used peaceful protests in the struggle for equal rights. A leader of the American Civil Rights movement, Dr. King delivered his iconic "I Have a Dream" speech at the Lincoln Memorial in 1963, and was named "Man of the Year" by *Time* magazine. In 1964, when he became the youngest (age thirty-five) to ever win the Nobel Peace Prize, he donated the $54,000 prize to the Civil Rights movement.

Although he was assassinated in 1968, his legacy of nonviolence and peaceful social change continues to resonate and inspire to this day. Numerous roads, parks, bridges, and buildings bear his name, in honor of his memory. In 1986, President Ronald Reagan signed legislation declaring the third Monday in January to be Martin Luther King, Jr. Day, a national holiday.

CHARACTER

"The content of your character is your choice. Day by day, what you choose, what you think, and what you do is who you become."

— Heraclitus
Greek Philosopher
c. 535 BC – c. 475 BC

The content of your character is not necessarily a choice, but rather a *result* of your choices; it is, in fact, the culmination of every choice you have ever made, whether they are public or a deep, dark secret known only to you. When it comes right down to it, you are the only person who knows the full scope and magnitude of your decisions, and your actions, and therefore only you can possibly know what kind of person you really and truly are; others can only speculate. I hope you are trying to be a better person, and to make better choices, because there is no harsher judge than the one staring back at you from the mirror.

A Greek philosopher born in what is now Iran, Heraclitus was known for his dictum that "Change is the only constant in life." He famously said that we cannot step in the same river twice, for while we may think it is the exact same river, it most assuredly is not; a great many things have changed, and in fact, simply putting a foot in the water has changed it.

January 17th

DOUBT

"When in doubt, don't."

— Benjamin Franklin
American Polymath
1/17/1706 – 4/17/1790

There isn't a human being who ever lived that didn't deal with doubt. From "To be or not to be" to "Will you marry me," we've all had to come to grips with making decisions without 100-percent certainty that we are making the right choice. Some questions (and answers) have monumental ramifications that require a good deal of thought; others we are willing to determine with the toss of a coin. In the latter, I wish you good luck; in the former, I have learned that, all else being equal, trust that little voice inside. . .

———————◇———————

Undoubtedly the most interesting and wizened of America's founding fathers, Ben Franklin was a celebrity around the globe. One of his biggest claims to fame came as a result of his studies of electricity, and in particular his life-saving invention, the lightning rod. Franklin's popularity at King Louis XVI's court resulted in some jealousy on the sovereign's part. Irritated by a countess's infatuation with Franklin, the king presented her with a chamber pot that had Franklin's face painted on the bottom. Nonetheless, Franklin was able to charm the king himself; enough so to secure the much-needed military aid that would prove instrumental in turning the tide of the Revolutionary War.

January 18th

CHOICE

"The power of choosing good and evil is within the reach of all."

— Origen
Egyptian Scholar, Christian Theologian
185 AD – 254 AD

There are times when we like to tell ourselves that we have no choice, that we have no other option but to say or do something that we don't particularly want to do; not because it is difficult (it is) or because it is unpleasant (it is), but because it is hurtful. When we face these kinds of dilemmas, we console ourselves with the idea that it was unavoidable, or that we chose "the lesser of two evils." The only way around this is to actually choose good, instead of evil, even when (especially when) our choice means the person on whom the most harm is visited is ourself.

———————◇———————

A child prodigy, Origen was a headmaster at a school in Alexandria by age seventeen and is considered the first Bible scholar. As an early Christian, Origen lived through times of turbulence and persecution. Barbarian invasions were creating instability throughout the Roman Empire, and his father, Leonidas, was beheaded for being a Christian. The most prolific theological writer of his time, Origen is best known for his *Hexapla*, an analysis of the Old Testament that took twenty years to complete, and *De Principiis* (First Principles), both of which were instrumental to the development of the early Christian canon.

January 19th

NOBILITY

"Put more trust in nobility of character than in an oath."

— Solon

Greek Statesman, Poet

640 BC – 558 BC

Anyone can make a promise, take a vow, or swear an oath, but so too can they break it. How sure are you of a person's integrity, their honor, or their decency? Does your assessment change according to what is at stake?

Virtue and decency are traits which develop over time, and we have either our own experience or the experiences of others to tell us on whom we should or should not rely. While we're on the subject, let's turn this inward: How noble is *your* character?

———◆———

Known as one of the Seven Wise Men of Greece, and The Lawgiver, Solon is credited with reforming the political structure of Athens and paving the way for democracy. As *archon* (annual chief ruler), Solon sought to legislate against the moral decay of Athens; to address the growing conflict between rich and poor; and to stem the accumulation of crushing debt. His chief economic reform, the "shaking off of burdens," included the elimination of all debts. He also ended the aristocratic monopoly of government, inserting a multi-tiered Council of Four Hundred, consisting of citizen-representatives whose level of political power and privilege was based on their income, not birth.

FRIENDSHIP

"Love is blind; friendship closes its eyes."

— Friedrich Nietzsche
German Philosopher, Cultural Critic
10/15/1844 – 8/25/1900

Everybody wants love. To be loved, to be in love; the universally accepted notion is that all you really need is love. But as wonderful as love is, you could make the argument that friendship is every bit as important to our psyche, and to our sense of self (and if we're honest, sometimes it's a whole lot healthier).

Love may indeed be blind — and deaf, and dumb — but a good and true friend will only ignore your faults for so long; at some point, a friend will tell you what a lover never would . . . and that's a good thing, because we all need people around us who will keep us honest.

———————◆———————

Two of Friedrich Nietzsche's most well-known commentaries on the human condition present a conundrum: If there is no objective order or structure in the world (nihilism), why do we strive so ambitiously to attain the highest possible position within it (the will to power)? The answer, of course, belies one of the most basic of human desires: It may not be much, but I want to be the master of it.

Nietzsche peered into many of the motives that drive our behavior —love, religion, morality — and his (sometimes harsh) conclusions have exerted a profound influence on thinkers and intellectuals for generations. His personal philosophy revolved around manliness, strength, and self-reliance; ironically, he suffered a mental breakdown in 1889, when he witnessed a horse being flogged in the streets of Turin, Italy. He never recovered, but his friends and family took care of him for the next eleven years, until he died in 1900.

SPIRITUALITY

"We can no more do without spirituality than we can do
without food, shelter, or clothing."

— Ernest Holmes
American Writer, Teacher
1/21/1887 – 4/7/1960

We may call it by different names, but each of us has a "spiritual" side. Some require rituals, or icons, or pageantry, while for others their temple is found under a canopy of sequoia trees. There is evidence across all strata and all times that we are seekers of the divine, the hallowed, the holy. We all appear to be searching for the same thing, but we call it by different names and we approach it from different routes. No matter who we are or what we are looking for, the process itself seems essential to our well-being.

———————◇———————

Ernest Holmes was the founder of a spiritual movement known as Religious Science, which studies the relationship between religion and science. In 1927, he wrote *The Science of Mind*, which integrated what he saw as universal truths that are present within each of the world's religious faiths. An offshoot of the New Thought movement, which was embraced and influenced by Ralph Waldo Emerson, the Science of Mind philosophy holds that spiritual awareness can expand exponentially, encompassing all of humanity. Holmes also espoused the belief that each of us can harness the power of our thoughts to create the life that we want, and that it is vitally important to avoid negative thoughts, because negativity brings us the life we do not want.

CONTEMPLATION

"Silence is the sleep that nourishes wisdom."

— Francis Bacon
English Statesman, Philosopher
1/22/1561 – 4/9/1626

No one ever learns more from themself than from others. It's true — the more we listen, the more we learn. The world likes to intrude, with its gadgets, schedules, crowds, commitments, and traffic of every conceivable variety. All of this is noise. Make a point of finding some time, and a quiet place, to be still and to contemplate what others have said, and what you think of it.

———◇———

Sir Francis Bacon was an extraordinarily accomplished philosopher, statesman, jurist, orator, and author, but it was his ideas about empiricism that helped to drive the scientific revolution of Elizabethan England. Specifically, Bacon challenged the widely held Aristotelian idea that, given enough time, all scientific truth could, in fact, be determined through endless discussion among learned men. Bacon argued, simply and forcefully, that obtaining real truths required the collection of objective evidence. In 1620 he published *Novum Organum*, which outlined how to go about acquiring that evidence, and kick-started the age of empiricism.

SOLITUDE

"One can acquire everything in solitude except character."

— Stendhal
French Writer
1/23/1783 – 3/23/1842

Given enough time for reflection, we can develop a great many traits, but character isn't one of them. Character involves consideration of, and interaction with, the interests of others, which means that we must learn to put others ahead of ourselves, on occasion. This is an extraordinarily good thing, since we aren't built for prolonged periods of solitude anyway, and if we aren't willing to compromise it is a sure and certain thing that we will end up being alone for far longer than we would like.

———————◇———————

Stendhal is one of 187 different pseudonyms used by Marie-Henri Beyle, who is best known for his penetrating analysis of his characters' inner demons and psychological makeup. His most famous works are *Le Rouge et le Noir* (The Red and the Black) and *La Chartreuse de Parme* (The Charterhouse of Parma).

In addition to writing novels, Stendhal also served for over a year as a lieutenant under Napoleon's command, and wrote a biography of the composer Rossini (*Vie de Rossini*). He is the source of the Stendhal Syndrome, in which one is overcome with palpitations, dizziness, and even hallucinations in response to unbearable beauty. He first described the symptoms as a travel writer, in his book *Naples and Florence: A Trip from Milan to Reggio*.

ENDURANCE

"Endurance is not just the ability to bear a hard thing,
but to turn it into glory."

— William Barclay
Scottish Theologian, Author
12/5/1907 – 1/24/1978

We cannot help but marvel at those who overcome tremendous burdens; those magnificent fighters who succeed despite truly remarkable afflictions. But as fantastic as their public glory may be, it is their private, internal story that interests me, because who else can be more proud of us, than us? Only we can know just how far we stretched ourselves, and fought and overcame those psychological matters, deep in our soul, or those physical barriers, heartless and unyielding, and all of those frightful things of which only we ourselves could possibly be fully aware. Yes, everyone may know how you escaped from the tunnel, but how many knew you were a lifelong sufferer of paralyzing claustrophobia?

Celebrate your victories, in public and in private. Only you know how truly epic your struggles are.

———————◇———————

William Barclay was a Professor of Divinity at the University of Glasgow for twenty-eight years. Although he was a popular and engaging theological "personality" — he was widely known for his many appearances on radio and television programs — Barclay is best known for his prolific writing: his commentary on the New Testament alone spans seventeen volumes. There were some controversies, however, as Barclay often challenged accepted Christian dogma. He rejected the perfection of scripture, for example, and refuted many of Jesus's miracles (maintaining that there were other, non-supernatural explanations).

Like Origen, Barclay was an avowed Universalist who believed that "in the end, all men will be gathered into the love of God." His works, though scholarly, were written with the "common man" in mind. In 1969, he was awarded the Order of the British Empire by Her Majesty Queen Elizabeth II.

SELF-RESTRAINT

"To enjoy freedom we have to control ourselves."

— Virginia Woolf
English Writer
1/25/1882 – 3/28/1941

We mustn't take freedom for granted, for although we are always free to choose, if we do not exercise proper restraint we will most assuredly find that there are limits to what will be tolerated by those with whom we share those very same rights.

———————◇———————

Virginia Woolf was one of the most creative and influential writers of the twentieth century. Her writing style was often a mix of free association, stream-of-consciousness, and intense, personal internal dialogue. Some of her best-known novels include *Mrs. Dalloway*, *To the Lighthouse*, and *Orlando*, each of which received critical acclaim and rave reviews.

Despite her many successes, in life as well as in love, Woolf suffered from bouts of deep depression. In 1941, she walked to the nearby Ouse River, filled her overcoat with stones, and drowned herself. She is reported to have said, of death, that it was the one experience she would not be able to describe.

January 26th

STRESS

"Man should not try to avoid stress any more than
he would shun food, love or exercise."

— Hans Selye
Hungarian-Canadian Endocrinologist
1/26/1907 – 10/16/1982

Can you imagine how stressful it would be, simply trying to avoid all forms of stress? Constantly trying to elude something that may or may not even occur? Madness. And here's the really crazy thing: Not all stress is bad for us. For example, stress can be a key survival tool. Fight, or flight? Stress is a determining factor.

Yes, it can be chaotic, and scary, but stress can also be a great motivator and a creative force. After all, where would we get our pearls if it weren't for the stress caused by a little grit in the nacre?

―――――――◇―――――――

Hans Selye was born in Hungary, but he was a man of the world. Fluent in eight languages, including English, he could also have conversations in another half dozen languages. He lived and worked in Czechoslovakia, the US, and Canada, and was widely regarded as one of the world's foremost authorities on endocrinology.

Selye is perhaps best known for his General Adaptation Syndrome, which describes how the body reacts to stress, and in particular how, over time, it can lead to ulcers, high blood pressure, and heart disease. He also sought to understand the influence of stress on a person's ability to recover from injury and disease.

In all, Selye wrote over 1,700 scientific papers on the subject of stress, as well as thirty-nine books. His *The Stress of Life* and *Stress Without Distress* were worldwide best-sellers and sold millions of copies. He has been called "the Einstein of medicine."

January 27th

COURAGE

"Courage is not simply one of the virtues, but the form
of every virtue at the testing point."

— C. S. Lewis
Irish Novelist, Poet, Academic
11/29/1898 – 11/22/1963

Each of us has it within ourselves to be strong, to persevere, to endure physical or emotional pain, but it takes real courage to push ourselves to the very brink, even over the edge, when we just don't think we can go any farther.

It's easy to stop short, to accept the status quo; no one will blame you, and everyone will say they understand. But that's not good enough. I wish you the courage to maintain your composure in the face of unfairness, to take that new job that scares you to death, to walk away from that abusive relationship, to stand up for someone who really needs a friend, and — most of all — to understand that you have a storehouse of courage to call upon whenever you need it. Trust me: You have it in you.

———————◇———————

Born in Belfast, Northern Ireland, Clive Staples Lewis was a prolific writer of both fiction and non-fiction. He is best known for his fantasy series *The Chronicles of Narnia*, and for his spirited defense of Christian principles. A scholar and intellectual, Lewis held academic positions at both Oxford and Cambridge universities. While teaching at Oxford, he joined a group of writers who called themselves The Inklings, and it was here that Lewis, known as "Jack" among his friends, met fellow fantasist J. R. R. Tolkien. While Tolkien was working on developing the myths of Middle Earth, he suffered from writer's block — sometimes lasting for a year or more. Lewis became his sounding board, and encouraged Tolkien to stick with it, and to doggedly work through his dry spells. The eventual result was *The Lord of the Rings*.

TEMPTATION

"No temptation can ever be measured by the value of its object."

— Sidonie Gabrielle Colette
French Novelist
1/28/1873 – 8/3/1954

We are seldom attracted by the true or subjective value of a thing, but by our own perception of its worth. What means nothing to one person can, after all, mean the world to another, for beauty (value) really is in the eye of the beholder.

It does not matter what others think of your desires; what truly matters is the importance that you place on them.

———————◇———————

Sidonie Gabrielle Claudine Colette Gauthier-Villars de Jouvanel Goudeket, known simply as Colette, was a French novelist whose best-known work, *Gigi*, was turned into both a play and a film. A supremely talented writer of highly descriptive (and slightly salacious) prose, Colette examined the joys and heartaches of love from a woman's point of view.

In life, as in her art, Colette had a soft spot for the ingénue, and her characters were often meditations on her own real-life experiences among the cads, vagabonds, and hedonists of turn-of-the-century Paris. She was nominated for a Nobel Prize in Literature in 1948, and was elected to the Legion d'Honneur in 1952.

TEMPERANCE

"Temperance is moderation in the things that are good
and total abstinence from the things that are foul."

— Frances E. Willard
American Educator, Suffragist
9/28/1839 – 2/17/1898

Few things are more difficult to maintain than self-restraint; we simply want what we want, even when we know that we shouldn't. If it weren't for outside influences — alcohol is a usual suspect, here — it would be much easier to listen to our conscience, and to heed our own counsel.

There is a great deal of pride to be found in making good choices, but alas, this is a lesson that is often learned in hindsight. Unless, of course, you learn it now.

———————◇———————

Frances Willard was the national president of the Woman's Christian Temperance Union for almost twenty years and a leader of the Prohibition movement. She was considered a radical for her pioneering stance against gender inequality and was a tireless advocate for those who were marginalized or disenfranchised — those who lived on the fringes of society. Her tireless efforts were instrumental to the eventual passing of both the 18th and 19th Amendments, which prohibited alcohol and granted women the right to vote.

A passionate and articulate speaker, Willard was in high demand as a lecturer, and in 1883, she spoke in every state in the U.S. She was reportedly one of the most famous women in the world, second only to Queen Victoria.

January 30th

ABSTINENCE

"Abstinence and fasting cure many a complaint."

— Danish proverb

It's kind of funny how often we complain about things over which we have no control, yet we do so little to control those things that are in our power. When it comes to affecting a positive change within a negative environment, the first step is also the easiest to grasp: Stop doing what is causing you harm!

———————◇———————

Danish proverbs, or *ordsprog* ("word-languages") are known for their fun-loving and common-sense approach to life's truisms.

HEALING

"Healing is a matter of time, but it is sometimes also
a matter of opportunity."

— Hippocrates
Greek Physician
460 BC – 370 BC

When it comes to healing, time is important, but sometimes so is distance. Get away from what is keeping that wound open.

———————◇———————

All freshly minted doctors take what is called the "Hippocratic Oath," named for (but probably not written by) the most famous and revered figure in the history of medicine: Hippocrates.

A forefather in the use of the scientific method, Hippocrates conducted experiments, collected data, and made observations in a methodical and rational manner, showing that disease and healing were natural processes, not a result of supernatural forces. Although the medical practices of Hippocrates's time were primitive by modern standards, the ethical code of professional conduct that bears his name continues to be honored to this day.

PURPOSE

"Everyone has a purpose in life and a unique talent to give to others.
And when we blend this unique talent with service to others, we experience
the ecstasy and exultation of our own spirit,
which is the ultimate goal of all goals."

— Kallam Anji Reddy
Indian Entrepreneur
2/1/1939 – 3/15/2013

There has never been a better time to be alive, in all of human history, than right now. By any measure, advances in technology, medicine, energy, and agriculture have increased both the standard of living and the overall lifespan for people all around the globe. If there is a downside to all of this remarkable progress, it is that amid these giant leaps for mankind, it can be difficult to find some kind of grand or exalted capital-P "Purpose" in our lives. But we mustn't despair; we must recalibrate. We aren't all queens, but even drones play a very important part in making our world a better place, and believe it or not, there is ecstasy in the mundane. Having a job, paying the bills, supporting a family, cultivating friendships — these are true successes. These are the things that give life Purpose, and they are worthy goals.

———————◆———————

Dr. Kallam Anji Reddy was a pharmaceutical researcher, entrepreneur, and philanthropist whose determination to make drugs more affordable made him a billionaire. He was known as a brilliant reverse engineer, who could take expensive new drugs and find ways to recreate them in a less expensive form. His Dr. Reddy's Foundation nurtures the poorest of the poor in India and Southeast Asia, teaching life skills, health and hygiene, career education, and entrepreneurship, in order to improve employability among the most disadvantaged.

February 2nd

CONSENSUS

"Consensus is what many people say in chorus
but do not believe as individuals."

— Abba Eban
Israeli Diplomat, Scholar
2/2/1915 – 11/17/2002

Consensus can be a funny thing, a strange and disorienting thing, because it can be attained devoid of reason, without proof, and without a single fact. Consider that "the consensus" once held that the earth was flat; that the universe revolved around our planet; that slavery was a good and proper thing.

The desire to fit in, to be a part of something — to belong — is a powerful, almost instinctual thing. However, it is far more important, and empowering, to maintain your integrity.

Never be afraid to say what you mean, and to stand your ground when the facts are on your side. Going along merely to get along leads nowhere.

———————◇———————

Born in South Africa and raised in England, Abba Eban was instrumental in the establishment of the state of Israel. Having served under Winston Churchill in WW II, he became a member of Israel's first provisional government, in 1946. The following year he gave an impassioned speech to the General Assembly, which led to Israel's recognition and admission to the United Nations. Eban brought a rational and objective eye to every issue, relying on fact, reason, and logic to carry the day.

MENTALITY

"We are always the same age inside."

— Gertrude Stein
American Novelist, Poet, Playwright
2/3/1874 – 7/27/1946

Once we get beyond childhood, and perhaps early adulthood, it does seem like we reach a certain mental age and never really stray too far from it. I think my internal age is somewhere around thirty-five: old enough to have learned some things; young enough to look for the humor in most things; and experienced enough to be grateful for every single thing.

What's *your* age?

———————◆———————

Gertrude Stein was born in Pittsburgh and raised in Oakland, but when she moved to Paris in 1903, she never looked back. An eccentric, she collected avant-garde art as well as artists. Considered an astute judge of talent, Stein could make or break an artist's reputation with a well-chosen remark.

Stein held court in her salon at 27 rue de Fleurus, on Paris's Left Bank. The eclectic group included expatriate writers Hemingway, Fitzgerald, and Ezra Pound, painters Picasso and Matisse, and her beloved ever-present white standard poodle, Basket.

Stein's most successful work, *The Autobiography of Alice B. Toklas*, was a quasi-memoir about her life in Paris, written in the voice of her life partner, Alice B. Toklas. Upon her death, in 1946, Stein was interred in Paris's Cimitière du Père Lachaise, alongside such luminaries as Oscar Wilde, Frédéric Chopin, Amedeo Modigliani, and more recently, Édith Piaf and Jim Morrison.

ASSUMPTIONS

"Appearances are often deceiving."

— Aesop
Greek Fabulist
620 BC – 564 BC

Have you ever made an assumption that was terribly wrong? What was it that caused you to do it? Was it based on appearances? Someone else's opinion? A long-held prejudice?

It's bad enough when we misjudge a thing, but even worse when we misjudge a person. If we don't have all the facts, we mustn't jump to conclusions based solely on appearances. Take the time to learn about that which you choose to judge.

———◇———

Although his exact date of birth is unknown, most of his existence is murky, and none of his actual writing has survived the millennia, it seems that almost every clever story that involves anthropomorphic animals or objects has been credited to Aesop's pen. As legend has it, he was born a slave but earned his freedom as a reward for being incredibly quick-witted and highly intelligent. While working for King Croesus, he apparently gave offense to some Delphians, who snuck a golden bowl from their temple into his luggage, so that it *appeared* Aesop had stolen it. He was summarily sentenced to death, and was thrown off a cliff.

DEDICATION

"Patriotism is not a short and frenzied outburst of emotion
but the tranquil and steady dedication of a lifetime."

— Adlai Stevenson II
American Politician, Diplomat
2/5/1900 – 7/14/1965

Every child has gotten mad at their parents, but over time, they came to understand that their anger was misplaced, or that it was a drop in the ocean compared to all the good that was done for them by those same parents. The same can be said for one's country; yes, things have been done that we disagree with, and we have been upset, but if we are honest, we have to admit that there have also been a great many good things done on our behalf.

Most relationships should be weighed in a similar fashion: over the long run. It isn't *what they said today* that matters; it's *what they have done over time*. It's also about what you have done, or not done. Are you as devoted to them and their happiness as they are to you and yours?

———◇———

Although Adlai Stevenson was a lifelong Democrat, his great-grandfather, Jesse Fell, was a founder of the Republican Party, a close friend of Abraham Lincoln, and the first to suggest that Lincoln be the new party's candidate for the presidency. A two-time presidential candidate himself, Stevenson ran, and lost, both times (in 1952 and 1956) to Republican Dwight D. Eisenhower.

Stevenson worked in the government for most of his life, including several federal appointments as well as serving as the 31st Governor of Illinois. He was a member of the delegation that drafted the charter for the establishment of the United Nations, in 1945, and he served as the United States Ambassador to the UN, from 1961 until his death in 1965.

REFLECTION

"I have always preferred the reflection of the life to life itself."

— Francois Truffaut
French Director, Screenwriter
2/6/1932 – 10/21/1984

Whether it's an image or a contemplation, there is always something lost and something found in a reflection — the sharp edges may be taken away, but the truth of a thing still remains.

There is a softness there; a quality that both helps and hinders our search. Sometimes what we see is better, more interesting, than the original. And, at other times it is a blessing that perhaps our recollection has been tempered by the act of remembrance itself, our memory fogged over by emotion.

For better or for worse? It's all in how you look at it.

Francois Truffaut was a devoted cinephile from the first time he saw a movie, having snuck into a theater at age eight. By age twenty, he was a film critic, and at twenty-three he tried his hand at directing. His disdain for traditional filmmaking would set the stage for what would become known as the New Wave movement, which sought to break away from the same old, tired, workmanlike productions that were common in French cinema. In 1974, Truffaut's film *Day for Night*, a film-within-a-film about filmmaking, won an Academy Award.

NORMALCY

"The only normal people are the ones
you don't know very well."

— Alfred Adler

Austrian Doctor, Psychotherapist

2/7/1870 – 5/28/1937

Have you ever heard the quip about supermodels? I refer to the comment (paraphrased): "Yeah, she's gorgeous, but somewhere there's a guy who got fed up with her crap."

It's really all about perceptions. We tend to look at those around us and buy into the idea that their lives are more (or less) normal than our own. Not only that, but we are also disposed to assign a higher value to their "normalcy" than to our own. Why is that? What is normal, anyway?

When you think about it, none of us are really normal. Each of us is loaded with all kinds of different quirks, foibles, and shortcomings — in addition to a whole lot of curiosity, empathy, and love. We are different. We are unique. We are wonderful. And we are prone to misjudgment.

———————————————

Alfred Adler, along with Carl Jung and Sigmund Freud, is thought to have had one of the most profound and lasting influences on the field of modern psychology.

After breaking with Jung over a difference of opinion, Adler developed what was called "individual psychology," from which sprang the term *inferiority complex*. He was also particularly curious about motivation and the forces which compel us, against all odds, to pursue our dreams. He called the determination to reach our full potential "striving for perfection."

In 1937, while on a lecture tour in Scotland, Adler died of a heart attack and was cremated. Somehow, his family lost his remains. They were found, seventy years later, and in 2007 his ashes were interred in his hometown of Vienna, Austria.

February 8th

PHILOSOPHY

"History is Philosophy teaching by examples."

— Thucydides
Greek Historian, General
460 BC – 395 BC

It has been said that those who don't learn from history are destined to repeat it, but it often seems that even those of us who have learned must still relive it, again and again, because we are trapped in the very same orbit as those who have not, cannot, or will not learn.

What is philosophy but learning from history: extracting all of the wisdom to be gained from the past — and all of those universal truisms — and then passing it on to those who would listen. It sounds a lot like parenting, doesn't it? And, like parenting, it seems that those for whom the advice would be most beneficial are very often those who are the least interested in heeding it.

But still, we try.

———◇———

Thucydides was an extraordinarily rational man. His *History of the Peloponnesian War*, written in 431 BC, is widely praised for its impartial analysis of a war in which he served as a general on the losing side. His failure to prevent the capture of the city of Amphipolis resulted in his exile — and the opportunity to study and write about the war.

Thucydides is also considered the father of the school of political realism, which holds that fear and self-interest are the primary drivers of tension between nation-states. He theorized that as new and powerful states begin to rise, it creates anxiety and apprehension among the existing powers, and that the growth of Athenian influence inevitably led to the war with Sparta.

February 9th

INTELLIGENCE

"Politeness decrees that you must listen to be kind;
intelligence decrees that you must listen to learn."

— Letitia Baldrige
American Etiquette Expert
2/9/1926 – 10/29/2012

The art of listening gets short shrift. We hear what is being said, and a competition erupts in our brain: a battle between processing what is being said and trying to come up with something witty to interject at the earliest possible opportunity. Which side usually wins?

Sometimes, perhaps most times, it doesn't really matter because what is being said isn't of great importance — it's just us; we're just chatting. But there are times when the speaker should command our full attention; when the subject demands our full consideration; when we need to shut down our own inner dialogue and listen intently and with purpose to the words being spoken. These are learning opportunities, and they can be very rare, especially if we aren't looking for them.

Letitia "Tish" Baldrige was a public relations executive, etiquette expert, and author of many books, but she is most famous for the time she spent as Jacqueline Kennedy's Social Secretary, helping the First Lady to plan the many official state dinners and social gatherings in the White House. She later served as secretary to American ambassadors in Paris and Rome (under Clare Booth Luce), and later started a public relations and marketing business.

Baldrige was considered an authority on contemporary etiquette and wrote a syndicated column on the subject. She said that consideration for others was the overarching tenet of etiquette, not a bunch of staid and unforgiving rules. The most important thing, she felt, was to always, *always* be kind.

February 10th

TRADITION

"Tradition does not mean that the living are dead,
it means that the dead are living."

— Harold Macmillan
British Prime Minister
2/10/1894 – 12/29/1986

We are creatures of habit. We like new and exciting things, but there is something comforting about routines; we even (grudgingly) accept schedules — when we aren't slaves to them.

Customs and traditions have a different feel, though, don't they? It's almost like we adhere to them because . . . well, because it's what we do; it's what everyone does. They are more than habit, more than routine. They are reassuring. They bind us not only to each other, but to those who came before, who also found value in them.

Conservative British politician Harold MacMillan served his country admirably, first in WWI as a soldier, then in WWII as undersecretary to Winston Churchill, and then as Prime Minister from 1957 to 1963. His grandfather founded the eponymous publishing house, Macmillan & Co., which published seven volumes of his memoirs, spanning the years from 1914 to 1963.

Incredibly, MacMillan's wife, Dorothy, had an affair with Tory politician Bob Boothby that lasted thirty years; even more incredibly, everybody knew about it — including the press — but no one said a word about it. The times were much different then.

February 11th

SUCCESS

"Our greatest weakness lies in giving up. The most certain
way to succeed is always to try just one more time."

— Thomas A. Edison
American Inventor, Businessman
2/11/1847 – 10/18/1931

Saying that the best way to succeed is to keep at it until you succeed is a bit like saying "I found it, and it was in the last place I looked." Well, of course it was. If you'd have kept on looking *after* you found it, people might have thought you were crazy.

But it's a point well-taken — too often we give up when we're right there, on the cusp of breaking through and finding what we're looking for. So often in life, success comes to those who want it the most, to those who are blessed with an extra helping of passion and tenacity.

Let 'em think you're crazy. Never give up.

———————◇———————

His grade-school teacher thought Thomas Edison was a "difficult" child, hyperactive and distracted by seemingly everything; she was right. Edison's mother, a teacher herself, took him out of school and taught him at home. She advanced a broad curriculum that went beyond science, math, and history; the two would study whatever piqued the interest of young Edison. Thus, she not only imparted knowledge, she taught him to *think*.

Thomas Edison always said that he was never discouraged, and never thought that he would not be successful in his quest to develop the first commercially viable electric light bulb. When he finally succeeded, after years of painstaking trials, a reporter asked him how it felt to fail a thousand times. Edison quipped that he didn't fail a thousand times, but that the light bulb was an invention that required a thousand steps.

EMPATHY

"Because a human being is endowed with empathy, he violates
the natural order if he does not reach out to those who need
care. Responding to this empathy, one is in harmony with
the order of things, with dharma; otherwise, one is not."

— Dayananda Saraswati
Indian Hindu Religious Leader
2/12/1824 – 10/30/1883

In a sense, we are all caretakers. We watch out for our friends, and family; for our neighbors, and for ourselves. For these, we do so out of love, but empathy is the reason we extend ourselves to strangers. The question is: Why?

The textbook definition of empathy will usually involve some kind of reference to a feeling of shared experiences. We all know what it is like to suffer, and it is this familiarity with suffering that drives us toward empathy; to render aid when we can, even unto strangers. It's what makes us human.

———————◇———————

Dayananda Saraswati spent almost half of his life as a wandering ascetic, travelling across India in search of religious truths. A follower of Vedic ideals, Dayananda sought equality and universal brotherhood for all of humankind. He is best known for his influential book, *Satyarth Prakash*, which helped to fuel the Indian independence movement. He is considered one of the architects of modern India.

RIGHTEOUSNESS

"The righteous say little but do much, but the wicked promise much
and perform not even a little."

— The Sages

When it comes to putting faith in others, there are generally two kinds of people: those who speak empty words and those whose actions speak louder than words.

We all have that one friend (or relative, or co-worker, or neighbor) who is always talking about their big plans that never seem to go anywhere, but if we are lucky, we also have at least one person in our lives who can be counted on to do what they said they would do.

Breaking promises doesn't necessarily make you wicked, but keeping promises does help to make you righteous among your peers.

Your word is an oath. Give it openly; honor it faithfully.

———————◇———————

The Sages are rabbis and scholars who have contributed to the collective wisdom of Jewish thought, opinion, and authoritative law, including the Old Testament.

February 14th

ELECTIONS

"Bad officials are the ones elected by
good citizens who do not vote."

- George Jean Nathan
American Drama Critic, Editor
2/14/1882 – 4/8/1958

When we select, we elect. We choose. We opt. We decide. In their song "Free Will," the rock band Rush makes the point that even when we choose not to decide, we have still actually made a choice. And it's true: Sometimes we take an action by not taking action, and avoidance is, in and of itself, an exercise in free will.

It is very important to understand that our choices always have consequences: Whether we are talking about voting for a candidate or where to go for dinner, if we don't speak up, we really can't complain about the outcome; our silence spoke for us.

———————◆———————

Born on Valentine's Day in Fort Wayne, Indiana, George Jean Nathan rose to prominence as an author, editor, and drama critic in New York City. Considered a fierce but fair judge of talent, Nathan is credited with setting the standards of theatrical criticism that are widely followed to this day. In his will, he established the George Jean Nathan Award for Dramatic Criticism, which remains one of the most distinguished (and richest) prizes in American theater. It is administered by his alma mater Cornell's English department.

February 15th

LEARNING

"I have never met a man so ignorant that
I couldn't learn something from him."

— Galileo Galilei
Italian Polymath
2/15/1564 – 1/8/1642

According to medieval French rabbi Shlomo Yitzchaki, also known as Rashi, wisdom consists of the knowledge one acquires from others. Does it really matter whether that knowledge comes from a distinguished scholar, or a dropout?

Don't be so quick to dismiss those whom you feel are your intellectual inferiors. Instead, embrace the idea that we can expand our knowledge and grow our wisdom through the most unlikely of sources — even from dropouts like Steve Jobs, Bill Gates, Oprah Winfrey, Wolfgang Puck, Walt Disney, Abraham Lincoln, Ted Turner, William Randolph Hearst, Russell Simmons, Charles Dickens, Ellen DeGeneres, Richard Branson, John D. Rockefeller, or the Wright brothers, just to name a few.

———————————◇———————————

Galileo was a philosopher, mathematician, and astronomer whose experimental processes led directly to the development of the scientific method. Famously, he figured out how telescopes worked, learned how to grind lenses, and soon produced a version that would magnify celestial bodies by twenty times. His discoveries revolutionized astronomy, proved that Copernicus was correct — the planets orbited the sun, not vice versa — and landed him in hot water with the Catholic Church. Pronounced a heretic, he spent the last ten years of his life under house arrest.

In 1991, Pope John Paul II acknowledged that the Church had erred in condemning Galileo nearly 360 years earlier. In 1995, NASA's *Galileo* became the first spacecraft to orbit Jupiter.

CHAOS

"Chaos was the law of nature; Order was the dream of man."

— Henry Adams
American Historian
2/16/1838 – 3/27/1918

There is a Yiddish proverb that says, "We plan, God laughs." Its humor belies a stone-cold truth, which is that our lives are susceptible to unforeseen and incredibly random events that have a way of showing us, often in stark and traumatic terms, just how little control we actually have over our lives. Change is inevitable; the only question is: What form it will take?

The Stoics had a fairly rational and pragmatic way of bringing Order to Chaos: First, accept that there are very few things (and these are mostly internal things) that we can actually control. Primarily, we can control only how we react to the things that happen around us, or to us, not the things themselves. Second, the Stoics teach that to be prepared for a thing — to have imagined it happening — is to reduce its sting. This isn't to say that we want to sit around and imagine horrible things happening all of the time, but there is a time and a place for these contemplations (and you've probably been there). Sadly, sometimes the only thing we can do is to plan for the worst while hoping for the best.

———————————◆———————————

Like so many of us, Henry Adams was baffled and bewildered by how quickly the world around us changes. His most famous work, *The Education of Henry Adams*, is an account of his struggle to come to terms with the changes wrought by scientific discoveries and technological advances during his lifetime. Although he self-published a few copies, it wasn't made available for public consumption until after his death, in 1918. It won the Pulitzer Prize in 1919.

CHARITY

"Every good act is charity. A man's true wealth hereafter is
the good that he does in this world to his fellows."

— Molière
French Playwright, Actor
1/15/1622 – 2/17/1673

Charity is a currency that comes in many forms. Time and money are the most commonly spent, but other acts of charity are equally valuable in their own right: pretending not to see or hear something in order to spare someone embarrassment; saying you are full so that someone you know is hungry will eat that last piece of pizza; quietly supporting someone who needs an ally but has none.

All acts of kindness and grace involve compassion, the cornerstone of charity and the clarifier of character, for what we do for one, we generally do for others. Let them one day say of you that the world is a better place because you were once in it; not for the millions you gave away but for the people you took in. After all, what do we leave behind but our good name?

———————◇———————

Known for his biting satire, Molière (Jean-Baptiste Poquelin) liked to skewer the pretentions and affectations of high society. Although many of those he ridiculed were openly hostile to his less-than-flattering depictions of them, Molière found a benefactor in King Louis XIV, who provided financial support and encouragement.

On this day, in 1673, Molière complained of illness while preparing to act in his play, *The Imaginary Invalid*. His wife and friends tried to stop him from performing, but he was more concerned with the stage workers who needed their daily wage, and the show went on. He died that evening.

REALITY

"We live, not as we wish to, but as we can."

— Menander

Greek Dramatist

342 BC – 291 BC

Who hasn't dreamed of being a rock star, of winning the lottery, of hanging out with a famous celebrity? Sure, we all have. From time to time, everyone imagines how wonderful it would be if only things were different: If only I had been born rich; if only I had been born beautiful; if only, if only, if only...

There is nothing wrong with a little wistful daydreaming. Fantasy is healthy, and Fantasy has a place in every person's life — but it is Reality that rules the roost.

Don't allow yourself to waste time or energy on the "if onlys." Life in the here and now is challenging enough, and although we'd all like to be a little richer, a little sexier, a little more this or a little more that, the reality is, this is who we are. For better or for worse, *this is where we are now*, and if we are going to be happy, we need to embrace it. It's all we have.

Like Molière, Menander was also a hugely popular comedic playwright. He wrote over one hundred plays, many of which became a part of the canon of European literature for nearly a thousand years after his death. Known for his love of aphorisms and proverbs, such as "Whom the gods love die young," Menander was reportedly quoted by Julius Caesar as he crossed the Rubicon, saying, "Let the die be cast."

EXTREMISM

"Extremism in the defense of liberty is no vice.
And moderation in the pursuit of justice is no virtue."

— Barry Goldwater
American Politician, Author
1/2/1909 – 5/29/1998

Is there anything more worthy of our utmost effort than ensuring our freedom? If our liberty is to be prized above all else, are there any limits to what should or may be done in resistance to those who seek to usurp it?

There is a fine line between extremism and anarchy, so it is important to distinguish between that which is supported by the rules of God and man, and that which is based on how we *feel* at a particular time. The trick is to know what is important to us, what is vital, long before a storm begins to gather and threaten it.

What are you willing to lose a friend over? For what would you willingly go to jail? For whom or what would you fight and die? Know these truly, and you know your Self completely.

Barry Goldwater served five terms as a senator from Arizona and ran as the Republican Party's nominee for president in the 1964 election. Running against incumbent Lyndon Baines Johnson (and the memory of JFK), Goldwater lost in a landslide. Nonetheless, the gruff, brusque, and plain-spoken Goldwater was credited with re-energizing the Republican Party, which would win seven of the next ten presidential elections.

REBELLION

"The thing worse than rebellion is the thing that causes rebellion."

- Frederick Douglass
American Abolitionist, Orator, Writer
2/14/1818 – 2/20/1895

Do we rebel against a thing simply because we don't agree with it? Or do we rebel because justice demands resistance against it? In either case, our reaction provides an insight into the strength of our own moral compass.

If our cause is righteous, so too must be our defense of it. No matter how good our intentions, we must not abandon the consistent application of fact, reason, and logic merely because we find that they are at odds with our indignation. That is the way of chaos, not character, and certainly not justice.

———————◇———————

Disguised as a sailor, twenty-year old Frederick Douglass escaped slavery by taking a train ride from Baltimore to Philadelphia. He had been determined to learn how to read and write as a child, and once settled in Massachusetts, he was soon delivering powerful speeches for the abolition of slavery.

A gifted orator, Douglass was welcomed in England, where he spent almost two years speaking in support of the abolitionist movement. His English friends eventually bought his freedom, raising the $700 needed to make him a free man.

A life-long proponent of equal rights in every quarter, Douglass fought just as hard for the women's suffrage movement as he did for the right of African-Americans to vote. In 1888, at the Republican Convention in Chicago, he became the first African American to receive a vote for the nomination to be a U.S. vice presidential candidate.

ESTEEM

"As love without esteem is capricious and volatile,
esteem without love is languid and cold."

— Jonathan Swift
Irish Satirist, Poet, Cleric
11/30/1667 – 10/19/1745

There are plenty of people in our life whom we respect, and even admire, even though they are merely surface relationships — a function of convenience, or happenstance. We often appreciate them for what they do, but not for who they are as individuals; we simply don't know them that well.

There are, on the other hand, people we know very intimately, and for whom we have great affection — but little to no respect. We can't help it; we care for these charmers in spite of their disrepute. But we know this much going in: these kinds of relationships aren't built to last.

Where there is love — real love — there is respect. If there is no respect, well . . . what exactly are you doing?

———————————◇———————————

Jonathan Swift's father, an attorney also named Jonathan, died a few months before he was born. His uncle, Godwin Swift, ensured that Jonathan received a first-rate education, providing the means for his nephew to receive a degree from Trinity College. Amid the political turmoil of the times, Jonathan left Ireland and moved to England, finding work as secretary for statesman Sir William Temple.

Swift fell in love with Esther Johnson, the daughter of Temple's housekeeper. Their relationship would last almost forty years. In 1726, almost sixty years old, Swift published *Gulliver's Travels*, which was a huge success. Shortly after its publication, Esther died. He spent the last thirty years of his life as Dean of St. Patrick's Cathedral, in Dublin, where he is buried next to Esther.

February 22nd

REPUTATION

"Associate with men of good quality if you esteem your own reputation; for it is better to be alone than in bad company."

— George Washington
American President, General
2/22/1732 – 12/14/1799

Our own reputation is one of those things that we seldom think about — until the precise moment when we realize its absolute value. Perhaps you want to ask a friend or a relative for a loan. Maybe your boss is considering who will be promoted. Perhaps there is a controversy, and an investigation ensues and somehow you are caught up in it. What do the actions you have taken in the past tell others about your character? Will their assessment be helped or harmed by the things you have said and done?

It takes a lot longer to build a reputation than to destroy it. Be someone with whom other high-character people choose to associate. It's never too soon to start building (or improving) your reputation.

———◆———

When it came time to choose who would lead the Continental army against the British, the one man whom everyone could agree on was George Washington. His experience, stature, and military bearing made him the obvious choice. After his nomination by John Adams, his appointment as Commander-in-Chief was unanimous.

When the war was over and the fledgling nation needed a leader, once again the choice was an easy one. Washington received every vote from the Electoral College (and remains the only president to have ever done so). When he stepped down after serving two terms as president, Washington quelled any talk of a monarchy and secured his well-earned reputation as a man of the utmost integrity.

STRENGTH

"I've never met a strong person with an easy past."

— Atticus

Roman Philosopher

110 BC – 35 BC

There is no way to develop strength except through trial. Just as muscles are strengthened through toil or exercise, so too is the mind. Woe, then, unto those who have lived a life devoid of strife, bereft of struggle, and to those who have avoided concepts or arguments that expose, challenge, and expand their worldview, for theirs is a life half-lived.

What little we know of the philosopher Atticus comes from snatches of his writing captured in Eusebius's *Preparatio Evangelica* (Preparation for the Gospel), which was written hundreds of years after Atticus lived and died. We can gather that he was a fairly open-minded fellow: He advocated simply letting people be who they want to be, saying, "It is better to be hated for what you are than to be loved for what you are not." He also suggested that each one of us must grab life by the horns, and learn to embrace the bitter as well as the sweet, for how could we possibly appreciate the latter without the former?

February 24th

DETERMINATION

"God grant me the courage not to give up what I think
is right even though I think it is hopeless."

— Chester W. Nimitz
American Admiral
2/24/1885 – 2/20/1966

It takes no small amount of resolve to stick to your principles when they seem to be under attack from every quarter; even when you know you are right, the temptation to surrender to the crowd can be overwhelming. But here's the thing: When you are right, it doesn't matter what anyone else *believes*, because deep down, you *know*; you know the facts are on your side, and just as important, you know how you will feel if you betray yourself in order to appease those who are lying to themselves.

Prudence may sometimes dictate silence for the sake of comity, but always be true to yourself and to your values — especially when you know you are right.

———————◇———————

Chester Nimitz was a sixteen-year-old boy when he entered the U.S. Naval Academy, and at twenty he was commanding a gunboat in China. Immediately following the attack on Pearl Harbor, in 1941, he was named commander in chief of the Pacific Fleet, and many of the most epic, hard-fought battles of WWII were won under his leadership, including those at Midway, the Coral Sea, the Philippines, Iwo Jima, and Okinawa. When all was said and done, Japan surrendered aboard his flagship, the USS Missouri.

In post-war America, Nimitz was hailed as a national hero, but he always insisted that he was just a representative of the many brave men who fought under his command.

LONGEVITY

"Youth is the gift of nature, but age is a work of art."

— Stanislaw Jerzy Lec
Polish Poet
3/6/1909 – 5/7/1966

I have always thought that one of the greatest blessings in life would be to get to experience all of the usual and familiar landmarks of a typical "long and fruitful" existence: the wonder of early childhood; the uncertainties of the teenage years; navigating the challenges of college; finding meaningful work; establishing a home of our own; getting married and having children, and watching them go through many of the same things we all do; retiring one day and trying to figure out what to do when we have both time and (hopefully) money. And although it may sound morbid, I've spent a good amount of time contemplating death and dying, and my hope is to be alert and aware enough to fully experience what *that* is all about. It's a part of this grand adventure, too, is it not?

Youth is a gift given to everyone, but age requires a good deal of determination and luck. Indeed, each of us has been young, but not all of us will get to be old, for longevity is a privilege that is denied to many. Therefore, never complain about growing old; be grateful, because every day is truly a gift.

Stanislaw Jerzy Lec was a poet who is probably best known for his philosophical aphorisms ("No snowflake in an avalanche ever feels responsible") published in his three-volume series, *Unkempt Thoughts*.

As a young man during WWII, Lec was imprisoned in a German work camp. After his second failed attempt to escape, he was sentenced to death; however, his third attempt was a success — he was able to overpower and kill his guard with the shovel he had been given to dig his own grave.

February 26th

GRACE

"When grace is joined with wrinkles, it is adorable. There is an
unspeakable dawn in happy old age."

— Victor Hugo
French Poet, Novelist
2/26/1802 – 5/22/1885

Hopefully, those of us who are lucky enough to reach a ripe old age
will find joy in having done so, for there are few things in life that are more
depressing than having to listen to a chronic complainer — especially when
coming from an old-timer; one of Life's lottery winners.

Gratefulness begets happiness, so be thankful for the blessing that is
growing old. Find your joy, and be someone else's inspiration; be that person
whom others want to be around, no matter how old you are.

Arguably the greatest of all French writers, Victor Marie Hugo gained
fame as a poet and artist long before his novels *The Hunchback of Notre Dame*
and *Les Miserables* were ever written. His first collection of poetry, *Odes et
Poésies Diverses*, was published in 1822 to wide acclaim and earned Hugo a
pension from Louis XVIII.

More poetry was forthcoming, as were numerous plays, but as Hugo's
literary reputation grew, his political leanings began to change. He ran for
election to the French National Assembly, where he pushed for universal suffrage, education, and the abolition of the death penalty. As a public official,
Hugo found that there was little time for writing; however, he did manage
to draft an outline of the work that would eventually become *Les Miserables*,
some fifteen years later.

Hugo was married to Adele Foucher for nearly fifty years, and they had
five children. Her death in 1868 brought about a profound sadness in Hugo,
but he was able to find consolation in Juliette Drouet, a former actress with
whom he had maintained a discreet affair for fifty years.

SORROW

"If we could read the secret history of our enemies, we should find in each man's life sorrow and suffering enough to disarm all hostility."

— Henry Wadsworth Longfellow
American Poet, Educator
2/27/1807 – 3/24/1882

No matter how much we despise even our very worst of enemies, our humanity compels us to extend a certain amount of compassion, and perhaps some small measure of forgiveness, should we recognize some exonerating truths behind their hurtful actions. It isn't always about us, strictly speaking, and with understanding and mercy comes release. Not theirs — ours.

Listen, my children, and you shall hear . . . about Henry Wadsworth Longfellow, in his day a poet of unequaled prominence, both at home and abroad. He is believed to have been the first American to be honored in Poet's Corner, in Westminster Abbey.

Although he spoke five languages and translated Dante's *The Divine Comedy* into English, Longfellow is probably best remembered for "Paul Revere's Ride" and "The Arrow and the Song." He wrote "Paul Revere's Ride" as a call for courage in the face of the looming Civil War. He was too old to fight, but he was not spared from the grief of this period: his wife, Frances, would die from burns suffered when her dress caught fire. Longfellow would not write for many years afterward.

CRUELTY

"Your own soul is nourished when you are kind;
it is destroyed when you are cruel."

— King Solomon
Israeli King
1010 BC – 931 BC

It is a fundamental, unavoidable truth that when we intentionally hurt others, we also hurt ourselves. The circumstances do not matter: every single time we deliberately inflict pain or suffering of any kind upon another living being, we diminish who we are. The sting of our guilt is merely the manifestation of our soul contracting.

And yet, how utterly sublime it is when we give of ourselves to others; when we know, deep down inside, that we have been a part of an exchange that goes beyond all of the ordinary, day-to-day interactions that play out, over and over again in our lives; when we recognize in a single, transcendent instant what it is to connect in a transformative and positive way with another soul.

We are free to choose whether we act out of spite or generosity. What will it be for you, today? Regret and remorse, or inner joy? Do something nice for someone today, and take note of how it makes you feel.

———————◇———————

King Solomon, son and heir of King David, is often considered to be one of the wisest people to have ever lived. It is said that once he became king, God appeared to Solomon in a dream and offered him anything he asked. Solomon asked for the ability to govern his people with wisdom and understanding, and God was so pleased with his choice that He also granted him great riches and longevity.

Solomon's name means "peace" or "peaceful" in Hebrew.

February 29th

DELIGHT

"Few delights can equal the presence of one whom we trust utterly."

— George MacDonald
Scottish Author, Poet, Minister
12/10/1824 – 9/18/1905

Whom do you trust completely, and without reservation? When was the last time the two of you had a meaningful conversation? Reach out! Say hello! Do what you can to keep your most precious friendships aglow.

Scotsman George MacDonald was an author, poet, and Christian minister. A writer who was well-known for his "fantasy" literature, MacDonald is said to have inspired many like-minded authors, such as J. R. R. Tolkien (*Lord of the Rings*), C.S. Lewis (*The Chronicles of Narnia*), and Madeleine L'Engle (*A Wrinkle in Time*). He also acted as mentor to Lewis Carroll (*Alice in Wonderland*).

MacDonald's ministerial career was marked by his persistent belief in divine presence, but not divine providence; he could not imagine a God Who would love some but not others.

March 1st

VALUES

"Some people are your relatives but others are your ancestors,
and you choose the ones you want to have as ancestors.
You create yourself out of those values."

— Ralph Ellison
American Novelist, Scholar, Critic
3/1/1914 – 4/16/1994

It is axiomatic that we cannot choose whom we are related to; it is what it is and there is absolutely nothing we can do about it. However, we do get to pick and choose those who are worthy of emulation — and it isn't always family members.

Take a moment to consider your values, and your principles, and how you came to embrace them. Chances are, your ideals have been shaped by those of your family, or perhaps your friends. Are any of your core values controversial? Have you ever "done the math" to see if they stand up to scrutiny? If not — if you are merely parroting someone else's opinion — what you have barely qualify as beliefs, and certainly not principles. Where is the value in that?

———————◇———————

Ralph Waldo Ellison, named after journalist and poet Ralph Waldo Emerson, was born in Oklahoma, attended the Tuskegee Institute in Alabama, was a researcher in New York City, wrote *Invisible Man* in Vermont, and was an American Academy fellow in Rome. He played the cornet and trumpet, studied music, and once dreamed of becoming a symphony composer. A worldly intellectual and Renaissance Man, Mr. Ellison brought his talents as a writer to bear on piercing the cultural and social mores of White America — and the attendant marginalization of minorities — from an African-American perspective.

HERITAGE

"We, of our time, have played our part in the perseverance, and we have
pledged ourselves to the dead generations who have preserved intact for us
this glorious heritage, that we, too, will strive to be faithful to the end,
and pass on this tradition unblemished."

— Eamon de Valera
Irish Political Leader
10/14/1882 – 8/29/1975

We often feel compelled to preserve and pass on our Traditions and
Heritage, in part because they work and are valued, and in part out of a sense
of duty to our immediate ancestors, who did the same. We'd all like to think
that the legacies we pass on are worthy of the effort, but that isn't necessarily
so — history is replete with examples of horrific customs and conduct that
seemed like a good idea at the time. What are we perpetuating today that will
be considered shameful in the future?

———————◇———————

Born in New York City to an Irish mother and a Spanish father, Eamon
de Valera was raised in Ireland and became the preeminent Irish Nationalist
statesman and political leader of the twentieth century.

As the elected leader of Sinn Fein, de Valera was largely responsible for
the violence associated with the so-called War of Independence. He eventually
turned away from militant republicanism, however, and worked to achieve
Irish independence through more traditional political means. He would be
instrumental in the establishment of the Irish Constitution, and in 1959 he
was inaugurated as President of Ireland, a position he held for fourteen years.

LETTING GO

"Knowledge is learning something new every day.
Wisdom is letting go of something every day."

— Zen proverb

There are a great many things vying for our attention, and it can be difficult to make time for the many worthwhile activities that satisfy our curiosity, nourish our intellect, or comfort our soul. Making a conscious effort to walk away from the pointless, mindless, and time-wasting activities that manage to dominate our lives is one way to make time for learning something useful; dumping those things that we cannot change and cannot control — yet worry endlessly about — is another.

———————◇———————

Zen is a school of Mahayana Buddhism that originated in China. With an emphasis on self-control, meditation, and the salvation of all sentient beings, Zen is less concerned with the accumulation of doctrinal knowledge and places more value on contemplating the inward-looking nature of our minds. We are then to use those insights for the benefit of mankind.

WONDER

"One of the secrets of life is to keep
our intellectual curiosity acute."

— William Lyon Phelps
American author, critic, scholar
1/2/1865 – 8/21/1943

We should always strive to maintain a sense of wonder about the world around us, and the people in it. This is a crazy, beautiful, awe-inspiring place, wherever you may be — and wherever you aren't. The more you learn, the more you know, and of particular importance is to take a minute, every so often, to just appreciate and ponder all of those great unknowns.

Be curious. Learning is good for you; it's good for your brain, and it feeds your soul. And look at you! You're doing it!

———————◇———————

William Lyon Phelps spent forty years at Yale, teaching contemporary literature with an emphasis on Russian novels. A wildly popular lecturer, his students often voted him Yale's MIP (Most Inspiring Professor). Mr. Phelps also wrote a syndicated newspaper column called "The Daily Thought" that was read by millions.

Now isn't *that* interesting?

OPINIONS

"New opinions are always suspected, and usually opposed, without any other reason but because they are not already common."

— John Locke
English Philosopher, Physician
8/29/1632 – 10/28/1704

There is a tendency to cling to the familiar, to embrace and even defend what we have become used to. New ideas, different ways of doing things, of seeing things; these are anathema to the Luddite reflex that lurks within the average mind. That isn't to say there aren't known knowns or that "if it isn't broke, why fix it" doesn't have its place, but just because we've always done a thing a certain way doesn't mean that we should never take a fresh look from time to time and challenge the status quo. Remember, conventional wisdom once held that computers had no place in the home. Aren't you glad that Bill Gates and Paul Allen had a different opinion?

———————◇———————

Considered one of the most famous philosophers and esteemed political theorists of the seventeenth century, John Locke was well-known among the Founding Fathers of the United States. His argument for a very limited government is rooted in the belief that human rights are bestowed by God, not man; that a government should therefore have only a very few and specific powers over its citizens; and that it is the duty of those so ruled to overthrow their government should these boundaries be corrupted. These were radical thoughts in Locke's day, and they were still radical nearly a hundred years later, when they were inserted into the Declaration of Independence and the U.S. Constitution.

ART

"The true work of art is but a shadow of the divine perfection."

— Michelangelo
Italian Sculptor, Painter, Architect
3/6/1475 – 2/18/1564

Michelangelo di Lodovico Buonarroti Simoni, or simply Michelangelo, is one of the greatest (if not *the* greatest) artists to have ever lived. His paintings are superb, and his sculptures are so lifelike you almost expect to see them breathe. Yet even as we marvel at his skill, at his otherworldly ability to capture the human form in astonishing detail, we know that he was in awe of God's flawless creations. That includes you.

Painter of the Sistine Chapel. Sculptor of David, *and* the Pieta. Chief architect of St. Peter's Basilica. Any one of these would make a most excellent epitaph — unless, of course, you were Michelangelo.

Michelangelo was no shrinking violet, full of false modesty; he was fully aware of his own greatness, but he also knew that he could not compete with perfection. And yet, he left behind a legacy of coming oh-so-tantalizingly close.

Speaking of competition: Did you know that the two most talented and renowned artists the world has ever known were both alive, plying their trades during the Renaissance, a few hundred miles apart, in Italy? It's true: During the late fifteenth and early sixteenth centuries, the lives of Michelangelo and Leonardo da Vinci overlapped, for about forty-five years.

March 7th

EQUALITY

"By nature all men are equal in liberty,
but not in other endowments."

— Saint Thomas Aquinas
Italian Friar, Philosopher
c. 1225 – 3/7/1274

Each of us are bestowed with strengths and weaknesses, privileges and frailties that are as unique as our souls. These are the things that make us different. Where we are the same lies in our freedom to choose if, and how, we will use our strengths to overcome our weaknesses.

———————◇———————

As the youngest of nine children, Thomas of Aquinas was able to observe the differences in individual abilities first-hand. As the son of a Count (Landulph), Thomas could undoubtedly see the difference between the haves and the have-nots. As a young scholar, he distinguished himself among his peers, and as a theologian he rejected the assumption that theology (faith) and philosophy (reason) were incompatible, asserting that "both kinds of knowledge ultimately come from God" and, in fact, prove the existence of God. The Catholic Church has long considered Thomas to be an important role model, and an exemplar for all who are studying for the priesthood.

PASSION

"Follow your passion. Nothing – not wealth, success, accolades or fame – is worth spending a lifetime doing things you don't enjoy."

— Rabbi Lord Jonathan Sacks
British Lord, Chief Rabbi, Philosopher, Author
Born 3/8/1948

It doesn't matter if our dreams are large or small, we seldom regret chasing them. What are you passionate about? More importantly: What are you doing about it?

———————◇———————

One of the world's leading intellectual figures, Jonathan Sacks is the author of numerous books on Jewish thought and is a global religious leader, philosopher, and moralist. A frequent and popular academic lecturer, the Cambridge- and Oxford-educated Rabbi has won several prestigious international awards, holds sixteen honorary degrees, and was knighted by Queen Elizabeth II in 2005.

March 9th

COMPOSURE

"Nothing baffles the schemes of evil people so much
as the calm composure of great souls."

— Honore-Gabriel Riqueti
French Noble, Count of Mirabeau
3/9/1749 – 4/2/1791

No small measure of the instigator's pleasure comes from seeing anger, aggravation, and tears on the faces of those they seek to torment. It isn't always easy to do, but the best way to dim that bulb is to deny them the satisfaction of seeing your pain. What is most helpful is to anticipate the provocation and then steel yourself against it. It is always easier to face a difficulty after having first considered its possibility.

———————◆———————

A Machiavellian master of intrigue, Honore-Gabriel Riqueti was a lifelong troublemaker and raconteur whose efforts to reconcile the French monarchy with the aims of the French revolution ended in dishonor and bloodshed. Known as much for his fiery oratory as his scandalous love affairs, Mirabeau (as he was known) died in 1791, at age forty-two, leaving this world just as the Reign of Terror was about to begin.

REACTION

"We cannot choose our external circumstances, but
we can always choose how we respond to them."

— Epictetus
Greek Stoic Philosopher
c. 50 AD – c. 135 AD

If ever there were a single sentence that encapsulates the essence of Stoicism, it is this one, in which Epictetus advises us to be ever mindful of the fact that the only real control we have over external events lies in how we respond to them. We tend to forget this simple fact, which often leads to highly emotional (yet altogether impotent) reactions. Knowledge is the beginning of Wisdom.

———————◇———————

Born a slave, Epictetus nonetheless overcame his circumstances and, through study and rank determination, became a lecturer, a teacher, and a philosopher of the first order. Known today primarily for *Discourses*, the four-volume compilation of his teaching, Epictetus was forced to leave Italy by the Roman Emperor Domitian, who banned all philosophers from the peninsula. Epictetus promptly established a school in Greece, where he spent the remainder of his life teaching and honing the philosophy of Stoicism.

GOD

"Every visible and invisible creature is an appearance of God."

— Johannes Scotus Eriugena
Irish Theologian, Philosopher
c. 815 – c. 877

Consider this: If you can think it, if you can imagine it, if you can visualize it in your mind's eye, you are one step closer to gaining an understanding of a thing's origin. And if you can but acknowledge the origin of all origins, you can ponder the endless variations in outcomes that are possible within the confluence of free will and divine purpose.

Put another way: If you are not the origin, then Who is?

———————◇———————

Johannes Scotus Eriugena was an Irishman who spent most of his life in France translating medieval texts and commentaries, including Plato. His religious beliefs were considered radical in his time, particularly his conviction that all things come from God, and his insistence that every individual has a personal and direct connection to God, with no need for the rituals and formalities of church doctrine. This led, inevitably, to his writings being banned by various Popes, well into the seventeenth century.

March 12th

ADDICTION

"Every form of addiction is bad, whether the narcotic be alcohol
or morphine or idealism."

— Carl Jung
Swiss Psychiatrist, Psychoanalyst
7/26/1875 – 6/6/1961

Is every addiction truly "bad?" What is addiction, if not highly focused devotion? And if we are devoted to a *good* thing, must that necessarily be a bad thing?

In truth, an addiction becomes bad only when it becomes an unhealthy or uncontrollable obsession. What obsesses you? Is it an honorable habit, or an illicit vice?

———◆———

While on staff at the Burghölzli Asylum of the University of Zürich, Carl Jung studied mental illnesses and developed the concepts of the introverted and extroverted personality types. If you have ever taken a Meyers-Briggs personality test, you are familiar with Jung's theory that we all tend to fall into one or more of the Thinking, Feeling, Sensing, and Intuition groups.

Between 1907 and 1912, Jung worked closely with Sigmund Freud. The two were close friends and collaborators, however, their professional relationship ended, in part due to Freud's unremitting insistence that all psychological neuroses are sexual in nature; Jung believed them to stem from a lack of spiritual development. It was this spiritual connection that caught the attention of Bill Wilson, the founder of Alcoholics Anonymous, who integrated spirituality into his program for the treatment of alcohol addiction.

CYNICISM

"Inside every cynical person, there is a disappointed idealist."

— George Carlin
American Comedian, Social Critic
5/12/1937 – 6/22/2008

It is easy to be a cynic. The sad truth is, too often we tell ourselves that being a skeptic, a naysayer, or a "doubting Thomas" is about being realistic, or worse yet, about being practical (groan). Where's the fun in that?

Sure, things don't always work out the way we want them to, but we mustn't let our failures end our dreams prematurely. Forge ahead! Try a new approach, and if that doesn't work, try a different one, and at last, when you are absolutely sure that it cannot and will not work, take pride in your effort, and pleasure in what you have learned. After all, life is about experiences, and you are ready for the next one.

George Carlin was a comedian noted for his darkly humorous, witty, and often scathing commentary on the human condition. He was particularly fond of skewering the peculiarities of the English language, religious mores, and social taboos in general. His observations, though crass and controversial at times, were genuinely thought-provoking; it wasn't that he was trying to convince the audience so much as he was trying to get them to *think*.

In 2008, Carlin was posthumously awarded the Mark Twain Prize for American Humor. They probably should have given it to him sooner.

ABSURDITY

"If at first the idea is not absurd, then there is no hope for it."

— Albert Einstein
German Theoretical Physicist
3/14/1879 – 4/18/1955

To achieve greatness is often a matter of going beyond the socially accepted norms, of pondering the unconventional, of embracing the counterintuitive. Consider the "firsts" in the culinary field, such as the first time someone saw an egg drop from a chicken's butt and decided to eat it. Or the first person to brew (and drink!) coffee collected from civet droppings. What were they thinking when they came up with bird's nest soup? How hungry was the first person who ever saw an oyster and decided to shuck that snotty mass from its briny shell? What about Rocky Mountain Oysters? Tripe? Haggis? Kimchi?

Don't be afraid to try something new, no matter how crazy it sounds. You always want to be safe, but do you always want to play it safe? Sometimes you just have to put yourself out there and risk being thought a fool. Don't sweat it. Everything is temporary.

Albert Einstein is considered the greatest physicist who ever lived, but he was working as a clerk in a Swiss patent office when he proposed revolutionary new ways of looking at Time, Space, Gravity, and Energy.

Although many of Einstein's theories were presented over a hundred years ago, the best scientific minds have been trying to prove (or disprove) them ever since. What has made it so difficult to either verify or deconstruct Einstein's theories is that we have often lacked the technology to precisely measure what he said is out there. As the means and opportunities have presented themselves through the years, however, we have discovered that, in almost every instance, he was right.

WILLPOWER

"Wise to resolve, and patient to perform."

— Homer
Greek Author
Ninth century BC – Eighth century BC

Careful planning and dogged persistence are the tools of every success. Once you have made up your mind, let nothing stand in your way.

———————◇———————

Homer is the name given to the mysterious author of *The Iliad* and *The Odyssey*, two larger-than-life poems that serve as twin pillars of Ancient Greek literature.

Are these the works of one man, a single poetic genius? Or are they the result of a team effort — a collaboration that stretched over hundreds of years? Although no definitive proof exists either way, the wisdom attributed to Homer through these works, through the ages, has become so prevalent that today he is mentioned in the same breath as Plato and Aristotle in the pantheon of philosophical superstars.

ACHIEVEMENT

" Trust yourself. Create the kind of self that you will be happy
to live with all your life. Make the most of yourself by fanning
the tiny, inner sparks of possibility into flames of achievement."

— Golda Meir
Israeli Prime Minister
5/3/1898 – 12/8/1978

Push yourself. It isn't enough to have dreams and make plans; you must
strive, and work, and do. Most of all, you have to *complete*. Cross that finish line!

———————————◇———————————

Born in Kiev, Russia, "Goldie" Meir immigrated with her family to
Milwaukee, Wisconsin in 1905. During World War II, she became an outspoken champion for a Jewish state and for Jewish immigration to Palestine,
long considered the Jewish homeland. A signer of Israel's declaration of independence, she served as Israel's Foreign Minister from 1956 to 1966. In 1969,
she became Israel's fourth Prime Minister, and one of the first women to lead
a nation in the modern era.

ASPIRATION

"Do for this life as if you live forever, do for
the afterlife as if you die tomorrow."

— Ali ibn Abi Talib
Arabian Islamic Leader
3/17/599 – 1/29/661

There is a story about a fifty-something man who confides in a friend that he'd like to study medicine, but that at his age it's a foolish dream. "By the time I finish my studies, and an internship, I'll be nearly sixty years old!" he laments.

His wise friend asks, "How old will you be if you *don't* finish your studies and undergo an internship?"

Chasing dreams is a lifelong pursuit. Some may be big, some may be small, but they all play an important role in propelling us ever onward, in making our lives interesting, and full. And sometimes, when we are dogged enough, and determined enough, we catch them.

Ali ibn Abi Talib was the cousin and the son-in-law of Muhammad, the last prophet of Islam. He was incredibly devoted to Muhammad and demonstrated his allegiance through numerous acts of bravery and prowess on the battlefield. At the same time, he was a pious man who wrote numerous works on religion and morality, playing a pivotal role in the development of Islam. He ruled as the Fourth Caliph from 656 to 661.

March 18th

EXCUSES

"Whoever wants to be a judge of human nature
should study people's excuses."

— Christian Friedrich Hebbel
German Poet, Playwright
3/18/1813 – 12/13/1863

It is amazing what we hope others will accept; even more astonishing is the belief that we somehow deserve more.

———————◇———————

Christian Hebbel was a poet and dramatist who often used the psychology of tragedy to dramatize historical events and characters in order to highlight how people and societies change and adopt (or adapt to) new moral values. His own life and choices would imitate his art, as he married for money — casually jettisoning his long-suffering mistress, with whom he had two illegitimate children — because, he explained, his first duty to the world was to share with it his poetic genius, which he could not do if he had to struggle for his (financial) existence.

AMBITION

"Intelligence without ambition is a bird without wings."

— Salvador Dali
Spanish Painter
5/11/1904 – 1/23/1989

Even without wings, a bird is still a remarkable creature. But, ah! What it *could* be!

Ambition alone does not correlate to greatness, nor is it a very reliable barometer of intelligence. Indeed, the yin to ambition's yang is action: genuine, concentrated effort; striving to meet one's potential in spite of all obstacles.

Question: Are you walking when you could be flying?

———————◇———————

With a full name that was every bit as surreal as his paintings, Salvador Domingo Felipe Jacinto Dalí i Domènech, 1st Marquess of Dalí de Púbol grabbed life by the horns, expressing himself across a wide variety of media, including sculpture, film, photography, and of course, those paintings.

Ever the showman, Dali played up his natural eccentricity and garnered publicity and attention wherever he went, often in grandiose and creative ways. Playing on his reputation as a haughty *artiste*, he famously remarked, "Each morning when I awake, I experience again a supreme pleasure — that of being Salvador Dali."

TIMING

"At times it is folly to hasten; at other times, to delay.
The wise do everything in its proper time."

— Ovid

Roman Poet

3/20/43 BC – c. 17 AD

Sometimes the better part of wisdom is to simply recognize when to take action and when to wait for things to come to you. Unfortunately, we don't always have the patience or the experience to make good decisions — which is why mistakes are often the price we pay for gaining wisdom.

All else being equal, there is almost always *something* that can be done to get you closer to the outcome that you desire. When King David was told that not he but his son, Solomon, would build the first Jewish Temple in Israel, what did he do? He started amassing all of the materials that would be needed for the Temple's construction.

It might take more time, but even baby steps will eventually get you to your destination.

Publius Ovidius Naso, or simply Ovid, is considered a giant of Latin literature. Born into wealth, he counted among his friends Horace and Virgil, and is probably best known for his 12,000-line poem *Metamorphoses*, an epic account of the history of the world from its creation to the deification of Julius Caesar.

In 8 AD, the emperor Augustus banished Ovid to Romania, for reasons that remain unclear (although there are hints of a peripheral involvement in the adultery of one of Augustus's granddaughters, who was also banished at the same time). He spent the rest of his life in exile, and died in 18 AD.

REVELATION

"A man never discloses his own character so clearly
as when he describes another's."

— Jean Paul

German Writer

3/21/1763 – 11/14/1825

We often wonder what others think of us, but if we listen closely to how our friends describe one another, we get our answer.

Johann Paul Friedrich Richter was a German satirist whose pen name, Jean Paul, was born of a deep admiration of the French writer Jean-Jacques Rousseau. A master of using humor and irony to veil his own (ultimately) sentimental assessment of humanity, he was easily moved to tears by emotional displays. The unexpected death in 1821 of his son, Max, marked the beginning of the end for Richter: he went blind in 1824 and died of edema in 1825. A monument to him still stands in Bayreuth, Germany.

SIN

"Let the one among you who is without sin
be the first to cast a stone."

— Jesus Christ
Jewish Preacher, Religious Leader
c. 1 AD – c. 33 AD

It seems nearly all of us possess an emotional and irrational instinct to point a finger at others when we see them err. Irrational, you say? Certainly. Indeed, we readily accept the notion that to err is to be human, and to be human is to err. But beyond the platitudes about no one being perfect, let us consider the logic we believe we are deploying when defending our own lapses in judgment: "So-and-so did the exact same thing!"

What, pray tell, does that have to do with our own actions?

Absolutely nothing.

Rationalizing one wrong by comparing it with another does not mitigate a thing; two wrongs will never make a right. Try this, instead: Accept that what you did was improper, admit it, and commit yourself to never make the same mistake again. Not only will it elevate your standing among those who would judge you, it will also take a weight off your soul.

———◇———

Jesus of Nazareth was a carpenter who became a preacher, a teacher, and a healer. Although he was crucified by the Romans, his followers believe he rose from the dead and ascended to Heaven. Jesus Christ, as he is known, is the central figure of Christianity, and Christians believe him to be the Son of God, the Messiah, and Savior of the World.

RESPECT

"There is no respect for others without humility in one's self."

— Henri Francis Amiel
Swiss Philosopher, Poet
9/27/1821— /11/1881

Self-esteem and self-confidence are good things, in the proper measure. What we must avoid is the idea that we are better than others and therefore have nothing to learn from them, to appreciate about them, or have in common with them.

There is always something we can relate to, or something to appreciate, in those we meet, no matter what our differences might appear to be. Sometimes it is that life can humble you. Respect the struggle.

Henri Francis Amiel was a professor of aesthetics and moral philosophy at the Academy of Geneva. He is best known for his masterwork *Journal Intime* (Private Journal), a revelatory diary of self-analysis that was published to international acclaim — posthumously. Possessing a great intellectual ability and having had a successful academic career, Amiel's *Journal* nonetheless paints a picture of an emotionally fragile man who is profoundly skeptical about the societal values of his time, as well as his own place in the world. He died thinking himself a failure, never fully aware of his own value.

CONTEMPT

"What I have known with respect to myself, has tended much
to lessen both my admiration, and my contempt, of others."

— Joseph Priestley
English Chemist, Philosopher, Theologian
3/24/1733 – 2/6/1804

Have you ever taken a dislike to someone, at first sight? You couldn't
quite put your finger on it, but there was definitely something about them
that rubbed you the wrong way.

It happens. Thankfully, these things often dissipate as quickly as they
appear — usually because the more we learn about others the more difficult
it is to dislike them. And, if we're honest, we'll acknowledge that we possess
many of the exact same character flaws and moral failings that we are so quick
to notice in others — being judgmental chief among them. So give them a
break, just as they are undoubtedly doing for you.

———————◆———————

Joseph Priestley was a man of far-ranging interests, in nearly all of which
he was an expert. He was a chemist, credited with the discovery of oxygen; a
theologian, who helped found Unitarianism; and a scientist, whose experiments
and writings on electricity would become the go-to text for over a century (Ben
Franklin encouraged him to publish his findings). He was also a respected
philosopher, educator, political theorist, and writer.

The English government found Priestley's defense of the American and
French revolutions to be seditious, and the press stirred up anger against him.
In 1794, a mob burned down his house, and Priestley fled to the United States,
where he discovered a form of government that was "relatively tolerable." When
he died in Northumberland, Pennsylvania, in 1804, his passing was mourned
by President Thomas Jefferson.

March 25th

SLOTH

"We excuse our sloth under the pretext of difficulty."

— Quintilian
Spanish-Roman Teacher, Rhetorician
c. 35 AD – c. 100 AD

It is a universal truth that it is often more difficult to avoid work than it is to just buckle down and get the job done. If you absolutely must exert yourself, if it's simply unavoidable, always choose to *do the work*; ultimately, it's the only option that will leave you with a sense of accomplishment — and self-respect.

A rhetorician is a writer or speaker whose goal is to inform, convince, and persuade their audience, and Marcus Fabius Quintilianus, aka Quintilian, was among the best who ever lived. A Roman born in northern Spain, Quintilian was Rome's top educator, serving under the Emperors Titian, Vespasian, and Domitian. He was the first teacher to receive a salary from the state and was responsible for educating Emperor Domitian's heirs.

Quintilian's long experience as an educator led him to believe that the process itself had a great effect upon one's direction in life; in effect, you become what you study and train to be. He also believed that we should never underestimate the power of good role models, writing, "Pupils, if rightly instructed, regard their teacher with affection and respect. And it is scarcely possible to say how much more willingly we imitate those we like."

March 26th

CONSEQUENCE

"You can do anything in this world if you are
prepared to take the consequences."

— W. Somerset Maugham
British Playwright, Novelist
1/25/1874 – 12/16/1965

They say, "Rules are meant to broken," and our prisons teem with those who feel the same way about laws. What is it that makes one person follow the rules, while another believes rules are for suckers?

It seems to me that the problem isn't that we are unwilling to accept the consequences of our actions, but that we too often fail to consider them in the first place. And, in many cases, it seems apparent that there has been precious little emphasis on the idea that we are responsible for everything we do — or don't do.

———————◆———————

William Somerset Maugham was a highly successful playwright, novelist, and short story writer widely known for his semi-autobiographical style and penchant for blurring the line between fictional and non-fictional characters. Maugham trained and qualified as a physician, but his first novel, *Liza of Lambeth* (published in 1897), was so successful that he gave up medicine to become a full-time writer.

During WWI, Maugham served in the ambulance corps and was eventually recruited by the British Secret Intelligence Service. He resumed his writing career after the war and is considered one of the most popular writers of his time. He is probably best known today for his novels *The Razor's Edge* and *Of Human Bondage*.

March 27th

MOTIVATION

"What makes bitter things sweet? Hunger."

— Alcuin
English Scholar, Clergyman, Poet
c. 735 – 5/19/804

Desperation of any sort is a powerful motivator. We do what we must, no matter the difficulty, and despite any hardships; no questions asked. Our reward? We get the privilege of trying to do better tomorrow.

———————◇———————

Charlemagne made a point of surrounding himself with the best and brightest minds of the age, and in the year 781 he invited Alcuin to join him at the Carolingian court at Aachen, in northern Germany. Alcuin, a scholar, clergyman, poet and teacher from York, Northumbria, accepted the invitation and was soon advising the king and educating his children.

Alcuin was a leading light of the ensuing intellectual and cultural awakening that is known as the Carolingian Renaissance. His prominence is best summed up by Einhard, Charlemagne's biographer, who called him "the most learned man anywhere to be found."

LUCK

"It's hard to detect good luck – it looks so much like something you've earned."

— Frank A. Clark
American Politician, Lawyer
3/28/1860 – 4/14/1936

Sometimes it seems like good ol' Lady Luck is right by our side, while at other times it seems like we are being hounded by what can only be called just plain bad luck. It might seem random, but there is a secret to making sure that we increase the former and reduce the latter: hard work.

Practice, preparation, passion, and persistence have done more to ensure "good luck" than all of the trinkets, charms, and superstitious routines put together. The truth is, we make our own luck, through our own determined efforts — or through laziness and neglect. So go ahead and celebrate your good fortune, when it comes. You've undoubtedly earned it.

———————◇———————

Frank Clark was born in Alabama, attended law school in Georgia, and was elected to Congress as a representative of Florida. He left office in 1925 and moved to Miami, where he opened a law practice. Three years later, President Calvin Coolidge called on him to serve on the U.S. Tariff Commission. In 1933, he became an attorney for the Bureau of Internal Revenue (known today as the IRS), where he worked until his death in 1936. He was seventy-six years old.

EXPECTATION

"High achievement always takes place in
the framework of high expectation."

— Charles Kettering
American Inventor, Engineer
8/29/1876 – 11/25/1958

Few can overcome the stigma of low expectations. Let's face it: Life isn't always fair, and sometimes we labor under an undeserved reputation for being second-string, a benchwarmer. For some of us, that's okay; we'll take what we can get. For others, such an assessment stings; it hurts our pride and we can't wait for the chance to prove everyone wrong. The question is: What are you doing to prepare yourself for the opportunity?

Don't sink to the level of someone's mistaken valuation of you or your abilities; rise to the challenge. Raise the bar on what you expect from yourself, and others will, as well.

———————◇———————

Charles Franklin Kettering was an American engineer, businessman, and a prolific inventor who held over 150 patents during his lifetime. He developed the first electric self-starter for the automobile, designed the first electronic cash register, and helped to develop the refrigerant Freon, used in refrigerators and air conditioners. He was also a co-founder of Dayton Engineering Laboratories Company (DELCO), and served as vice president and director of research at General Motors for twenty-seven years. He was also interested in medicine, and in 1945 he and longtime General Motors head Alfred P. Sloan established the Sloan-Kettering Institute for Cancer Research in New York City. The small-town Ohio farm boy was posthumously inducted into the National Inventors Hall of Fame in 1980.

PERSPECTIVE

"Wise are they who have learned these truths: Trouble is
temporary. Time is tonic. Tribulation is a test tube."

— William Arthur Ward
American Writer
c. 1921 – 3/30/1994

It is a tall order, trying to convince yourself to not worry about things.
We are programmed, it seems, to fret and agonize over the issues and people
and events that intersect with our lives; however, the first step toward maintaining our sanity is to accept that our worrying about a thing will not actually
impact it in any tangible way; we are, in fact, the only thing that is affected
by our anxiety.

Don't waste a moment worrying unduly about things over which you
have no control. The difficult part, of course, is making that distinction. The
Stoic philosopher Epictetus said that the only thing we have control over is
our reaction to external events, and I like that; I believe that. However, I prefer
my mother's short-but-sweet consolatory dictum: "Things always work out."
She swore by that statement, and I do, too.

———————◇———————

William Arthur Ward is one of America's most quoted and broadly published writers of inspirational aphorisms. Born and raised in Louisiana, Ward
joined the U.S. Army as a private in 1942, served in the Philippines, and
attained the rank of captain. After the war, Ward graduated from McMurry
University in Abilene, Texas before receiving a master's degree from Oklahoma
State University. Returning to Texas, Ward became a college administrator at
Texas Wesleyan College, in Fort Worth, and served on the Board of Directors
of numerous organizations, including the Rotary Club, the Red Cross, and
the Boy Scouts of America.

READING

"The reading of all good books is like a conversation
with the finest minds of past centuries."

— Rene Descartes
French Mathematician, Philosopher
3/31/1596 – 2/11/1650

While academic instruction is a highly effective method of imparting information and ideas, there is not a more democratic means available, to *everyone*, than to learn by reading. If you know how to read, you possess the key to the doorway of knowledge. If you want to learn about astronomy, there are books about astronomy. If you want to learn about agriculture, you can read all there is to know about agriculture. Interested in the history of Ancient Rome? There are books for that. Solar power? Plate tectonics? English literature? Yes, yes, and yes; we have the information you seek. All you have to do is read.

René Descartes was a French polymath. A mathematician, a scientist, and a philosopher, he also had a law degree and practiced medicine. And he read. A lot.

Considered the father of modern Western philosophy, Descartes is probably known to most people for his declaration, "I think, therefore I am" (*Cogito, ergo sum* in Latin). His universal method of deductive reasoning, based on mathematics, led to the development of a new scientific method grounded in experimentation and observation, and collecting empirical data, not opinion or intuition.

Descartes believed that human beings are virtuous at heart and are at their best when they seek and act upon the truth; his work helped humanity to find it.

April 1st

BELIEF

"For I do not seek to understand in order to believe, but I believe in order to understand. For I believe this: unless I believe, I will not understand."

— Anselm of Canterbury
Benedictine Monk, Philosopher
c. 1033 – 4/21/1109

More often than we like, we find that we must make decisions, in matters large and small, based primarily on what we simply *believe* to be true. When no technical data exists to tell us whether we can reliably refute or corroborate what stands before us, we must choose to either go with what our intuition is telling us, or reject it out of hand.

While empirical data is nice — it assures us that our choice is logical, and it validates the idea that we are on the right track — sometimes the only thing we have to go on is a simple, persistent belief. And sometimes it is enough.

———————◆———————

Anselm was an Italian-born Benedictine monk, philosopher, and theologian of the Catholic Church who was canonized as a Saint upon his death. He served as Archbishop of Canterbury from 1093 to 1109, and is best known for his celebrated argument (the *Proslogion*) that God exists and is "the supreme good."

LANGUAGE

"To have another language is to possess a second soul."

— Charlemagne
Francian King, Holy Roman Emperor
4/2/742 – 1/28/814

Studying a foreign language helps to provide a deep and abiding insight into how others view the world we share. Words, and the manner in which they are structured (etymology), reflect a culture's history and give us an understanding of their outlook on life, work, family, friendships, and even beauty.

Knowing a language different from your own allows you to experience an existence that is different — separate, yet familiar — from everything that you take for granted. It also shows us how very much we all have in common.

Io studio italiano. Studi una lingua straniera?

———————◇———————

Charlemagne, or Charles the Great, was a warrior king who established the most powerful Christian kingdom of the Middle Ages. Originally comprised of France, Luxembourg, the Netherlands, and western Germany, Charlemagne's empire grew to encompass almost all of Western Europe, leading some to call him the father of Europe. He promoted education and learning — he could speak Latin and understood Greek, as well as other languages — and was the driving force behind the First Renaissance.

Charlemagne was crowned Emperor of the Romans by Pope Leo III on December 25, in the year 800, at St. Peter's Basilica in Rome. He died in 814 and was buried at the cathedral in Aachen, in western Germany.

April 3rd

BLAME

"A man can fail many times, but he isn't a failure
until he begins to blame somebody else."

— John Burroughs
American Naturalist, Essayist
4/3/1837 – 3/29/1921

Everybody fails. There is not a single person alive who has not failed at least once. The differences between us lie in how we react to our failures, and they are twofold: whether we get back up when we fall, and whether we take responsibility ourselves or try to shift the blame onto others. In the end, it isn't about our plan, or our effort, or our outcome; it's about our character.

Today, we would call John Burroughs an environmentalist. Long active in the conservation movement, he lived and wrote much like Henry David Thoreau, and he considered Walt Whitman to be an inspiration as much as any mountain, field, or stream. An avid fly fisherman, he was friends with fellow outdoorsmen Teddy Roosevelt and John Muir.

Burroughs wrote about nature for over half a century, much of it from his farm in the Hudson River valley. His best-known works include *Wake-Robin*, *Birds and Poets*, and *Signs and Seasons*. The John Burroughs Association, established to honor his remarkable legacy of in-depth study and exceptional writing on nature and natural history, continues to this day.

April 4th

MODESTY

"Modesty seldom resides in a breast that is
not enriched with nobler virtues."

— Oliver Goldsmith
Irish Novelist, Playwright, Poet
11/10/1728 – 4/4/1774

It's one thing to know that you are capable, or even exceptional; it is quite another to call attention to that fact yourself.

Always let others sing your praises. A person who is accomplished yet humble is doubly admired.

------◇------

Oliver Goldsmith was a study in contradictions. He attended medical school in Edinburgh but abandoned medicine to become a writer. He wrote incredibly erudite prose, and yet was also a gifted poet. He is known for the novel *The Vicar of Wakefield*, the play *She Stoops to Conquer*, and the poem "The Deserted Village."

Unsophisticated and not particularly attractive — he was considered ugly by some — Goldsmith was nonetheless beloved by his friends and contemporaries, most of whom considered him an odd and eccentric man. Although he was a confident and polished author who reached millions, he was utterly inept and ineloquent in social situations. Having become rich and successful, he found himself constantly in debt due to his own extravagance. Through it all, Goldsmith maintained an unfailingly gracious view of humanity and the human condition.

ACCOUNTABILITY

"Few things can help an individual more than to place responsibility
on him, and to let him know that you trust him."

— Booker T. Washington
American Educator, Author, Orator
4/5/1856 – 11/14/1915

There is a light inside each and every one of us, and it seldom glows brighter than when we are given the opportunity to be useful, to contribute toward a common goal, to validate a faith freely placed in us. If you want to see somebody work for you, really *get after it*, surprise them by assigning them an important task — with the leeway to get the job done as they see fit and with full responsibility for the outcome. Whether you're a three-year-old or a thirty-year veteran, nothing motivates us like being given the chance to show what we can do.

Booker Taliaferro Washington was the author of five books and an advisor to presidents, but he is probably best known as the founder of Tuskegee University and for being one of the foremost voices of the African-American community for twenty-five years.

Born into slavery in Virginia, Washington put himself through school and became a teacher after the Civil War. In 1881, he founded the Tuskegee Normal and Industrial Institute, an agricultural college in Alabama, and in 1901 he became the first African-American to have dinner at the White House with the president (Theodore Roosevelt).

Consistently espousing values of hard work and strong moral character, Washington was a tireless champion of human rights until his death in 1915.

April 6th

OPPORTUNITY

"The ladder of success is best climbed by
stepping on the rungs of opportunity."

— Ayn Rand
Russian-American Novelist, Philosopher
2/2/1905 – 3/6/1982

Opportunity can be a surreptitious thing — you just never know where or when it will present itself. The best piece of advice I ever received is to treat everyone with dignity and respect and a smile on your face, and to do all that you can do to help them when you can. Whether you are a company's janitor or its CEO, you never know when you will need help — and trust me, you are going to need help.

You would be surprised how often it turns out that the smallest kindness you did (or did not do) for someone will be remembered when you are in trouble and they are in a position to help. It may not always seem like it at the time, but your behavior — being a "good citizen" — is an opportunity generator, and the person you help the most is usually yourself.

———◆———

Ayn Rand is best known for her novels *The Fountainhead* and *Atlas Shrugged*, and for her staunch defense of capitalism, which she believed is the only truly moral social system.

Born in St. Petersburg, Russia, Rand witnessed the Russian Revolution in 1917 and the subsequent birth of the Union of Soviet Socialist Republics (USSR). Her father, a successful pharmacist, had his shop confiscated by the Communists, which infuriated Rand. In 1926, she managed to escape under the pretext of a brief visit to family in America. She never went back, and in 1931 she became an American citizen.

Rand is also associated with Objectivism, a philosophy that advocates for the use of reason, independent thinking, individual rights, and free-market capitalism.

April 7th

CONFLICT

"Difficulties are meant to rouse, not discourage.
The human spirit is to grow strong by conflict."

— William Ellery Channing
American Theologian
4/7/1780 – 10/2/1842

What do you do when difficulties arise? Do you fold like a house of cards, or do you make an effort to address your problems like a grown-up?

We all have issues. We all have challenges. We all have responsibilities, and we all face uncertainties. What sets us apart is how we react to our individual trials, and what we learn from our tribulations. Once you accept that things are going to happen, that you are going to have to take action to fix what is broken, to right what is wrong, you are halfway home.

Problems are opportunities for accomplishment. And every triumph, every *effort*, is another brick in your wall. Keep on building. Let's see what you can do.

———————◇———————

After graduating first in his class at Harvard, William Ellery Channing studied for the ministry and was ordained in 1802. The following year he was called to preach at Boston's Federal Street Church, where he would serve as minister for nearly forty years.

Considered one of Unitarianism's leading theologians, Channing was a passionate and articulate champion of human rights, and a dynamic speaker whose views on social reform were as well-received overseas as they were in the United States. His books were translated into several languages and it was believed that Alexis de Tocqueville, John Stuart Mill, Max Weber, and Queen Victoria were among his most avid readers.

UNCERTAINTY

"Uncertainty is the only certainty there is, and knowing
how to live with insecurity is the only security."

— John Allen Paulos
American Mathematics Professor
Born 7/4/1945

It is a simple thing to understand: We have relatively little control over most of the things that happen in our lives. That is the nature of life. What we do have is the ability to reason; to differentiate; to estimate the overall likelihood of different events actually occurring — and how much time and worry we should expend on those possibilities.

Don't allow the "what-ifs" to consume your every waking thought. You'll be fine — and if not, you'll deal with that, too.

———————◇———————

A prolific author and popular public speaker, mathematics professor John Allen Paulos has written numerous scholarly papers on probability, logic, and the philosophy of science. Paulos has been published in the *New York Times*, *The Wall Street Journal*, *American Scholar*, *Forbes*, and the *London Review of Books*. He has also written monthly columns for ABC News, the *Scientific American*, and *The Guardian*, and has lectured extensively on the importance of mathematical literacy — in particular, statistics and probabilities.

PROCRASTINATION

"There is no such thing as a long piece of work,
except one that you dare not start."

— Charles Baudelaire
French Poet, Essayist
4/9/1821 – 8/31/1867

On a certain level, procrastination can feel pretty good. All we have to do is convince ourselves that we have plenty of time, that we'll get started "later," that it isn't a big deal anyway, and besides, if it doesn't get done, well, the consequences really aren't all *that* bad.

The problem with shirking our responsibilities is that things pile up; what was once a manageable schedule is now a calendar of red letter days, each one a fire threatening to burn out of control.

Some call it laziness; some call it leisure. In either case, *earn* your free time — and ditch that nagging pressure.

Charles Pierre Baudelaire was a French poet who is perhaps best known for *Les Fleurs du mal* (The Flowers of Evil), which some consider one of the most influential poetry collections of the nineteenth century. Baudelaire also worked as an essayist, art critic, and translator, and it was while working to translate the poetry of Edgar Allen Poe that Baudelaire discovered how similar the two of them were. Solitary by nature and given to moods of intense melancholy, he was amazed to find that the American writer's temperament so thoroughly mirrored his own.

Baudelaire was known as an extravagant spendthrift, and he burned through half of his inheritance in two years. Many of his works were published posthumously, too late to save him from the accumulation of debt that hounded him for much of his life.

HYPOCRISY

"The only vice that cannot be forgiven is hypocrisy.
The repentance of a hypocrite is itself hypocrisy."

— William Hazlitt
English Writer, Critic, Philosopher
4/10/1778 – 9/18/1830

Most of us are fairly quick to pardon our fellow man. We readily accept that "everyone makes mistakes," and that "to forgive is divine." And if the offender demonstrates a modicum of contrition, well, we're usually ready to move on. However, when it comes to forgiving those who have betrayed their own high-flown (and oft-repeated) principles, we take a special joy in knocking them off of their high horse. And the sad and simple truth is, we seldom let them forget it.

Hypocrisy is a betrayal of character. Never give others the chance to reconsider the person you have convinced them you are.

———————◇———————

William Hazlitt was an exceptionally talented English writer, critic, painter, and philosopher, considered by some to be on par with Samuel Johnson and George Orwell.

As a boy, Hazlitt went to the New College at Hackney, a Unitarian seminary, but he lost his faith, left the school, and decided to study philosophy. By 1798, he had moved to Paris and taken up painting. He became good enough to earn a paltry living by painting copies of the "Old Masters" that hung in the Louvre.

In 1812, married and broke, Hazlitt took a job in London, at the *Morning Chronicle*, where he quickly earned a reputation as a brilliant essayist and a leading Shakespearean critic. Percy Bysshe Shelley, John Keats, and William Wordsworth were counted among his friends and admirers.

Hazlitt's career took off, but it would be marked by a series of personal and professional setbacks, much of them attributed to drinking. He developed stomach cancer and died in 1830. His last words were, "Well, I've had a happy life."

APPETITE

"Subdue your appetites, my dears, and
you've conquered human nature."

— Charles Dickens
English Author
2/7/1812 – 6/9/1870

To some extent, we are all slaves to our desires. No matter how hard we try, it seems there are certain people and particular things that we simply cannot resist; certain urges that we consistently struggle to defy. Yet try we must, for we are not barbarians, and it is our struggles that make us human.

To say that Charles John Huffam Dickens was an English writer would be an understatement of monumental proportions. The creator of some of the world's best-known fictional characters is universally acclaimed as a literary genius and is quite possibly the greatest novelist of all time.

As prolific as he was influential, Dickens wrote one best-seller after another, including *Oliver Twist, A Christmas Carol, David Copperfield, Great Expectations*, and *A Tale of Two Cities*. His books were extraordinarily popular during his lifetime, and are still widely read today.

Dickens suffered a stroke and died in 1870, leaving behind one final, albeit unfinished novel, *The Mystery of Edwin Drood*. In spite of his wishes, he was buried in Poet's Corner at Westminster Abbey, where hundreds of thousands of people lined up to walk past his body.

April 12th

COURTESY

"Courtesies of a small and trivial character are the ones
which strike deepest in the grateful and appreciating heart."

— Henry Clay
American Lawyer, Politician
4/12/1777 – 6/29/1852

What may seem to the giver to be nothing may in fact be everything to the receiver. If you've ever had "one of those days," when everyone and everything seemed to be going against you, and someone showed you the smallest kindness, just when you needed it most, then you know exactly what I mean.

Henry Clay, Sr. was a lawyer and statesman who represented Kentucky in both the United States Senate and the House of Representatives. He was also one of those people who seemed to have a knack for not only brushing up against history, repeatedly, but also for having an impact upon it.

As a young lawyer, Clay represented Aaron Burr, who was accused of treason in 1806 for planning to carve out a new empire in the Spanish-held American southwest. Clay believed his client was innocent, and Burr was acquitted, but Clay would find out later that Burr was guilty. Livid, he never spoke to Burr again.

As a member of the House of Representatives, Clay helped President Madison lead the country into war with Britain in 1812, and in 1814 he helped to negotiate the Treaty of Ghent, which ended the war.

In 1824, as Speaker of the House, Clay's support of John Quincy Adams ensured that Adams would win the presidency during a run-off election, defeating John C. Calhoun, Andrew Jackson, and Clay himself.

On June 29, 1852, Clay succumbed to tuberculosis. His body was laid in state in the Capitol rotunda, the first ever to receive that honor.

April 13th

RIDICULE

"Resort is had to ridicule only when reason is against us."

— Thomas Jefferson
American President
4/13/1743 – 7/4/1826

Saul Alinsky called ridicule "man's most potent weapon," because a quick and clever insult is generally a good distraction. It buys time; it gains support among at least some of the audience; and it deflects attention away from a simple truth: that you are losing the fight.

If you want to debate the issues, come armed with the facts; make use of reason; and apply logic. Most of all, be respectful. The reputation you save is undeniably your own.

———————◇———————

Thomas Jefferson was an American Founding Father and the third president of the United States, serving from 1801 to 1809. Although he is often credited with being the author of the Declaration of Independence — a distinction he would insist upon for the rest of his life — Jefferson didn't do it alone. The Second Continental Congress appointed a committee of five to draft a declaration. The co-authors included John Adams, Benjamin Franklin, Roger Sherman, and Robert Livingston. Jefferson was tasked with the physical act of writing the document, which underwent a number of revisions before being presented to the Congress on July 1, 1776. The first signatures were added, in earnest, on July 4th.

On July 4th, 1826, both Jefferson and Adams died on the same day — exactly fifty years after the signing of the Declaration of Independence. Unaware that Jefferson had died that morning, Adams's last words were "Jefferson lives."

Thomas Jefferson was buried at his beloved estate, Monticello. His grave is marked by an obelisk with an epitaph he wrote for himself.

INDIFFERENCE

"The most destructive criticism is indifference."

— E. W. Howe
American Novelist, Editor
5/3/1853 – 10/3/1937

If silence can speak volumes, indifference is a universal translator. Nothing says more with less than indifference, and what it says (quite succinctly) is this: I could not possibly care any less about it, about you, or about your opinion.

Indifference can exasperate an enemy and devastate a friend. Use it sparingly.

———————◇———————

Edgar Watson Howe was a novelist, editor, and iconoclast of the late nineteenth and early twentieth centuries. His best-known novel is *The Story of a Country Town*, which painted a realistic portrayal of life in a small Midwestern town. He would have known a lot about the subject, having grown up in Wabash County, Indiana, before moving with his family to Bethany, Missouri.

By age twelve, Howe was an apprentice printer, and at nineteen he took the reins as the publisher of *The Golden Globe*, a newspaper in Golden Colorado. Known as much for his pessimism as his witty editorials, a collection of his journalistic essays was published in 1933, with the title *The Indignations of E. W. Howe*.

In 1937, Edgar Howe died and was buried in Atchison, Kansas, where he had founded the *Atchison Daily Globe* sixty years earlier.

April 15th

AUTHORITY

"Nothing strengthens authority so much as silence."

— Leonardo da Vinci

Italian Artist, Polymath

4/15/1452 – 5/2/1519

When we fail to protest overreach, we fortify the perceived authority of the action and embolden the tyrant behind it. Acquiescence implies consent. Don't look the other way; if something is wrong, if someone has assumed a power not granted, say something — or be prepared to live with the consequences.

Leonardo da Vinci was an Italian polymath of the Renaissance. Perhaps best known for the *Mona Lisa*, or *The Last Supper*, or even *The Vitruvian Man*, his genius endures, but the man himself remains a mystery five hundred years after his death.

While he left behind over fifty notebooks, many of which provide exquisitely detailed renderings of his inventions, as well as copious notes on his many scientific inquiries, Da Vinci divulged little personal information. Historians have speculated that he was a vegetarian (for humanitarian reasons), and that he may have been homosexual (he was accused but acquitted of sodomy when he was twenty-two). He was said to have been amiable but aloof; stylish, graceful, and generous.

Of course, we do know that Da Vinci had an insatiable curiosity about virtually everything, from science and engineering to literature and languages. Alas, Da Vinci's various interests often sidetracked him, and he left behind a great many unfinished projects. "Art is never finished," he declared, "only abandoned."

COWARDICE

"Courage is often lack of insight, whereas cowardice
in many cases is based on good information."

— Peter Ustinov
English Actor, Writer, Director
4/16/1921 – 3/28/2004

For all intents and purposes, courage and bravery are synonymous. However, it is actually bravery that involves an action (or reaction) based on instinct, with no regard for danger, while courage is doing something even when we know it is dangerous. In any case, sometimes it isn't what we see, or hear, but what we feel. We are blessed with intuition for a reason — always trust your gut, and never be afraid to be afraid. Fear can save your life.

———————◇———————

Sir Peter Alexander Ustinov was an actor, screenwriter, director, and comedian who was equally at home playing a role on film, directing an opera, giving voice to an animated character, or acting in a play. A skilled story-teller and humorist, his talents for vocal mimicry and physical comedy made him a popular guest on late-night talk shows. He appeared in over a hundred film and television productions, and won two Best Supporting Oscars: one for his role in *Spartacus* (1960) and one for his role in *Topkapi* (1964).

Ustinov had ancestral connections to Russian nobility, as well as to the Ethiopian Royal Family. Fluent in Russian, French, German, and Italian, he served as a Goodwill ambassador for UNICEF and received that organization's Medal for Distinguished Service in 1993.

MINDFULNESS

"The only true source of politeness is consideration."

— William Gilmore Simms
American Poet, Novelist, Historian
4/17/1806 – 6/11/1870

To be mindful of others is to simply be aware of the impact our own conduct has on those around us. Too often we act without thinking, our actions mere reflexes, tripped by the selfish and greedy impulses hard-wired into our psyche. But there are other things lurking in our consciousness: the desire for friendship, the need for companionship, and an understanding that compassion and cooperation underpins them both.

We can't always help ourselves, but if we take a moment, we often find that in being considerate of others, we are doing just that.

———————◇———————

William Gilmore Simms was a poet, novelist and historian. Simms was a prominent writer in the pre-war South, and Edgar Allan Poe declared him "the best novelist America had ever produced." Many of his stories follow the trajectory of the American South, from colonial times into the antebellum period. His best known works include *The Yemassee, The Partisan*, and *The Golden Christmas*.

Before the war, Simms worked as an editor for several South Carolina newspapers and served in the State Legislature from 1844 to 1846. When the war ended, his home and library destroyed by Sherman's army, Simms nearly worked himself to death, taking on every writing and editing job he could find in order to support his impoverished family.

EMOTIONS

"The degree of one's emotions varies inversely
with one's knowledge of the facts."

— Bertrand Russell
British Philosopher, Nobel Laureate
5/18/1872 – 2/2/1970

Emotions have a time and place, but never allow them to cloud your ability to think critically and speak clearly. No matter how strongly you feel about an issue, you will never be able to persuade others if you are armed only with emotions. The facts always speak for themselves, and do so much more eloquently, and effectively, than feelings.

———————◇———————

Bertrand Arthur William Russell, 3rd Earl Russell, was a British philosopher, mathematician, historian, and writer (he won the Nobel Prize for Literature in 1950). Although best known for his work in mathematical logic, Russell is widely considered to be one of the founders of modern analytic philosophy (which also relies heavily on logic).

A social critic and political activist, Russell self-identified as a liberal, a socialist, and a pacifist, but he also confessed that he had never really committed to any of these ideologies "in any profound sense." It was during WWI that Russell first became involved in anti-war activities, and in 1918 he spent six months in prison for writing anti-war propaganda. He would be imprisoned again, in 1961, aged eighty, for inciting people to civil disobedience during his involvement in anti-nuclear protests. He was also opposed to, and protested against, the war in Vietnam.

INSTINCT

"The very essence of instinct is that it's followed independently of reason."

— Charles Darwin
English Naturalist, Biologist, Geologist
2/12/1809 – 4/19/1882

Sometimes it is best to trust your instincts, because sometimes your instincts are all you have. And sometimes, they are all you need.

———◇———

Charles Robert Darwin was an English naturalist, geologist and biologist, best known for developing a theory to explain the biological adaptation and subtle transformation of creatures over time, usually in response to environmental change.

On December 27, 1831, Darwin boarded the HMS Beagle, a Royal Navy research ship, to begin a five-year voyage of discovery that would take him around the world. When he returned to England in 1836, Darwin began to write a multi-volume book describing the exotic plants and animals he had seen. The trip would spur Darwin to reconsider and reexamine everything he knew about scientific evidence. Gradually, these thoughts led to the development of a new and highly controversial theory about the origin and evolution of life on Earth, which was published in his ground-breaking book, *On the Origin of Species by Means of Natural Selection*, in 1859.

Although initially met with skepticism and derision, eventually his "theory of evolution" gained worldwide acceptance and is known today simply as "Darwinism." Charles Robert Darwin died in April 1882, and was buried at Westminster Abbey.

April 20th

CENSORSHIP

"Once you permit those who are convinced of their own superior rightness
to censor and silence and suppress those who hold contrary opinions,
just at that moment the citadel has been surrendered."

— Archibald MacLeish
American Writer, Poet
5/7/1892 – 4/20/1982

In a free and open society, the right of citizens to say what they think,
feel, and believe is as fundamental as the right to associate with whom you
wish, to be treated fairly under the law, and to have a reasonable assumption
of privacy. Those whom you cannot criticize, and with whom you cannot
disagree, are not your fellow citizens; they are your masters.

———————◇———————

After serving with the Yale Mobile Hospital Unit in France during WWI,
Archibald MacLeish returned to Harvard Law School, where he graduated at
the head of his class. He spent the next three years practicing law in Boston
before he and his wife, Ada, moved to Paris, joining a coterie of expats that
included Ernest Hemingway, F. Scott Fitzgerald, Cole Porter, Gertrude Stein,
and Dorothy Parker.

Considered a modernist poet, Archibald MacLeish is best known for his
poems "Ars Poetica," "The End of the World," "Eleven," and "Not Marble
Nor the Gilded Monuments." In 1933, he would win a Pulitzer Prize for
Conquistador, and his *Collected Poems 1917–1952* would win another Pulitzer
in 1953. He won a third Pulitzer Prize, for his play *J.B.*, in 1959. As a Professor
of Rhetoric and Oratory at Harvard, MacLeish taught creative writing and
poetry until he retired, in 1962.

April 21st

GRIEF

"Grief is the price we pay for love."

— Queen Elizabeth II
English Queen
4/21/1926 ~

If everything has a cost, and the cost of a thing is commensurate to its value, then we rightly should pay a very high price indeed for love. And the thing is? We do. We surely do, and we gladly do. Again, and again, and again.

———◇———

Elizabeth Alexandra Mary Windsor was born in London, the first child of the Duke and Duchess of York. In 1936, her parents became King George VI and Queen Elizabeth when her father's brother, King Edward VIII, abdicated the throne to marry Wallis Simpson, an American divorcee.

Elizabeth began to take on public duties during World War II, and she became Queen when her father died in 1952. Married to Prince Philip since 1947, they have four children. Their oldest, Prince Charles, is first in line to succeed the Queen, who has served as a constitutional monarch for nearly seventy years — the longest tenure in the history of the United Kingdom.

April 22nd

RELIGION

"Religion is the recognition of all our duties as divine commands."

— Immanuel Kant
German Philosopher
4/22/1724 – 2/12/1804

If you are a religious person, there are certain moral imperatives, and certain cultural and social norms, that seem to be shared across almost all belief systems: the idea that life is sacred, that theft is wrong, that we should love our neighbor. Our obedience to these or similar aphorisms is, in a very real sense, an homage to the One of our chosen faith.

Even if you are not a religious person, and do not believe that the rules that guide our behavior are divine in origin, chances are you do agree with and/or consent to them because, if nothing else, it is readily apparent that they foster a more civilized life — for believers and non-believers alike.

———————◇———————

Immanuel Kant is considered a central figure in modern philosophy. He maintained that it is the human mind that constructs the framework of human experience, and that reason is the foundation of morality.

According to Kant, each individual acts according to their own subjective maxims: highly personalized rules or policies — "imperatives" — which express a desired goal or outcome. While we may be inconsistent in the actual pursuit of our desires, as rational human beings our default pre-disposition is to pursue them in a moral fashion.

Kant also postulated that we are inextricably tied to the idea of what he called "the highest good," a world in which complete virtue and complete happiness exists. He theorized that the pursuit of this ideal requires first and foremost that we believe it is attainable, which would naturally necessitate a belief in the immortality of the soul and the existence of God.

SCORN

"Of friends, however humble, scorn not one."

— William Wordsworth
English Poet
4/7/1770 – 4/23/1850

Friendship freely given has inestimable worth, just as being a false friend comes at an incalculable cost. If you do not genuinely care about those in your inner circle, let them go; part amicably, for it is better to end a relationship cleanly and with dignity than for either to labor under false pretenses. That road leads to enmity and contempt.

In 1795, William Wordsworth became friends with fellow poet Samuel Taylor Coleridge. The two soon began working together on *Lyrical Ballads*, an anthology of their poetry that included Wordsworth's "Tintern Abbey" and Coleridge's "Rime of the Ancient Mariner." Published in 1798, the duo's work helped to launch the English Romantic movement. Their circle of friends included fellow poets Percy Bysshe Shelley, John Keats, and George Gordon (Lord) Byron.

In 1843, Wordsworth became England's eleventh poet laureate. His epic autobiographical poem, *The Prelude*, which he worked on for over fifty years and would span fourteen books, was published upon his death, in 1850.

POVERTY

"As for poverty, no one need be ashamed to admit it;
the real shame is in not taking practical measures to escape it."

— Pericles
Greek General, Statesman, Orator
c. 494 BC – c. 429 BC

No one worth knowing really cares about what is in your wallet, what kind of car you drive, or how much you have in your bank account. The measure of a person's worth is never about their financial means, or the lack thereof. It is, and always will be, about their character. And the thing is? Character is something that the richest man can't buy for all the money in the world, and the poorest man doesn't have to spend a penny to possess.

It is what we do in this life, and how we go about it, that really matters.

———————————◦———————————

According to the historian Thucydides, Pericles was considered "the first citizen" of democratic Athens. A well-known and influential Greek statesman, orator, and general, Pericles was also a prominent patron of the arts and a leading politician who used his influence to fund vast cultural projects in Athens, including the construction of the Parthenon, the Erechthelon, and the temple of Athena Nike.

In the summer of 430 BC, an epidemic broke out and devastated the Athenians. Historians are unable to identify the disease with any certainty, but it is generally thought to have been typhus or typhoid fever. Pericles lost two sons during the epidemic, and he himself would succumb to it the following year.

April 25th

SECURITY

"It's an old adage that the way to be safe is never to be secure...
Each one of us requires the spur of insecurity to force us to do our best."

— Harold W. Dodds
American President of Princeton
6/28/1889 – 10/25/1980

Security — economic security, in particular, but also physical and emotional security — tends to erode our sense of urgency, about almost everything. Security makes us lazy, in other words, and it also makes us less aware, less curious, and less interested in seeking out new opportunities.

The simple truth is, the more satisfied we are with the status quo, the more complacent we become. Conversely, look at what a little desperation will do: If you need firewood to warm your house, guess what? You'll learn to love chopping wood.

———————————◆———————————

Harold Willis Dodds was the fifteenth President of Princeton University. Born in Utica, Pennsylvania, he received his Bachelor's degree at Grove City College in 1909 and began his teaching career at a public school. He continued his education, earning a Master's degree at Princeton in 1914 and a PhD at the University of Pennsylvania in 1917. During World War I, Dodds worked in the U.S. Food Administration, and returned to teaching after the war, at Western Reserve University. During this time, he became involved with the National Municipal League, and was soon advising the President of Nicaragua, helping to ensure their elections were free and fair. Dodds returned to Princeton in 1925 to take a job as a professor, and in 1933 he was appointed president, a position he held until he retired in 1957.

PUNCTUALITY

"Better three hours too soon than a minute too late."

— William Shakespeare
English Poet, Playwright, Actor
4/26/1564 – 4/23/1616

There is nothing more valuable than time — undisputedly our most precious commodity — yet how often we waste it, lose track of it, or sleep through it. We take our time for granted, and that is certainly our prerogative, but here's something else to ponder: Have you ever taken a moment to consider what it means to squander someone else's time?

William Shakespeare, the "Bard of Avon," is considered England's national poet and is universally acknowledged as the greatest writer to ever use the English language. He wrote thirty-seven plays, including *Hamlet*, *Romeo and Juliet*, *Macbeth*, *The Taming of the Shrew*, and *Richard III*. He also composed 154 sonnets. "Shall I compare thee to a summer's day?" and "To me, fair friend, you never can be old" are a couple that may be familiar to you.

The cause of Shakespeare's death is unknown, although some scholars have speculated that he may have died of typhus. His plays continue to be staged all over the world, validating his friend (and fellow playwright) Ben Jonson's proclamation that Shakespeare "was not of an age, but for all time."

DIGNITY

"How can a rational being be ennobled by any thing
that is not obtained by its own exertions?"

— Mary Wollstonecraft
English Writer, Philosopher
4/27/1759 – 9/10/1797

We place far more value on the things we make than on the things we buy, and the same is true of the things we earn versus the things that are given to us. Surely we appreciate a thoughtful gift from a friend or family member, but sentimentality aside, most of us also understand the value of dignity. While it is imperative to give when we can, and take when we must, self-respect dictates that we eschew charity when we are fully capable of making our own way in life.

Mary Wollstonecraft was a writer, philosopher, feminist, and fervent activist for women's equality. Although she wrote novels, a history of the French Revolution, a hugely successful Scandinavian travelogue, and even a children's book, she is best known for *A Vindication of the Rights of Woman*, a book that was considered highly controversial in its time. What was so scandalous? Wollstonecraft put forth the idea that women are not fragile, defenseless creatures, and that the use of such antiquated ideas to deny women the same (equal) educational opportunities that were afforded to men did irreparable harm to the dignity of both sexes.

Wollstonecraft had two daughters. In 1797, she delivered her second daughter, Mary (who would become the celebrated author of *Frankenstein*). Wollstonecraft would die, ten days later, due to complications of childbirth.

CURIOSITY

"Satisfaction of one's curiosity is one of the
greatest sources of happiness in life."

— Linus Pauling
American Scientist, Humanitarian
2/28/1901 – 8/19/1994

Have you ever been in a situation where you aren't supposed to move — or worse yet, where you can't move — and all you can think about is how desperate you are to move? How wonderful it would be, your mind says, to stretch that leg, to yawn that yawn, to blink, to swallow. Indeed, curiosity is that irresistible itch, that tantalizing mental puzzle that will not go away until you solve it. You may as well go for it; you won't be satisfied until you do.

———————◦———————

Linus Carl Pauling was born with a mind full of questions, and he spent a lifetime chasing down the answers. His inquisitive nature led to a great many important discoveries in a variety of different disciplines, including chemistry, medicine, psychiatry, and nutrition, and he is credited with being the founding father of molecular biology. He was the author or co-author of more than a thousand papers and books, including *The Nature of the Chemical Bond*, which is widely acknowledged as being one of the most influential scientific books ever written.

Pauling is generally considered to be one of the two greatest scientific minds of the twentieth century (the other being Einstein), and *New Scientist* called him one of the twenty greatest scientists of all time. He was also a winner of the Nobel Peace Prize. In fact, he is the only person ever to be awarded two unshared Nobel Prizes: one for Chemistry, in 1954, and another for Peace, in 1962.

April 29th

INTRIGUE

"If you pass something every day and it has a little character,
it begins to intrigue you."

— Frank Auerbach
German-British Painter
4/29/1931

Explore things: objects, ideas, historical events; anything that grabs your interest. Going beyond the headline, delving a little deeper into a subject, demonstrating a little intellectual curiosity: This is how you grow your Self.

———◇———

Frank Helmut Auerbach was born in Berlin, but his parents, who would later perish in a concentration camp, were able to get him out of Germany, sending him to England in 1939. Known as a figurative artist — his work is recognizable, based on real people and objects as opposed to abstract art — Auerbach often paints the same people and street scenes over and over again. His technique is unique, in that he often paints an image, scrapes it off his canvas, and then repaints it, the result being a multi-layered piece of textured art.

Most of Auerbach's exhibitions have been in Europe, but his work has been shown around the world. In 2016, his "Head of Gerda Boehm," once owned by David Bowie, fetched $4.7 million at auction. Mr. Auerbach continues to live and work near Camden Town, in northwest London.

April 30th

ZEAL

"Never let your zeal outrun your charity.
The former is but human, the latter is divine."

— Hosea Ballou
American Theologian
4/30/1771 – 6/6/1852

It's one thing to talk about doing good deeds — even the thought of helping someone else makes us feel better about ourselves — but as we know, it is quite another thing to actually follow through. That's the sweet spot, for giving is itself a gift given twice.

You have it in you to make a difference, large or small. Extending a hand mustn't always be of a monetary nature; after all, some of us are struggling to make ends meet ourselves. What we do have, however, is time, talent, and energy. The trick is to have *determination*, as well.

———◇———

Hosea Ballou is one of the founders of American Universalism. Born and raised a Baptist, he converted to Universalism in 1789. He started preaching in 1791, and was officially ordained in 1794. He led several small-town congregations — in Vermont, New Hampshire, and Massachusetts — before he was named pastor of the Second Universalist Church of Boston, in 1817.

In addition to sermons, hymns, and theological essays, Ballou edited two Universalist journals and is perhaps best known for his book, *A Treatise on Atonement*. Written in 1805, Ballou's views were considered radical for their time, as he sought to break away from Calvinism and the Trinitarian doctrine. Insisting that scripture should be interpreted through the use of logic and reason, Ballou maintained that an infinite God loves human beings beyond measure; that He wants to see them happy; and that humans are incapable of truly offending God.

REWARD

"He who hasn't tasted bitter things hasn't earned sweet things."

— Gottfried Leibniz

German Philosopher, Polymath

7/1/1646 – 11/14/1716

It isn't that we must endure pain or suffering in order to *earn* our happiness, but those who have borne the former certainly do tend to have a greater appreciation for the latter. Perhaps there is a lesson here. Perhaps it isn't about getting what we think we deserve, but about being grateful for each and every little thing that comes our way, even when it is bittersweet.

Gottfried Wilhelm Leibniz was a philosopher and polymath, and one of the great thinkers of the seventeenth and eighteenth centuries. He is credited with making substantial contributions in the fields of logic, mathematics, physics, geology, and philosophy, among many others.

Sent to Paris on a diplomatic mission in 1672, Leibniz met many of the major intellectual figures of the time, including the Dutch mathematician Christiaan Huygens, who became Leibniz's mentor. It was during his time in Paris that Leibniz began to formulate his ideas for differential calculus — a field in which Isaac Newton was simultaneously toiling. He also designed a machine capable of making rudimentary calculations involving addition, subtraction, multiplication, and division.

Leibniz is regarded as one of the last universal geniuses. His contemporary, Denis Diderot, remarked that "Perhaps never has a man read as much, studied as much, meditated more, and written more than Leibniz." Gottlob Frege, thought by many to be the father of analytic philosophy, said of Leibniz, "He is virtually in a class of his own."

May 2nd

CRITICISM

"I praise loudly. I blame softly."

— Catherine the Great
Russian Empress
5/2/1729 – 11/17/1796

As a leader, one of your primary goals is to motivate those around you — and to keep them motivated. There are few better ways to accomplish this than to extend compliments in public and to keep criticisms private.

The word "criticism" has a generally negative connotation because many view it as a personal attack, when in reality it is a tool, a blueprint to be used to drive improvement. The next time you are critiquing someone's effort, be sure to temper the former and emphasize the latter.

———————⚬———————

Catherine II, also known as Catherine the Great, was born Princess Sophie of Anhalt-Zerbst, the eldest daughter of an impoverished Prussian (German) prince. She ascended to the throne when her husband, Peter III, was ousted during a rebellion she led against him. As Empress of Russia, Catherine would become the country's longest-serving female leader (1762 – 1796).

Although she wasn't particularly good-looking, Catherine was intelligent, energetic, and possessed of considerable charm — enough to maintain a lifelong correspondence with Voltaire. One of Europe's most enlightened rulers at the time, Catherine was well-read, a champion of the arts, and determined to steer her country toward the cultural and philosophical influences of Western Europe. Under her leadership, Russia became a major player on the European stage, and to this day Catherine II remains a source of national pride for many Russians.

POLITICS

"Politics have no relation to morals."

— Niccolo Machiavelli
Italian Diplomat, Philosopher, Historian
5/3/1469 – 6/21/1527

Despite all campaign promises to the contrary, and no matter how much we want to believe in the character of our candidate, politics are about getting things done, and morals are often the first sacrifice of an ambitious politician. It's almost as if they believe they are two separate beings: the politician, and the person. They aren't separate, and neither are we.

Niccolò di Bernardo dei Machiavelli, whose name is synonymous with intrigue, deceit, and cunning, was an Italian diplomat, politician, philosopher, historian, and writer of the Renaissance period. Often called the father of modern political science, Machiavelli's most famous work, *The Prince*, was published posthumously (in 1532) and it sealed his reputation as an amoral pragmatist.

Machiavelli's life was Gump-ian in its breadth of brushes with the rich, famous, and powerful. As head of the Florentine Republic's chancery, he often went on diplomatic missions that resulted in meetings with members of the French court, the court of the Holy Roman Emperor, the Borgias, and various Popes or their representatives. In 1513, he managed to get on the wrong side of the Medici family and was imprisoned, tortured, and eventually sent into exile. It seems he should have taken his own advice, and not "offend[ed] a prince and later put faith in him."

HABIT

"Habit is a cable; we weave a thread of it each day,
and at last we cannot break it."

— Horace Mann
American Educator, Politician
5/4/1796 – 8/2/1859

It is our routines and habits, and our customs and traditions, which define who we are, at our core. A wise person will examine their routines, from time to time, to make sure that their habits aren't leading them into harm; the last thing we want to do is to knit ourselves into a straightjacket.

Few did more in establishing and promoting the early American public school system than Horace Mann. A member of the Whig Party, Mann believed that education should be free and universal, non-denominational, and staffed by well-trained professional teachers.

Mann was a lawyer in Dedham, Massachusetts who gained renown for his legal acumen and oratorical skill. His political career began in 1827 when he won election to the Massachusetts House of Representatives. In 1837 he served as Secretary of the Massachusetts State Board of Education. Declaring that a republic will not remain free if its citizens are ignorant, Mann helped to initiate a vigorous reform movement of the public education system. Many of his innovations, including the ringing of bells between classes, are still in place today.

In 1848, Mann was elected to take the seat of former President John Quincy Adams, who had collapsed in the U.S. House of Representatives and died two days later. Like Adams, Mann was a fierce enemy of slavery.

In 1853, Mann accepted the presidency of Antioch College, a post he held until his death in 1859.

May 5th

LIFE

"Life can only be understood backwards; but it must be lived forwards."

— Soren Kierkegaard
Danish Philosopher, Poet, Theologian
5/5/1813 – 11/11/1855

Looking back is easy; at what we should have done and, just as likely, what we should not have done. There isn't much we can do about the past, and we can't know the future. The only real option we have is to be more mindful of the choices we are making in the here and now, knowing that one day we will be looking back on them — with pride, or regret.

———————◇———————

Soren Aabye Kierkegaard was a philosopher, theologian, poet, and social critic who is best known as the "father of existentialism." A profound and pro-lific writer, Kierkegaard often brought his intellect to bear on Christians, and Christendom, using creative re-imaginings of biblical figures to demonstrate their modern relevance. He also asserted that the only valid critique is one in which an entire life is examined, not merely the adherence to a particular philosophy. The question was: Although they talked the talk, did they walk the walk? In Kierkegaard's view, it is the totality of individual choices that will be judged by God.

INSULT

"The first human who hurled an insult instead of a stone
was the founder of civilization."

— Sigmund Freud
Austrian Neurologist, Psychoanalyst
5/6/1856 – 9/23/1939

The desire to retaliate can swamp our reason and overwhelm our senses, resulting in an almost completely autonomous, reflexive reaction. When we are wronged, we want revenge — and the sooner, the better. Such is human nature. However, have you ever snapped at someone, only to realize a moment later that it was an accident, or worse, that they weren't responsible for your pain? Could you have felt any worse about it?

It takes courage to de-escalate a situation. The good news is, we can overcome our instincts, and we can curb our desire for retribution; the first step is to understand that the actions we take in anger have a tendency to boomerang, bringing still more anger, and still more pain, often upon ourselves.

———————◇———————

Sigmund Freud is the founder of psychoanalysis, a "talking cure" in which a psychoanalyst attempts to identify and treat a patient's pathological behavior through an ongoing dialogue. Freud's breakthrough came while he was studying neuropathology at the Salpetriere clinic, in Paris, and it occurred to him that the root of psychological disorders may be mental instead of physical — rooted in the mind, instead of the brain. Working with patients classified as "hysterics," Freud realized that the act of talking seemed to provide a cathartic release for the patients, often freeing them of the emotional obstructions responsible for their irrational behavior.

TIME

"The butterfly counts not months but moments, and has time enough."

- Rabindranath Tagore
Indian Polymath, Nobel Laureate
5/7/1861 – 8/7/1941

Do you ever feel like there aren't enough hours in the day? Everyone does, from time to time, but what happens next? We either panic, or we prioritize; often we do both.

The truth is, with a little planning, there is always enough time to do what is most important to us, with those who are most important to us.

———————◇———————

Rabindranath Tagore wrote poetry, plays, short stories, and essays, and composed songs as well as paintings. He was known for his use of colloquial prose in Bengali literature, often writing poignant tales of "humble lives and their small miseries." Having spent a good amount of time in England as well as in his native India, Tagore's work is largely credited with introducing Indian culture to the West and vice versa. In 1913, Tagore became the first non-European to receive the Nobel Prize for Literature, and in 1915 he was awarded a knighthood. He is considered one of India's most talented and influential creative artists of all time.

SUFFERING

"The reward of suffering is experience."

— Harry S. Truman
American President
5/8/1884 – 12/26/1972

President Truman's words echo those of the Stoic philosopher Seneca, who said "A gem cannot be polished without friction, nor a man perfected without trials." It seems that woe and misery are largely unavoidable, and sometimes the best we can do is to learn from our tribulations so that we are prepared to face them if and when they should return.

———◇———

As soon as he took office as the 33rd President of the United States, upon the unexpected death of Franklin D. Roosevelt, Harry S. Truman faced one crisis after another. He did so with grace and aplomb.

America had been at war on two fronts, and shortly after Germany surrendered, Truman warned Japan that they must surrender or face "utter devastation." His plea was summarily rejected, forcing Truman to make the excruciating decision to drop atomic bombs on Hiroshima and Nagasaki. The Japanese surrendered on August 14th, and the war was officially over on September 2nd, 1945.

Truman was also known for his domestic policies, including the Fair Deal, but world affairs would continue to require his attention: the blockade of Berlin by the Soviet Union required a massive airlift of food and supplies; the U.S. was involved in escalating tensions in Korea; and the Cold War was beginning to intensify.

Through it all, Truman steered a steady course, and when it was over, he and his wife Bess left Washington, DC and drove home together, to their beloved Missouri.

ANIMOSITY

"Those whose character is mean and vicious
will rouse others to animosity against them."

— Xun Kuang
Chinese Confucian Philosopher
c. 310 BC – c. 238 BC

Have you ever noticed how those around you tend to mirror your expressions and body language? They do: If you smile, they smile; if you frown, they frown; and if you seem upbeat and positive, they will fall in line and follow your lead.

In our interactions with others, we usually get what we give. What are you putting out there?

———————◇———————

Xun Kuang, widely known as Xunzi, was one of three great Confucian philosophers of the classical period in China (the other two were Confucius and Mencius).

Although little is known of his early life, we do know that he lived during the Warring States period (475 – 221 BC), and that he was a contributor to the Hundred Schools of Thought. He was a prolific writer and much of his work, written in his own hand, survives to this day. There is also a book, called the *Xunzi*, which shares his name and has been attributed to him.

Xunzi's view of Confucianism is a bit darker than his contemporaries, who trusted in the innate goodness of human beings. Xunzi, on the other hand, believed that humanity's natural tendencies were inherently evil, and that societal norms were the primary civilizing influence, responsible for taming the immoral impulses that are present in all of us.

May 10th

INTENTIONS

"Our intention creates our reality."

— Wayne Dyer
American Philosopher, Author, Speaker
5/10/1940 – 8/29/2015

Our actions are defined first and foremost by our vision of the end we have in mind. Simply put: We do what we intend to do, whether according to a plan or "unintentionally" spurred by our subconscious desires. It is important, therefore, to carefully consider what it is that you hope to achieve, because honorable intentions translate into respectable actions a whole lot easier than dishonorable plans are abandoned.

———◇———

Wayne Walter Dyer was a philosopher, a motivational speaker, a self-help guru, and the author of thirty books. He is probably best known for his first book, *Your Erroneous Zones*, which has sold an estimated thirty-five million copies. The book spent sixty-four weeks on the *New York Times* bestseller list (1976/77) and is among the best-selling books of all time.

Dyer ran a private therapy practice, and was a high school guidance counselor in his hometown of Detroit. In the 1970s, he joined the faculty at St. John's University, in New York City, as a professor of counseling psychology. Soon, his lectures on positive thinking began to draw an audience beyond the students enrolled there.

In 2009, Dyer was diagnosed with chronic lymphocytic leukemia. He stated publicly that he felt he could eliminate the disease from his body through positive thinking. When he died in 2015, his Facebook page posted a coroner's report, which stated that "he did not have a trace of leukemia in his body."

EDUCATION

"There is no end to education. It is not that you read a book, pass an examination, and finish with education. The whole of life, from the moment you are born to the moment you die, is a process of learning."

— Jiddu Krishnamurti
Indian Philosopher, Speaker, Writer
5/11/1895 – 2/17/1986

Some are perpetual learners who constantly seek knowledge and wisdom, while for others knowledge is mostly a matter of happenstance: learning is merely a series of trials; ignorance the root of most errors. The former experience fewer traumas because of what they know; the latter experience more trauma because of what they don't.

———————◇———————

Born in Madanapalle, a small town in southern India, Jiddu Krishnamurti was groomed to become the World Teacher, or Maitreya, a guide who inspires humanity to align social priorities in order to create a more just and noble world. Instead, Krishnamurti broke with Theosophy and disavowed the ideas of organized religions, politics, and so-called gurus, calling all ideologies idiotic. He spent his life encouraging people to free their minds in the pursuit of truth.

May 12th

TRUST

"You may be deceived if you trust too much,
but you will live in torment if you don't trust enough."

— Frank Crane
American Minister, Speaker
5/12/1861 –11/5/1928

For most of us, trusting our fellow man is our default position: We generally take people at their word, and sometimes we get stung. It seems we can choose to trust everyone and risk being taken advantage of, on occasion, or we can trust no one and risk living a life of loneliness and seclusion. Which kind of world do you choose to live in?

Dr. Frank Crane was a Presbyterian minister, speaker, and popular columnist who was best known for his "Four Minute Essays," "If I Were Twenty-One," and "Everyday Wisdom." He was taking a trip around the world when he died, suddenly and unexpectedly, in Nice, France.

SINCERITY

"Sincerity is the way to heaven."

— Mencius
Chinese Philosopher
c. 372 BC – 289 BC

While there is no guarantee that sincerity is based on truth, or even reason, when all else fails, we tend to choose sides or make decisions based on little more than the perception of earnestness that we detect in our friends and family.

Sometimes we pay a price for going with our intuition, but it is far better to be the one who errs by putting trust in a friend than to be the one who loses a friend by abusing their trust.

Mencius was a philosopher whose contributions to the development of orthodox Confucianism earned him the title "second Sage" (after only Confucius himself). Above all, he believed in the innate goodness of humanity, and that every ruler had an obligation — a mandate from Heaven, no less — to provide for the material, day-to-day existence, as well as the moral and educational needs, of the common people. Although his campaign was unpopular among the Chinese princes — this was the age of Warring States (475 – 221 BC) — Mencius would tirelessly exhort them to honor their solemn duty to the Chinese people.

CONDEMNATION

"Someone has said that it takes less mental effort
to condemn than to think."

— Emma Goldman
Lithuanian Activist, Writer
6/27/1869 – 5/14/1940

Our prejudices and preconceptions often lead to snap judgments: we try, convict, and condemn people in the blink of an eye. These are tough forces to overcome because our first impressions are often based on past experiences — in other places, in other times, and with completely different people.

It's amazing how wrong we can be. However, if you make an effort to be aware of your biases, you can slow them down, take a closer look, and make a more nuanced and rational assessment. Easier said than done, for sure, but try.

───────────◇───────────

Emma Goldman was a political activist, an anarchist, and writer. Born in Lithuania and raised in Kaliningrad and St. Petersburg, Russia, she was known as "Red Emma," both for her heritage and her politics. Lionized as a free-thinker by the Left and denounced as a dangerous radical by the Right, she was a fiery speaker who could draw thousands. She inspired assassins, incited riots, and advocated violent revolution in both the United States and Europe as part of her anarchist political philosophy.

Goldman's U.S. citizenship was revoked in 1908, and in 1917 she was sentenced to two years in prison for agitating against World War I. When she was released in 1919, she was declared a subversive alien and was deported to the Soviet Union. She wrote about her experiences in her book, *My Disillusionment in Russia*.

HONESTY

"Confidence in others' honesty is no light testimony of one's own integrity."

— Michel Eyquem de Montaigne
French Philosopher
2/28/1533 – 9/13/1592

Nothing speaks more urgently to our assessment of someone's character than hearing them engage in gossip, rumor, or innuendo. These are the habits of low-integrity people, and should be recognized as such. If this is the esteem they extend unto others, what does it say about the regard they hold for you?

———————◇———————

Michel Eyquem de Montaigne is one of the most widely respected philosophers of the French Renaissance. He is known for his open-minded search for truth, and the autobiographical essays he wrote to document it.

As a member of the Parliament of Bordeaux, de Martaigne established a remarkable friendship with Etienne de la Boétie — a judge, writer, and philosopher. He called their relationship perfect and indivisible, and when La Boétie died unexpectedly, of dysentery, it was a devastating loss. One of his earliest essays, "On Friendship," is a stirring meditation on their closer-than-brothers relationship.

In 1570, de Montaigne retired to his family estate and dedicated himself to reading, meditating, and writing. By 1580, the first two books of his *Essays* were published (he would later publish a third). The *Essays* were very popular, and Voltaire, Jean Jacques Rousseau, and Gustav Flaubert were counted among his many admirers.

May 16th

POWER

"The measure of a man is what he does with power."

— Plato
Greek Philosopher, Teacher
c. 428 BC – c. 348 BC

Why is it that the folks least suited for power are so often the ones who crave it? You know the type: They have marginal people skills, yet they want to be in charge of people; they make poor choices, yet want to make all of the decisions; their life is a mess, yet they want to control the lives of everyone around them.

As a general rule, be wary of those who are eager or desperate for power, for it is a certainty that incompetence and misery will follow.

———————◇———————

Plato was a philosopher in Classical Greece. A disciple of Socrates, he founded the Academy, in Athens, where he taught through the use of probing questions, forcing his students to think analytically and defend their principles, often leading them to concede that many of their beliefs were unjustifiable. His most famous student at the Academy — which is widely considered to be the first institution of higher learning in the Western world — was Aristotle.

Plato's entire body of knowledge has survived intact for over 2,400 years. His *Dialogues* — philosophical discussions between two or more participants — were usually centered around a specific theme, such as justice, ethics, virtue, or friendship, and were written in the manner of ordinary conversations. As a literary device for his *Dialogues*, Plato used Socrates as the main speaker, to initiate penetrating inquiries in order to challenge, provoke, and ultimately to educate his students.

May 17th

GLORY

"Love of glory can only create a great hero;
contempt of glory creates a great man."

— Charles Maurice de Talleyrand
French Bishop, Diplomat
2/2/1754 – 5/17/1838

Indeed, there are times when a hero is needed; however, there are a great many more times when ordinary, selfless *people* are needed. The funny thing about those who don't worry about getting credit is that they are usually the ones who get it, and deservedly so.

———————◇———————

Charles Maurice de Talleyrand-Périgord was a bishop, a diplomat, and a statesman known for his tenacious (and often self-serving) skill as a negotiator, as well as his extraordinary aptitude for political survival.

A club foot derailed Talleyrand from his dream of military service, and he turned to the church. In 1770, he entered the seminary of Saint-Sulpice, in Paris, where he studied theology, read philosophy — and took his first mistress. There were other scandals, but Talleyrand graduated and was ordained.

In 1779, Talleyrand was appointed vicar general by his uncle, Alexandre. However, what he really wanted was the much more lucrative position of bishop, and when he was named Agent-General of the Clergy, in 1780, he engaged in a vigorous defense of the (often controversial) privileges of the Catholic Church. In 1788, he was appointed Bishop of Autun.

Talleyrand continued to live a charmed life: he emerged unscathed from The Terror of the French Revolution; served under Napoleon; helped to overthrow Napoleon; and replaced him with a Bourbon monarch. He saw the last King of France, Louis-Philippe, installed on the throne in 1830.

THE FUTURE

"The future starts today, not tomorrow."

— Pope John Paul II
Polish Pope
5/18/1920 – 4/2/2005

Don't allow yourself to get caught up in the dreaming instead of the doing. Get started already; there is no time like the present to launch your future.

———◆———

Pope John Paul II was born Karol Józef Wojtyla on May 18, 1920, in Wadowice, Poland. As a boy, he liked to play soccer, and was an exceptional skier and a strong swimmer. In 1938, he began to study philosophy at Krakow's Jagiellonian University. Although he dreamed of a career as an actor in the theater, Wojtyla would soon be drawn to religious studies. He would eventually earn a master's and doctoral degrees in Sacred Theology, and was formally ordained in 1946. More ordinations would follow, as he was named bishop of Ombi in 1958 and archbishop of Krakow in 1964, and was made a cardinal by Pope Paul VI in 1967. Finally, in 1978, Karol Józef Wojtyla would take the name John Paul II when he was named the 264th Pope — the first non-Italian pope in more than four hundred years.

As the leader of the Catholic Church, John Paul II traveled the world, spreading his message of faith and peace in more than a hundred countries. He also spoke out against Communism, and his voice, along with those of American President Ronald Reagan and British Prime Minister Margaret Thatcher, would be instrumental in bringing the Cold War to a close.

John Paul II served as Pope and sovereign of Vatican City until his death, in 2005, at age eighty-four. It is estimated that over three million people stood in line at St. Peter's Basilica to pay their respects to this beloved Pope.

PERCEPTION

"Logic will never change emotion or perception."

— Edward de Bono
Maltese Philosopher, Physician
Born 5/19/1933

The differences between objective (or critical) thinking and the purely subjective realm of "feelings" are stark, for it is a cold, hard truth that there is no shortage of people who reject facts, proof, reason, and logic for the warm embrace of groupthink. The question is: Do you know the facts behind your principles, or has your mind been co-opted by mere opinion?

Born into an aristocratic Maltese family that prized education, Edward Charles Francis Publius de Bono is a Maltese physician, psychologist, philosopher, author, inventor, and consultant. He graduated from St. Edward's College in Malta at the age of fifteen, and then obtained a medical degree from the University of Malta. He became a Rhodes Scholar at Christ Church, Oxford, where he acquired a Master's Degree in psychology and physiology. De Bono then went on to earn a Ph.D. in medicine from Trinity College, Cambridge; a Doctor of Design degree from the Royal Melbourne Institute of Technology; and a Law degree from the University of Dundee.

De Bono has held faculty positions at the universities of Cambridge, Oxford, London, and Harvard, and in 2005 was nominated for the Nobel Prize for Economics. In his spare time, De Bono has written eighty-two books that have been translated into forty-one languages. He is also known for coining the term "lateral thinking," and his deliberate thinking techniques have been used in organizations such as IBM and Dupont.

CONTENTMENT

"I have learned to seek my happiness by limiting my desires,
rather than in attempting to satisfy them."

— John Stuart Mill
British Economist, Philosopher
5/20/1806 – 5/8/1873

Where there are too many desires, there are too few resources to satisfy them: Time, money, energy, emotion; all are spent from our treasury in pursuit of what too often amounts to temporal cravings that offer only a fleeting and too often unsatisfying end. Prioritize your dreams, and put what is of lasting importance first.

John Stuart Mill was a philosopher and economist who made extensive contributions to social theory, political theory, and political economy. If there is a single thread that runs through the heart of Mill's theories, it is that understanding can be attained only through empirical observations, which must then be interpreted using logic and inference. In other words, reason is at the heart of all knowledge.

As a young man, Mill took a job as a junior clerk with the British East India Company, for whom he would work for the next thirty-five years. By the time he retired, in 1858, he was Chief Examiner of Correspondence, an executive position roughly equivalent to Undersecretary of State.

A month into his retirement, Mill's wife Harriet — the love of his life — died while they were traveling in France. Mill buried her in Avignon, and subsequently purchased a house close to the cemetery, where he would live for the rest of his life.

CAUTION

"How prone to doubt, how cautious are the wise!"

— Alexander Pope
English Poet
5/21/1688 – 5/30/1744

You mustn't take at face value anything you read, nor trust everything you hear. Always ask yourself: Do I have the whole story, or only a fragment of it?

———————◆———————

Alexander Pope was an eighteenth-century writer and poet. His best known works are probably *The Rape of the Lock*, *An Essay on Man*, and *An Essay on Criticism*.

A precocious child prodigy, Pope was largely self-educated. This was because his religion, Catholicism, precluded his admittance to university. He did receive some training by Catholic priests, and he managed to attend some Catholic schools near his home in London, but it was through his own determined efforts that he would become a learned man.

Physically, Pope had several ailments that would torment him his entire life. A curvature of the spine, coupled with a tubercular infection, made him somewhat frail and impeded his growth; as an adult, he was only four feet, six inches tall. He also suffered from frequent and severe headaches. Despite his physical impairments, Pope was said to have borne them with grace, and he presented an attractive overall appearance.

A quick-witted and ingenious satirist, Pope reveled in skewering the foppery of his times and is remembered for his epigrams, such as "To err is human, to forgive, divine," and "For fools rush in where angels fear to tread." Listed among the most frequently quoted writers in *The Oxford Dictionary of Quotations*, Pope is second only to Shakespeare.

FORTUNE

"Fortune truly helps those who are of good judgment."

— Euripides
Greek Dramatist
c. 481 BC – c. 407 BC

We don't tend to correlate good decision-making with good fortune, but we should, because the former most assuredly informs the latter. If you find yourself lamenting your "bad luck" more than occasionally, perhaps it is time to reexamine your decision-making process.

———————◇———————

Euripides was a tragedian playwright of classical Athens. He is credited with writing more than ninety plays, nineteen of which have survived from antiquity. His most famous tragedies include *Medea*, *The Bacchae*, and *Hippolytus*.

Euripides was known for taking a traditional tale and standing it on its head, exploring the darker, more passionate, and more fallible sides of Greek gods and heroes, infusing their stories with non-traditional plot elements like insanity and revenge. His female characters were often strong and capable, and equally as courageous as any of the male roles.

Euripides also had a knack for inserting commentary and dialogue pertaining to contemporary events or philosophical ideas, which his characters would debate on stage. *The Trojan Women*, for example, was written during the Peloponnesian War, and the dialogue suggests that the loss of life and the sacrifices inherent in any war make for a bittersweet victory, whoever the victors are.

For daring to introduce new concepts, and new ways of looking at people and events, Euripides came to be known as the most intellectual of the tragedians. It makes you wonder what his friend Socrates thought about that.

APOLOGIES

"To apologize is to lay the foundation for a future offense."

— Ambrose Bierce
American Writer, Poet
6/24/1842— 1914

Apologies are necessary to the maintenance of any relationship, for they replenish the trust and restore the equilibrium that is essential to each and every bond that we enter into.

If you give offense, apologize. If you take offense, forgive. Repeat often.

———————◆———————

Ambrose Gwinnett Bierce was a writer, journalist, and Civil War veteran, and the author of sardonic short stories often based on death and the macabre. He is best known for his short story *An Occurrence at Owl Creek Bridge*, as well as *The Devil's Dictionary* (also known as *The Cynic's Word Book*).

Bierce was raised in Kosciusko County, Indiana. When the Civil War began, he volunteered and saw action in battles at Shiloh, Chickamauga, and Kennesaw Mountain, where he was seriously wounded.

After the war, Bierce moved to San Francisco and took a job at the *News Letter*. He soon married, and the newlyweds moved to London, where his first three books were published. They returned to San Francisco when Ambrose was offered a job as a columnist for the *San Francisco Examiner*. There, the sharp-tongued Bierce specialized in confronting dishonest politicians, clergymen, social climbers, frauds, and hypocrites of every stripe.

In 1913, Bierce moved to Mexico, which at the time was in the middle of a revolution being led by Pancho Villa. He was never heard from again, his disappearance a mystery worthy of one of his short stories.

FIDELITY

"Fidelity is a gift not a requirement."

— Lilli Palmer
German Writer, Actress
5/24/1914 – 1/27/1986

There are few things we value more than faithfulness, and few things that are less devastating than betrayal. Unfortunately, we cannot make others be loyal or true; fidelity is either given freely or not at all.

Lilli Palmer was an actress and writer. In addition to her native German, she was also fluent in French and English. She studied drama in Berlin, however, as Hitler consolidated power in Germany, her parents, Rose Lissman, an Austrian Jewish actress, and Alfred Peiser, a German Jewish surgeon, relocated the family to Paris.

Palmer soon found work in British films, and in 1943 she married Rex Harrison. They had a son, Carey, and in 1945 they moved to America. Rex and Lilli found success, often acting together in Broadway plays and in feature films. However, a scandal would soon engulf the couple when Harrison's lover, Carole Landis, committed suicide in 1948.

Palmer worked with many of the major stars of her time, including James Mason, Louis Jordan, Gary Cooper, and William Holden. In 1959, she was nominated for a Golden Globe award for her work opposite Clark Gable in *But Not for Me*. In 1960, she was awarded a star on the Hollywood "Walk of Fame."

Palmer wrote an entertaining autobiography, *Change Lobsters – and Dance*, which turned out to be a best-seller. She also wrote four novels and a short story collection, and was a talented painter.

May 25th

RESISTANCE

"We gain the strength of the temptation we resist."

— Ralph Waldo Emerson
American Essayist, Philosopher
5/25/1803 – 4/27/1882

Do we really gain strength by resisting temptations? Yes, in many ways. Intellectually, we learn that we are stronger than our desire. Morally, we reinforce our sense of virtue. Spiritually, we are reminded of what it is to be righteous.

What is strengthened the most through resistance? Our character.

———————◇———————

Ralph Waldo Emerson was an essayist, lecturer, philosopher, and poet. He is best known as a leader of the Transcendentalist movement, and for his essay "Self-Reliance."

Emerson came from a long line of clergymen, and he, too, would follow that path. After graduating from the Harvard School of Divinity, he became a pastor in the Unitarian church. He married Ellen Tucker in 1829, but her death from tuberculosis, in 1831, triggered a crisis of faith, and Emerson soon left the church.

In 1832, Emerson sailed to Europe, where he met with several literary figures, including Thomas Carlyle, Samuel Taylor Coleridge, and William Wordsworth. Carlyle, in particular, had a lasting effect on Emerson, as his insights on the power of the individual would help to shape Emerson's own philosophy, which was centered on the personal nature of spirituality.

When he returned home in 1833, Emerson surrounded himself with kindred spirits who shared his sensibilities. Among these friends was a young man named Henry David Thoreau, who would further refine Emerson's philosophy while living in the woods by Walden Pond.

May 26th

COMMITMENT

"Commitment and credibility go hand in hand."

— Zbigniew Brzezinski
Polish-American Diplomat, Advisor
3/28/1928 – 5/26/2017

Never squander an opportunity to demonstrate that you are as good as your word. Always do what you say you will do, because your good name and character are attached to every pledge and promise that you make.

———◇———

Upon completing his PhD at Harvard, Zbigniew Kazimierz Brzezinski worked as a professor of government and as a research fellow at Harvard's Russian Research Center. In the early '60s, he took a similar position at Columbia University, and it was during this time that Brzezinski first acted as a foreign affairs adviser, first for President John F. Kennedy, and then under Lyndon B. Johnson.

In 1975, Brzezinski met presidential candidate Jimmy Carter, and agreed to be his foreign affairs adviser during the campaign. When Carter was elected President, Brzezinski served as his national security adviser. His tenure was marked by a few successes, but the administration's handling of the Iranian Revolution and subsequent hostage crisis would prove catastrophic for Carter. Despite doubts among the intelligence community, Brzezinski counseled support for the Shah of Iran. Consequently, when the revolution toppled the Shah, and the US embassy was overrun, there were few diplomatic options available for negotiating the release of American hostages. The appearance of weakness and ineptitude crippled Carter's chances for reelection in 1980, and he lost to Ronald Reagan.

May 27th

FAILURE

"People in their handlings of affairs often fail when they
are about to succeed. If one remains as careful at the end as he was
at the beginning, there will be no failure."

— Lao Tzu
Chinese Philosopher, Founder of Taoism
d. 531 BC

Everybody loves a good comeback — a last-ditch, last-second, super-human combination of focus and exertion that defies the odds and wins the game. Everyone, that is, except the one who has lost due to another's steely determination — or their own lapse in concentration.

Never presume that a thing is done is until it is done. Never coast to the finish line; *accelerate!*

———————————————

Lao Tzu, also known as Laozi, was an ancient philosopher and writer. He is the reputed author of the *Tao Te Ching* (the Book of the Way), and the founder of Taoism. A central tenet of Taoism is that simplicity is at the heart of virtue, which is perhaps why Lao Tzu is credited with saying that "the more laws one makes, the more criminals one creates."

Much of what we know about Lao Tzu is anecdotal. In truth, it is unknown whether Lao Tzu was an individual or an amalgam of many different philosophers. Even the name Lao Tzu is not a personal name but an honorific title meaning "Old Sage" or "Old Master." There is a story, credited to the historian Sima Qian, about Confucius meeting Lao Tzu and coming away from the encounter so impressed that he immediately dedicated his life to the study of philosophy. Although it is considered apocryphal, and the two would diverge significantly in thought, the story accords the highest possible esteem to Lao Tzu for his influence upon the greatest of all Chinese philosophers.

SADNESS

"Bad things do happen; how I respond to them defines my character and the quality of my life. I can choose to sit in perpetual sadness, immobilized by the gravity of my loss, or I can choose to rise from the pain and treasure the most precious gift I have— life itself."

— Walter Anderson
American Painter, Writer
9/29/1903 – 11/30/1965

We all experience sorrow, but we mustn't allow our grief to overwhelm us, for there is much of life still to live. Would those we mourn want to see us waste what they have just lost?

Born in New Orleans, Louisiana, Walter Inglis Anderson's artistic abilities were evident at an early age. His parents encouraged his early efforts and sent him to study art, first in New York and then in Philadelphia. He won a Packard Award for his animal drawings, and a Cresson Traveling Scholarship allowed him to spend a summer in France. He was fascinated by the cave paintings at Les Eyzies and the influence of the primitive images there would be apparent in some of his later works.

In 1937, Anderson was diagnosed as schizophrenic, and the next three years were spent in treatment. It was a sporadic process, undertaken in fits and starts, because Anderson would escape from every mental hospital in which he was placed. He fled from one by knotting up his bed sheets and climbing through a window. He left behind drawings of birds in flight on the walls, drawn with soap.

He finally did recover, and today Anderson is best known for his watercolors, ink illustrations, linoleum block prints, and the murals he painted for the Public Works Administration during the Great Depression.

LAUGHTER

"I have seen what a laugh can do. It can transform almost unbearable tears into something bearable, even hopeful."

— Bob Hope
American Actor, Comedian
5/29/1903 – 7/27/2003

Sometimes we laugh when we shouldn't, it's true; and sometimes it is said that from laughter we are dying. Sometimes we laugh just because we need to, and sometimes we laugh just to keep us from crying. Whatever the reason, please find a way, sometime today, to enjoy a little laughter.

———————◇———————

Comedian Bob Hope — American entertainer and comic actor known for his rapid-fire delivery of jokes, snappy one-liners, and wisecracks — was born Leslie Townes Hope in the Eltham district of southeast London. At the age of four, his family moved to the United States, and settled in the Cleveland, Ohio area.

Hope began his career in show business as a dancer and comedian, first on the vaudeville circuit, and then on Broadway. In the 1940s, he teamed up with popular crooner Bing Crosby for the first of seven "Road to . . ." comedies. The two played a pair of likeable con artists: Bing was the smooth talker, and Bob was the smart-talking coward. Their antics would prove to be box-office gold, and the two would maintain a lifelong friendship.

Hope had a deep respect for the men and women who served in the military, particularly during wartime. Hope made numerous trips overseas to entertain the troops as part of a USO delegation, and he and his wife, Dolores, spent many of their Christmases with the troops. In 1997, an act of Congress designated Hope an "Honorary Veteran."

May 30th

METAPHYSICS

"We are what we think. All that we are arises with our thoughts.
With our thoughts, we make the world."

— Buddha
Nepali Ascetic, Sage
c. 623 BC – c. 544 BC

The family dramas of my childhood certainly *shaped* my world, but as I grew, I was determined that they would not *be* my world; they would remain in my past, and my future — where I lived, who I saw, and how I spent my time — would be centered on Tranquility. Amazingly enough, it worked.

Think about what you want, and what you don't want, and start building your world. You are already doing it, after all.

———————◇———————

Gautama Buddha, also known as Siddhartha, or simply the Buddha ("Awakened One" in Sanskrit), was an enlightened being who discovered the path to freedom from suffering, followed it to its end, and then taught it to the world. His teachings form the foundation of Buddhism, one of the world's major religions.

According to Buddhist doctrine, the universe is the product of karma, the spiritual principle of cause and effect, wherein an individual's actions today have a direct effect on what will happen to them tomorrow: Good deeds contribute to good karma and future happiness, while bad deeds lead to bad karma and future suffering. Most Buddhist traditions are characterized by an emphasis on overcoming past suffering in order to attain Nirvana, a state of enlightenment that breaks the (otherwise) endless cycle of death and rebirth.

ARROGANCE

"Arrogance diminishes wisdom."

— Arabian proverb

You can always learn something from someone, and to dismiss an opportunity to gain knowledge or understanding is not only egotistical, but foolish. A wise person knows this. Now you do, too.

———————◆———————

Arabian proverbs highlight centuries spent in pursuit of wisdom. They tend to lean toward inspiration as well as education.

June 1st

PRINCIPLES

"Principles and rules are intended to provide a thinking man
with a frame of reference."

— Carl von Clausewitz
Prussian General
6/1/1780 – 11/16/1831

Always respect the law, whatever it might be, but understand that sometimes there are extenuating circumstances that can make a rule or regulation
inconvenient at best, and dangerous at worst.

———◇———

Born into a Prussian family with claims to nobility, Carl Philipp Gottfried
von Clausewitz joined his country's military as a twelve-year old lance-corporal;
finished first in his class at the Institute for Young Officers in Berlin; and rose
to the rank of Major General. His best-known work, *Vom Kriege* (On War), was
unfinished when he died, but is nevertheless one of the most highly regarded
treatises on military strategy ever written.

Upon his graduation from the military academy, Clausewitz was appointed
adjutant to Prince August Ferdinand. In 1806, when Napoleon invaded and
defeated Prussia, both he and the Prince were captured. In the ensuing peace
negotiations, Prussia lost half of its territories and was compelled to become
an ally of Napoleon. In 1812, when the Prussian army was pressed into service
during Napoleon's ill-fated invasion of Russia, Clausewitz resigned his commission and joined the Russian service. He would be instrumental in the defense
of Russia and would help to negotiate the Convention of Tauroggen, which
formed the coalition of forces (Russia, Prussia, and the United Kingdom) that
would eventually defeat Napoleon at Waterloo.

IGNORANCE

"The wise man doubteth often, and changeth his mind; the fool is obstinate, doubteth not; he knoweth all things but his own ignorance."

— Akenaton
Egyptian Pharaoh
c. 1380 BC – c. 1335 BC

Sometimes we have doubts even when we are fairly certain; that is normal. At other times, it is astonishing how truly wrong we can be about something that we believe to be unquestionably true (or false). This is 100% preventable, because ignorance can be cured; you just have to address your stubbornness.

———————◇———————

Akhenaten, also known by his earlier name, Amenhotep IV, was an Egyptian pharaoh. His reign, which lasted seventeen years, is noted for the abandonment of traditional Egyptian polytheism in favor of monotheism; for his marriage to Nefertiti; and for the (strong) possibility that he was the father of Tutankhamun, who ascended the throne following Akhenaten's death.

The reforms instituted by Akhenaten centered on worshipping Aten, a Sun-god who was often depicted as a disc in the sky, with rays extending to earth. Monuments and icons with the names of other Egyptian gods were erased or otherwise obliterated, which was not always greeted with approval by the average Egyptian. As King, Tutankhamun found favor with the people by returning things to the way they had been before Akhenaten's reign.

June 3rd

SELF-ASSURANCE

"A well-adjusted person is one who makes
the same mistake twice without getting nervous."

— Alexander Hamilton
American Founder, Statesman
1/11/1757 – 7/12/1804

Everybody makes mistakes. Even geniuses err. It's when you keep making the same mistake, again and again, *and again*, that you might want to consider swapping some confidence for some diligence.

Alexander Hamilton was an illegitimate teen from the British West Indies who became one of America's most accomplished founders.

Having arrived in America on a scholarship funded by his employers, Hamilton abandoned his studies when the Revolutionary War broke out. He joined General George Washington's army, and eventually became his aide-de-camp. Anxious to get into the fight, Washington assigned Hamilton the leadership of three infantry battalions at the battle of Yorktown; their victory effectively ended the war.

Writing under the pen name Publius, Hamilton wrote fifty-one of the eighty-five essays that comprised *The Federalist Papers*, the goal of which was to promote the ratification of the United States Constitution. It did, and as a member of the Continental Congress, Hamilton signed the Constitution.

Hamilton envisioned a mighty, industrial country. Toward that end, he helped to create the Bank of North America, served as the first Secretary of the Treasury, and established the United States Mint. He also founded the Customs Service, and launched the Coast Guard to ensure that all tariffs were collected.

On July 11, 1804, Hamilton was mortally wounded in a duel with Aaron Burr, and he died the following day. His wife, Elizabeth Schuyler, would live another fifty years. She never stopped promoting the achievements and legacy of her husband, whom she referred to as "my Hamilton."

STUBBORNNESS

"Obstinacy is the result of the will forcing itself
into the place of the intellect."

— Arthur Schopenhauer
German Philosopher
2/22/1788 – 9/21/1860

If facts are "stubborn things," so too are our own prejudices and assumptions. How many times have you said or done something based on how you felt instead of what you knew?

It is a terribly easy thing to fall back onto long-held beliefs; we're at ease there. But the shrewder thing is to know the facts, and then act accordingly. It may not be as comfortable, but it's way more satisfying.

———————◆———————

Arthur Schopenhauer was a philosopher who is best known for his 1818 book, *The World as Will and Representation* (Die Welt als Wille und Vorstellung). In his masterwork, Schopenhauer proposes that the mind sees the foundation of everything — literally, the entire world — based wholly on our will, a force which drives our actions through simple, instinctual, and often irrational impulses, driven by individual perceptions of "our" world — the world as each individual sees it.

Sometimes referred to as "the philosopher of pessimism," Schopenhauer was among the first of the nineteenth-century philosophers to assert that the universe is not a rational place. Although he did not achieve widespread acclaim in his lifetime, he had a lasting influence among leading thinkers across a fairly broad spectrum, including Friedrich Nietzsche, Carl Jung, Richard Wagner, Gustav Mahler, Leo Tolstoy, George Bernard Shaw, Erwin Schrödinger, and Albert Einstein.

STRUGGLE

"Prolonged endurance tames the bold."

— Lord Byron
English Nobleman, Poet, Politician
1/22/1788 – 4/19/1824

The world can wear down even the bravest among us. Sometimes you've just got to stop struggling, and stop fighting. Take a break and catch your breath; once you regather your strength, you can redouble your efforts (or reconsider your options).

George Gordon Byron, or Lord Byron, was an English nobleman, peer, and poet who was known as much for his sexual escapades (and attendant notoriety) as for his brilliant use of the English language. Among his most famous works are the poem "She Walks in Beauty," the poetic travelogue "Childe Harold's Pilgrimage," and the autobiographical "Don Juan," which he never finished.

Byron died while providing aid to the Greeks during their war of independence with Turkey, contracting a fever that killed him at the age of thirty-six. His talent, physical beauty, and untimely death all contributed to Byron's lasting reputation as the epitome of a romantic poet-hero. He remains a leading figure of English literature, and continues to be widely read to this day.

June 6th

STUDY

"Order and simplification are the first steps
toward the mastery of a subject."

— Thomas Mann
German Novelist, Nobel Laureate
6/6/1875 – 8/12/1955

It seems obvious, doesn't it? Yet how often do we choose to avoid even attempting to learn something new, merely because it seems too difficult, too complicated, or too time-consuming? Too often.

If it interests you, pursue it. A journey of a thousand miles. . .

———————◇———————

Paul Thomas Mann was a writer and social critic whose early novels, in particular *Buddenbrooks*, earned him the Nobel Prize for Literature, in 1929. Widely praised for his keen insights into the intellect and psychology of the characters he drew, Mann gave credit to the philosophers Schopenhauer and Nietzsche, as well as the composer Wagner, for helping him to fully develop them.

Mann's best-known works include *The Magic Mountain*, *Death in Venice*, and *Doktor Faustus*. He is widely regarded as the greatest German novelist of the twentieth century.

FANATICISM

"Fanaticism consists of redoubling your effort
when you have forgotten your aim."

— George Santayana
Spanish Writer, Philosopher
12/16/1863 – 9/26/1952

There is nothing quite like dealing with the unrelentingly unreasonable; they believe what they believe — what they *want* to believe — and no amount of logic or proof will ever sway them from their chosen path.

It's one thing to be fervent; it's quite another to be fanatical. It is a difference with a distinction, an opinion bereft of judgment, which often hides in plain sight.

———————◇———————

Jorge Agustín Nicolás Ruiz de Santayana y Borrás, known in English as George Santayana, was a philosopher, writer, poet, and briefly, a Harvard professor. Although his books were widely admired and influential, he is most often remembered for aphorisms, like "Those who do not remember the past are condemned to repeat it," and "Only the dead have seen the end of war."

A Spaniard by birth, Santayana was raised in the United States and considered himself to be an American, although he spent his later years in Europe and died, in Rome, with a valid Spanish passport.

MODERATION

"Moderation in temper is always a virtue,
but moderation in principle is always a vice."

— Thomas Paine
English-American Activist, Revolutionary
2/9/1737 – 6/8/1809

Attenuating our more aggressive and self-centered behaviors is certainly commendable, but at the same time, there are certain values that are worth fighting (and dying) for. Just make sure they're the right ones.

———————◇———————

Thomas Paine was a political philosopher, a writer, and a revolutionary who supported both the war in America and the uprisings in France. In 1776, he published *Common Sense*, the first pamphlet to publicly advocate for American independence from England. Paine's argument, that free men ought to live under a representative government instead of being subject to the whims of an aristocratic monarchy, was instrumental in convincing the colonists to go to war against the most powerful military on earth.

Once the Revolutionary War got underway, Paine enlisted and served under General George Washington. As a witness to the dreadful conditions the Continental Army was facing, Paine wrote a series of pamphlets called *The American Crisis*, the first of which opens with his most famous line: "These are the times that try men's souls."

Paine himself would undergo a series of trying times: During the French revolution, he would make an enemy of Robespierre, spend time in a French prison, and miraculously avoid the guillotine. His reputation was irreparably damaged, however, when he ridiculed Christianity in his notorious pamphlet, *The Age of Reason*, written in part while he was in a Paris jail. For this, only six people attended his funeral, in 1809.

GOSSIP

"It is just as cowardly to judge an absent person as it is wicked to strike
a defenseless one. Only the ignorant and narrow-minded gossip,
for they speak of persons instead of things."

— Lawrence G. Lovasik
American Theologian, Writer
6/22/1913 – 6/9/1986

We all have that one friend or colleague who just loves to gossip. They always know who did what, and with whom, and they seem to derive some kind of perverse pleasure from sharing other people's secrets. Never forget that these "friends" have no boundaries, and that everything you share with them will most assuredly be shared with others — friends and enemies alike.

Father Lawrence G. Lovasik was born in Tarentum, Pennsylvania and did a good deal of missionary work in America's coal and steel regions. A prolific writer of religious books and pamphlets, Lovasik said that his goal in life was to "make God more known and loved through my writings."

Upon his graduation from Divine Word Major Seminary, in 1938, Lovasik was sent to the Gregorian Papal University in Rome for additional theological studies. In August, he was ordained to the priesthood of the Society of the Divine Word. For the next forty years, Father Lovasik would work as a missionary throughout the eastern United States, and conduct religious retreats throughout the world.

June 10th

COHORTS

"When we ask for advice, we are usually looking for an accomplice."

— Saul Bellow
Canadian-American Writer
Nobel Laureate & Pulitzer Prize Winner
6/10/1915 – 4/5/2005

It isn't always advice we seek, so much as we just want someone to tell us that what we are doing is perfectly rational — even if only marginally so.

And, those who provide affirmation *before*, are duty bound to provide commiseration *after*.

———————◇———————

Saul Bellow was born to Russian-Jewish emigres in Montreal, in 1915, and was raised in the slums of Chicago's West Side. Bellow said he grew up as a rude and "thick-necked" hoodlum, but he rose from his humble beginnings to earn a Bachelor's degree, with honors, from Northwestern University in 1937. After graduating, he did some graduate work at the University of Wisconsin before enlisting in the Merchant Marine during World War II. It was during this time that he completed his first novel, *Dangling Man*, a semi-autobiographical tale about a young man waiting to be drafted for the war.

Bellow is widely considered to be one of the greatest authors of the twentieth century, and he is certainly one of the most decorated. He was awarded the Pulitzer Prize for Fiction; won the Nobel Prize for Literature; is the only writer to win the National Book Award for Fiction three times; was presented with the Congressional National Medal of Arts; and received the National Book Foundation's lifetime Medal for Distinguished Contribution to American Letters.

Bellow's best-known works include *The Adventures of Augie March, Seize the Day, Henderson the Rain King*, and *Humboldt's Gift*.

June 11th

COMMUNICATION

"The reason why we have two ears and only one mouth is that
we may listen the more and talk the less."

— Zeno of Citium
Cypriot Founder of Stoic Philosophy
c. 334 BC – c. 262 BC

It is often said that the best communicators are those who listen well. Being a good listener is more than just being quiet and hearing what is being said; it also requires no small amount of empathy. Try to put yourself in the speaker's shoes: really pay attention, and focus on what they are saying *right now*, instead of what you are planning to say next.

———◇———

Zeno of Citium was the founder of the Stoic school of philosophy, which he taught in Athens starting in about 301 BC. Stoicism emphasizes virtue and ethics, and teaches that happiness lay in conforming the will to reason. In addition, the Stoic accepts fate, with the tacit understanding that no matter what happens, there is no point in complaining about it.

Zeno was praised by the Athenians, who admired him for his self-restraint and determination to live the values that he taught. His philosophical system would eventually be embraced by Seneca, Epictetus, and Marcus Aurelius, as Stoicism gained influence throughout the Roman Empire. Even the apostle Paul would meet with the Stoics of his day, in Athens, as would other early Christian writers, who often used Stoic concepts and terminology to broadly fashion the metaphors they used to promote an understanding of their new faith.

LOVE

"What love we've given, we'll have forever.
What love we fail to give, will be lost for all eternity."

— Leo Buscaglia
American Motivational Speaker
3/31/1924 – 6/12/1998

Life is short, and just as troubling, it is unpredictable. We never know if we will have another chance to tell those we love how we feel about them. Have you considered that this moment, *right now*, may be the last time you ever see each other?

Always take the opportunity to tell someone that you love them.

Felice Leonardo "Leo" Buscaglia, PhD, was an author, motivational speaker, and professor at the University of Southern California. Known as Dr. Love, the Love Merchant, and the Hug Doctor (a man famously stopped his car on a busy street in downtown Toronto, got out, and embraced Buscaglia in a hug), he inspired and encouraged people from all over the world to love each other unconditionally.

Dr. Buscaglia wrote several best-selling books, including *Love, Living, Loving and Learning, Loving Each Other*, and *Born for Love*. His underlying message, "Love conquers all," was not meant to be a trite catchphrase, but rather to serve as a reminder for people to act on their love of and for others.

The Leo Buscaglia Foundation is still active today. Its mission is building community spirit by helping people to help others.

By the way, did you know? Felice means "happy" in Italian.

SEX

"Sex is a momentary itch, love never lets you go."

— Kingsley Amis
English Novelist, Poet, Critic
4/16/1922 – 10/22/1995

We often stumble into sex when what we are really looking for is love. While sex is a truly marvelous thing, it is often a fleeting connection, soon relegated to the back rooms of ramshackle memory. Love, on the other hand, is constructed of far sturdier materials: it is designed to endure, built to last, and destined for eternity — whether sex is involved, or not.

Sir Kingsley William Amis was a novelist, poet, critic, and teacher.

During World War II, Amis served as a commissioned officer in France, Belgium, and Germany. After the war, he returned to Oxford to complete his studies and, following his graduation in 1947, he married and took a job teaching at the University College of Swansea, in Wales. In 1954, his first novel, *Lucky Jim*, was published. It was a critical and commercial success, and made him a household name in Great Britain. His ear for dialogue, mixed with a satirical take on 1950s British society, was hugely popular with the public, and the book won the 1955 Somerset Maugham Award for Fiction. Over the next forty years, Amis wrote over forty books, but *Lucky Jim* remains his most popular work. It was eventually translated into twenty languages.

In 1981, Amis was named a Commander of the Order of the British Empire (CBE), and in 1990 he was knighted by Queen Elizabeth II. Amis died, following a stroke, in 1995. His last years had been spent living with his ex-wife and her husband, who had agreed to take care of him until his death.

GRATITUDE

"When it comes to life, the critical thing is whether you take things
for granted or take them with gratitude."

— G. K. Chesterton
English Writer, Philosopher
5/29/1874 – 6/14/1936

One of the secrets to inner peace and happiness is to cultivate an attitude
of gratitude. It starts with being thankful for every single thing you have,
including this very moment.

You have more than most, certainly more than many, and every breath
you take is literally a blessing. Say it out loud: I am grateful!

One of the most gifted and prolific writers of all time, Gilbert Keith
Chesterton was well-versed in poetry, philosophy, journalism, history, theology,
politics, art, economics, drama, and just about anything else one might wish
to discuss . . . at great length. It seems that the gregarious G.K. had something
to say about virtually every topic — and he was very good at expressing what
he thought, *ad nauseam.*

It is difficult to overstate Chesterton's influence. A partial list of his
colleagues, contemporaries, and admirers who were influenced by him would
include Ernest Hemingway, Evelyn Waugh, Gabriel Garcia Marquez, Marshall
McLuhan, Agatha Christie, Orson Welles, Mohandas Gandhi, C.S. Lewis, and
Kingsley Amis. George Bernard Shaw said of him: "The world is not thankful
enough for Chesterton."

Over the course of his life, Chesterton wrote over a hundred books and
made contributions to hundreds more; he wrote novels, plays, and poems, and
yet he is probably best known to most people for his series of short stories,
The Father Brown Mysteries.

June 15th

SELF

"The more you know yourself, the more patience you have
for what you see in others."

— Erik Erikson

German-American Psychoanalyst

6/15/1902 – 5/12/1994

For good or ill, our personality traits define who we are; they determine how we relate to the world, and how others relate to us.

What is your default mentality? Are you boastful, or humble? Rash, or thoughtful? Entitled, or appreciative? If you want to change the perception that people have of you, for the better, strive to be the latter.

Erik Homberger Erikson was a psychoanalyst known for his theories on the interactions of psychology and individual identity, and the intersection of psychology with history, politics, and culture. He is probably most famous for coining the phrase "identity crisis."

After immigrating to the US, Erickson joined the faculty of the Harvard Medical School, and in 1936 he left to join the Institute of Human Relations at Yale. A few years later, he moved his clinical practice to San Francisco, and in 1942 he became a professor of psychology at the University of California, Berkeley.

In 1950, Erickson published his views on psychosocial development in *Childhood and Society*, proposing that there are eight stages of development, each presenting its own demands and challenges, each of which must be overcome in order to advance to the next stage, which continues into old age. He continued to write about these stages as he grew older, including *The Life Cycle Completed: A Review*, in 1982, and *Vital Involvement in Old Age*, in 1986.

June 16th

VIRTUE

"Virtue is more to be feared than vice, because its excesses
are not subject to the regulation of conscience."

— Adam Smith
Scottish Economist, Author, Philosopher
6/16/1723 – 7/17/1790

Anything that has no governor ought to be watched, for a great many paths to Hell have been paved with the good intentions of those who believed the virtue of their aims was sufficient to rationalize any behavior spent in the attainment of them. "Meaning well" does not always end well.

———◆———

Often called the Father of Economics, the Father of Free Trade, and the Father of Capitalism, Adam Smith was an author, philosopher, and an economist who pioneered the idea that the measure of a country's wealth should not be judged by the gold in its treasury, but by the total output of its production and commerce. This measure is referred to today as Gross Domestic Product (GDP).

Smith was well-known to and widely read by the Founding Fathers of the United States, who would embrace many of his ideas in the establishment of their fledgling economy. Today, that economy is the largest in the world (and has been for a very long time).

Smith is best known for writing *An Inquiry into the Nature and Causes of the Wealth of Nations*, in which he asserts that free-market economies are the most productive and beneficial to their societies. His theory about an "invisible hand" at work within capitalist societies refers to the many benefits that arise, tangentially, from the natural pursuit of one's own self-interests, and that while these are often the result of an instinctive desire to help others, they are just as often unwitting or unintended.

June 17th

WEALTH

"Prosperity is the measure or touchstone of virtue, for it is less difficult
to bear misfortune than to remain uncorrupted by pleasure."

— Tacitus
Roman Senator, Historian
c. 54 AD – c. 120 AD

We all possess wealth, in one form or another. Whether we are gifted with talent, empathy, wisdom, love, or friendships, each of us is blessed in our own way. Being wealthy is another kind of blessing, but one that comes with its own set of challenges. The more you have, the more you tend to want — and the more frequently temptations seem to present themselves.

It isn't what we have, but what we do with it that counts. Share your gifts — whatever they might be — with the world around you.

Publius Cornelius Tacitus was a senator, an orator, and a historian of the early Roman Empire. Only one copy of each of his major works — the *Annals* and *Histories* — survives, nonetheless giving us valuable insights into the reigns of the emperors Tiberius, Claudius, and Nero, as well as those who reigned in the Year of the Four Emperors.

Tacitus also wrote the *Germania*, which detailed the lands, laws, and customs of the various Germanic tribes, and hinted at the problems they could cause if they united against Rome. His father-in-law, Agricola, was the general responsible for much of the Roman conquest of Britain, which Tacitus chronicled in a biography.

All told, Tacitus's detailed account of the Empire's history stretches from 96 AD to 14 AD.

EMBARRASSMENT

"It is the answers, not the questions, that are embarrassing."

— Helen Suzman
South African Politician, Activist
11/7/1917 – 1/1/2009

When someone asks you about your stance on an issue, will you be embarrassed by your answer? Probably not — unless your response betrays an ignorance that you'd just as soon keep hidden.

Anticipating questions is no more difficult than answering them. If you *think*.

Helen Suzman was a South African parliamentarian, an anti-apartheid activist, and an outspoken advocate for the country's non-white majority. Known for her strong public criticism of apartheid, she was unyielding in her opposition to all forms of racial discrimination. In 1974, as a Member of Parliament, Suzman went to the prison on Robben Island, where she spoke with political prisoners and met Nelson Mandela. She would be by Mandela's side when, as President, he signed South Africa's new constitution, in 1996.

Suzman retired from Parliament in 1989, after serving for thirty-six years. She went on to serve as the president of the South African Institute of Race Relations, from 1991 to 1993. In 1994, when South Africa held its first democratic elections, she was a member of the Independent Electoral Commission, which monitored the electoral process.

Suzman's activism resulted in numerous awards, including the United Nations Human Rights Award in 1978, and the Medallion of Heroism in 1980. In 1989, Queen Elizabeth II made her a Dame Commander of the Order of the British Empire. She was also nominated for the Nobel Peace Prize twice.

June 19th

SHAME

"The only shame is to have none."

— Blaise Pascal
French Polymath, Theologian
6/19/1623 – 8/19/1662

Shame exists whether we acknowledge it or not; it's just that, sometimes, it is others who feel it for us.

―――――――――◆―――――――――

Blaise Pascal was a French mathematician, physicist, inventor, writer and a Catholic theologian.

A child prodigy, Pascal was educated by his father, a tax collector in Rouen who was admired for his own mathematical abilities. As a seventeen-year-old, Pascal wrote an essay on geometry, which brought him acclaim among the best mathematical minds of the era, not least of whom was Rene Descartes. A few years later, he constructed a mechanical calculator (to help his father with his tax computations), which brought him even more fame. From there, Pascal turned to the natural and applied sciences, conducting experiments on hydrodynamics, barometric pressure, and vacuum — which today is quantified in units of measure called *pascals*.

Pascal was also a brilliant writer, who used his gifts to defend Christian precepts even though he did not always agree with Church doctrine. For Pascal, it was all very simple: one could not separate morality from spirituality.

Although he was one of the most celebrated minds of his time, and he was not above taking pride in his accomplishments, Pascal did hint in his private notes that he was a bit embarrassed by the abundance of his talents.

Pascal died in Paris, a month shy of his thirty-ninth birthday. It has been speculated that he had stomach cancer, tuberculosis, or both. His last words were "May God never abandon me."

DEFIANCE

"You are remembered for the rules you break."

— Douglas MacArthur
American General
1/26/1880 – 4/5/1964

When we break a rule and the result is successful, we like to claim that it is "the exception that proves the rule." When we act in defiance of the rules, and we fail, we blame the rules.

———————◆———————

Douglas MacArthur was an American five-star general best known for his command of Allied forces in the Pacific Theater during World War II.

Born into a military family that served on both sides of the Civil War, MacArthur graduated with honors from the United States Military Academy at West Point, in 1903. He received numerous promotions over the next decade, and when World War I broke out in Europe, Colonel MacArthur earned a reputation as a capable war-time leader.

By 1935, tensions were simmering in the Pacific, and MacArthur, now the Commander of all U.S. Forces in the Pacific, was sent to establish a defensive position in the Philippines. When the Japanese successfully invaded the Philippines, following the attack on Pearl Harbor, MacArthur publicly spoke out against President Roosevelt's decision to give priority to the war effort in Europe rather than the one being fought in the Pacific.

By the end of the war, President Harry S. Truman had appointed MacArthur Supreme Allied Commander. However, when war began in Korea, MacArthur once again criticized his boss, the president — and an exasperated Truman relieved him of command, effectively ending his military career.

June 21st

SERENITY

"God grant me the serenity to accept the things I cannot change, the courage to change the things I can, and the wisdom to know the difference."

— Reinhold Niebuhr
American Theologian, Professor
6/21/1892 – 6/1/1971

The beginning of serenity can be found in accepting that we have very little control over external events, and in having the maturity and the fortitude to make changes within ourselves.

As a professor at Union Theological Seminary for more than thirty years, Karl Paul Reinhold Niebuhr was an influential commentator on politics and public affairs, and one of America's leading public intellectuals. Today he is probably best remembered as the author of "The Serenity Prayer" (above), a popular invocation that has long been the mantra of Alcoholics Anonymous.

Niebuhr was a man of shifting allegiances: a committed socialist in his youth, he became an anti-communist Democrat in middle-age; a former pacifist, he rallied Christians to fight against Hitler; as a vocal critic of American exceptionalism, he nevertheless accepted the Presidential Medal of Freedom in 1964. Lastly, there is his "Christian Realism," a political theology which asserts that Heaven could never be established on Earth due to the persistence of humanity's evil inclinations. At the same time, however, Niebuhr also proclaimed that there are "indeterminate possibilities" for humanity, provided we do not presume to know with absolute certainty all of the answers to every difficult question we face.

CIRCUMSTANCE

"I am more and more convinced that our happiness or unhappiness depends far more on the way we meet the events of life than on the nature of those events themselves."

— Wilhelm von Humboldt
Prussian Philosopher, Statesman
6/22/1767 – 4/8/1835

Life is a series of events that we can neither anticipate nor control; however, it is not the events themselves, but our reaction to them, that sets the tone. A positive attitude is an asset under any circumstance.

———————◇———————

Friedrich Wilhelm Christian Karl Ferdinand von Humboldt was a philosopher, linguist, and diplomat. He theorized that language reflects both the culture and individuality of the speaker, and that each of us perceives the world essentially through the language of our culture. He is credited with developing the so-called "Humboldtian education ideal," a model for systematic education that was eventually adopted by numerous countries, including the U.S. and Japan. He was also instrumental in the founding of the Friedrich Wilhelm University at Berlin, which in 1949 was renamed Humboldt University.

Humboldt served in several diplomatic posts, including ambassadorships to Rome and Vienna, where he worked to forge alliances during the Napoleonic Wars. In 1815, following the defeat and abdication of Napoleon, Humboldt was one of the signatories of the Treaty of Paris, which signaled the end of hostilities.

June 23rd

RESILIENCE

"In order to succeed, people need a sense of self-efficacy, to struggle together with resilience to meet the inevitable obstacles and inequities of life."

— Albert Bandura
American Psychologist
born 12/4/1925

It may not seem like it, but our struggles against the "obstacles and iniquities of life" are the grit that makes the pearl, the dust that polishes the gem. Take pity on those who have suffered no trials, for without adversity we are all dim, dull creatures.

———◇———

Albert Bandura is a psychologist and originator of social cognitive theory (SCT), which holds that there are a number of "social" avenues for the acquisition of knowledge, including through media, social interactions, and observing the actions of others. He is probably most famous for his groundbreaking study on aggression, the so-called Bobo doll experiment, which showed a correlation between the behaviors of preschool-age children and the observed actions of adults. After seeing researchers verbally abuse an inflatable clown, the children then mimicked the abusive behavior. Ultimately, this research led to stricter governmental regulation regarding the exposure of children to violence on television and in advertising.

In 1977, Bandura was the first to demonstrate that a person's perception of their own competence and ability has a direct effect on whether they will attempt to do a thing, the level of energy they are willing to dedicate to completing the task, and how they feel about themselves as they are doing it.

DEPRIVATION

"No man is more cheated than the selfish man."

— Henry Ward Beecher
American Theologian, Abolitionist
6/24/1813 – 3/8/1887

A selfish person deprives him- or herself at least as much as they deprive others, for while they may believe that they end up with more by giving less, there are actually very few things which bond us one to another like the gratitude and appreciation of a gift freely given.

Henry Ward Beecher was a highly successful preacher, lecturer, and social reformer known for his support of the abolition of slavery and his emphasis on God's love and mercy. Beecher believed that the success or failure of a sermon was determined only by whether or not it produced a moral change in the listener. His oratorical skill and use of humor and colloquialisms made him one of the most influential Protestant ministers of his time.

Although Beecher was married, he was very popular among the ladies, and there were constant rumors of extramarital affairs. A scandal erupted in 1874 when the sixty-one-year-old Beecher was sued by a former friend who claimed Beecher had committed adultery with his wife. He was exonerated after appearing before two church tribunals, and the civil suit filed against him resulted in a hung jury.

June 25th

LIBERTY

"The 'Enlightenment,' which discovered the liberties,
also invented the disciplines."

— Michel Foucault
French Philosopher, Historian
10/15/1926 – 6/25/1984

Liberty requires boundaries, whether self-imposed or at the insistence of a civilizing authority, for freedom without restraint is anarchy.

———————◇———————

Paul-Michel Foucault was one of the most influential (and sometimes provocative) scholars of the post-World War II period. His work, which examined the relationships between knowledge and power, and the ways they are used as controlling mechanisms in society, often spanned several disciplines at once, including history, sociology, psychology, and philosophy. At the time of his death, Foucault was widely regarded as one of the most prominent intellectuals in France.

MOOD

"I don't wait for moods. You accomplish nothing if you do that.
Your mind must know it has got to get down to work."

— Pearl S. Buck
American Writer, Pulitzer Prize winner
Nobel Laureate
6/26/1892 – 3/6/1973

If we sit around waiting for a reason to get something done, we often find ourselves sitting, and doing nothing, for a very long time.

Moods and "inspiration" are for love-play and poets; what you need is *focus*. Stop giving yourself excuses and start taking care of business.

Pearl Sydenstricker Buck was an American writer and novelist. Raised primarily in the Chinese village of Chinkiang, by her Presbyterian missionary parents, most of Buck's work would center around China and Chinese culture. Her second novel, *The Good Earth*, highlights the life of a Chinese peasant family. It was an immediate best-seller and won Buck the Pulitzer Prize in 1932. A prolific and popular writer, Buck became the first American woman — and just the fourth woman overall — to win a Nobel Prize, in 1938.

Buck had a soft spot for children. Her daughter, Carol, suffered from developmental disabilities, and she and her second husband, Richard Walsh, adopted six other children through the years. She also took a lead role in several humanitarian efforts. In 1941 she founded the East and West Association, whose mission was to protect Asian Americans against racial intolerance; in 1949, she started an adoption agency, called Welcome House, which specialized in the placement of Asian-American children; and in 1964, she established the Pearl S. Buck Foundation to "address the issues of poverty and discrimination faced by children in Asian countries."

ANCESTRY

"There is no king who has not had a slave among his ancestors,
and no slave who has not had a king among his."

— Hellen Keller
American Author, Activist, Lecturer
6/27/1880 – 6/1/1968

Bloodlines mean very little. It is up to each of us, as individuals, to carve our own path and make our own way irrespective of our genealogical inheritance.

Helen Adams Keller was an author, political activist, and lecturer who overcame many disabilities to become a world-renowned champion of the disadvantaged.

Although born with her senses of sight and hearing, Keller contracted an illness that left her deaf and blind before her second birthday. In 1886, Keller was examined by Alexander Graham Bell, who referred her to the Perkins Institution for the Blind, in Boston, where she was introduced to twenty-year-old Anne Sullivan, a recent graduate and teacher who would remain by her side for almost fifty years. Sullivan's teaching methods would help Keller break through the isolation and loneliness of her profoundly dark and silent world. Their hard work and persistence paid off — in 1904, Keller graduated, cum laude, from Radcliffe College, becoming the first deaf-blind person to earn a Bachelor of Arts degree.

Soon after her graduation, Keller became an advocate for many of the social and political issues of the day, and in 1909, she joined the Socialist Party. In 1920, she co-founded the American Civil Liberties Union.

During her lifetime, Keller received many honors, including honorary doctoral degrees from universities around the world. In 1964, she was awarded the Presidential Medal of Freedom, and she was elected to the Women's Hall of Fame in 1965.

DEBATE

"Insults are the arguments employed by those who are in the wrong."

— Jean-Jacques Rousseau
Swiss-French Writer, Philosopher
6/28/1712 – 7/2/1778

Insults. Invective. *Ridicule.* These are small things for small minds.

Be humble when the argument is won, and gracious when it is lost, for this is how reputations are made, kept, or lost.

Born in Geneva, Jean-Jacques Rousseau was a philosopher, writer, political theorist, and composer. Although he was perhaps the least educated among the best-known philosophers, Rousseau was undoubtedly among the most influential. He made people look at things in new and different ways, suggesting for example, that parents should consider educating their children with the goal of cultivating their natural tendencies; that we should embrace our friends and family with our emotions, instead of maintaining the stiff and overly polite expressions that were popular in his time; and that it was possible reject religious dogma while still embracing religious sentiments.

The cornerstone of Rousseau's thought was that people are essentially good; it is only the progression of the sciences and arts that has caused the corruption of virtue and morality. He was not against progress and advancement, per se, but was merely pointing out the pitfalls that come with increasing sophistication. His thoughts and ideas — about freedom, beauty, and purpose — would be a spark of inspiration and a harbinger of change, from the furies of the French Revolution to the Age of Enlightenment and the dawn of Romanticism.

June 29th

ACTION

"The time for action is now. It's never too late to do something."

— Antoine de Saint-Exupery
French Writer, Poet, Aviator
6/29/1900 – 7/31/1944

So, you've thought about it. Maybe you've looked into it. Maybe you've even developed a half-hearted plan to start thinking about planning for it —but then you tell yourself that it can't be done; that it will never work; that you couldn't possibly do it, because you're too young, too old, too busy, too tired, too broke, or too scared. Hey, welcome to the club!

Just like opinions, we all have excuses. The thing is? We usually regret the things we didn't do more than the things that we did. Those things just cut a little bit deeper into the psyche. You simply have to ask yourself: Am I more afraid of a temporary failure, or a lifetime of regret?

Antoine Marie Jean-Baptiste Roger, count of Saint-Exupery, was a writer, poet, journalist, and aviator whose adventures in the sky fueled his literary work. Although most of his novels are known for heroic airborne exploits that usually end in death, he is best remembered for his novella, *The Little Prince*, a poetic fable that reminds us to cherish life's simple pleasures. The book has been translated into over three hundred languages and was voted the best book of the twentieth century in France. Saint-Exupery won several of France's highest literary awards and also received a U.S. National Book Award.

In 1912, Saint-Exupery took his first airplane ride, and it was love at first flight. He would somehow survive many harrowing aircraft accidents, but in 1944, he took off for a reconnaissance mission over occupied France and never returned. Sixty years later, his plane was found in the Mediterranean Sea, near Marseille. It is presumed that he was shot down by an enemy aircraft.

June 30th

WELFARE

"Our ideal is to make her ever stronger and better and finer, because in that way alone, as we believe, she can be of the greatest service to the world's peace and to the welfare of mankind."

— Henry Cabot Lodge
American Politician, Historian
5/12/1850 – 11/9/1924

The "she" that Mr. Lodge refers to is, of course, the United States. But it begs the question: Is there a single "person," one lone individual, who can have a singular impact on their family, their community, or the whole world?

You bet there is. You've just read half of a book brimming with examples. If you need one more, go look in a mirror.

———————◇———————

Henry Cabot Lodge was a Republican Congressman and historian from Massachusetts. A member of the prominent Lodge family, he failed in his first attempt for a seat in Congress, but succeeded in 1886. He was noted for his efforts to ensure voting rights in the South, and later for his foreign policy battles with President Woodrow Wilson, particularly over the Treaty of Versailles and Wilson's desire to enjoin the United States to the League of Nations: Lodge was deeply concerned about the League and potential conflicts with American interests.

Lodge had a PhD in history from Harvard University, and several of his biographies were published in the popular American Statesmen Series, including *Alexander Hamilton, Daniel Webster,* and *George Washington.* In 1895, *Hero Tales from American History* was published — co-written with Theodore Roosevelt. Lodge remained interested in history and wrote about major figures and events for the rest of his life.

VANITY

"Vanity is the quicksand of reason."

— Amantine Dupin (George Sand)
French Novelist
7/1/1804 – 6/8/1876

If your filter is vanity, you will always err on the side of your own opinion, not necessarily the facts. If you seek the truth, know that pride and arrogance will always be impediments to your search.

———◇———

Amantine Lucile Aurore Dupin, who went by the pseudonym George Sand, was a novelist and memoirist. She is known as much for her romantic affairs, which included composer and pianist Frederic Chopin, as she is for being one of the most prolific female authors in the history of literature (she wrote over seventy novels and plays).

Having grown up in her grandmother's country home, Dupin developed a life-long love of the countryside and the "simple" country folk who inhabited it. Most of her so-called "rustic" novels are informed by those seminal years and are essentially idealized versions of real-life incidents related to her life there.

Dupin adopted the nom de plume George Sand in 1832, for her novel *Indiana*, in which an unhappy heroine questions the social conventions of the day (and her marital responsibilities) in order to find love. The book brought her immediate fame and launched a long and prosperous career, capped some forty years later with *Tales of a Grandmother*, a collection of stories she wrote for her grandchildren.

July 2nd

SELF-CONTROL

"A cadet will not lie, cheat, or steal, nor tolerate those who do."

— West Point Cadet Honor Code

We don't give ourselves the credit we deserve when we exhibit restraint, perhaps because it often surprises us when we do.

In an age where justification and gratification have usurped common sense and common decency, try to be less surprised when you do the right thing by making a habit of doing the right things.

———————◇———————

The United States Military Academies have been educating, training, and inspiring men and women of character for over two hundred years.

INTEGRITY

"Start with what is right rather than what is acceptable."

— Franz Kafka
Czech Novelist
7/3/1883 – 6/3/1924

In life, it is often more difficult to stand up for the morally correct than to acquiesce to the politically correct. This is because we have been conditioned to hide behind None of My Business, Go Along to Get Along, and Everybody Else is Doing It.

Don't be fooled. Right is right, and no matter how much public opinion may indicate otherwise, being a stand-up person is what matters the most to the opinion that matters the most: your own.

Franz Kafka was a novelist and short story writer, best known for *The Metamorphosis*, a surreal tale of a traveling salesman who awakens to discover he is a giant insect.

Widely considered to be one of the major figures of twentieth-century literature, Kafka's work usually depicted an average man pitted against some sort of overwhelming force, often with little explanation or resolution. His mixture of anxiety and despair amid nightmarish predicaments examined the psychology of man and how far he could go before breaking.

Kafka's own life was a shadow of his fiction. An introvert, he found personal relationships difficult to maintain, and as a result suffered from social isolation. Physically frail, he pushed himself to exhaustion, working long days for an insurance company and interminable evenings writing his fiction. In 1917, worn down and suffering from tuberculosis, he was forced to take an early retirement.

Kafka died in 1924. The majority of his work was published posthumously, by a friend who had promised that he would burn his writing.

HONOR

"No person was ever honored for what he received.
Honor has been the reward for what he gave."

— Calvin Coolidge
American President
7/4/1872 – 1/5/1933

It is said that we honor the memory of the dead, and of the fallen, with remembrances of their contributions to our country, to our community, and to ourselves.

Each of us will die, and when that day comes, most of us hope to be thought of fondly, and with kindness. The question is: For what will you be remembered tomorrow by those who know you best today?

John Calvin Coolidge, Jr., was a Republican lawyer from Vermont who served as the governor of Massachusetts before becoming the 30th President of the United States. He was the Vice President under Warren G. Harding, who died of a heart attack while in office. When news of Harding's death reached him in the middle of the night, while he was visiting family in Vermont, Coolidge had his father, John Calvin Coolidge, Sr., administer the oath of office. His father was a notary public, and this remains the only instance where a U.S. president was sworn in by his own father.

Nicknamed "Silent Cal" for his thoughtful demeanor, Coolidge was a pro-business, low-tax, small-government conservative who famously said, "The chief business of the American people is business." It was during his presidency that the country saw the rapid economic growth that came to be known as "The Roaring Twenties."

Calvin Coolidge was the only American president born on the Fourth of July, but three other presidents — Adams, Jefferson, and Monroe — passed away on this date.

DISAPPOINTMENT

"See your disappointments as good fortune.
One plan's deflation is another's inflation."

— Jean Cocteau
French Writer, Director, Poet
7/5/1889 – 10/11/1963

The concepts of "good" and "bad" are, if nothing else, fluid and dynamic. It is often unclear, initially, if a thing is positive, negative, or a bit of both. The real truth is that most of the time, only time will tell.

Jean Maurice Eugene Clement Cocteau is widely regarded as one of the most important and influential creative figures of the Parisian avant-garde. A multitalented artist, Cocteau was a writer, a poet, a painter, a playwright, and a filmmaker. He is perhaps best known for his novel *Les Enfants Terribles*, and his film *Orpheus*, which is based on his play of the same name. He is also known for having decorated the Villa Santo Sospir in Saint-Jean-Cap-Ferrat, and for painting frescoes on various public buildings, including churches. The set and costumes for his ballet, *Parade*, were designed by his friend, Picasso.

In his epic poem, "L'Ange Heurtebise," Cocteau engages in battle with an angel named Heurtebise, who is believed to represent Cocteau's close friend, fellow writer Raymond Radiguet, who died of typhoid at age twenty-one. Heurtebise had previously made an appearance in *Orpheus*, as did Radiguet, in the form of Jacques Cegeste, a handsome young poet who is killed when he is run down by motorcyclists. He is later transformed into a guardian angel.

July 6th

COMPASSION

"If you want others to be happy, practice compassion.
If you want to be happy, practice compassion."

— Dalai Lama
Tibetan Monk
7/6/1935

Like most acts of loving-kindness, showing compassion to others gives as much comfort to those who offer it as it does to those who receive it.

The term Dalai Lama is a title given to the spiritual leader of the Tibetan people. It is believed that the Dalai Lama is continually reincarnated as the physical manifestation of the compassionate bodhisattva, or "Buddha-to-be."

The current Dalai Lama was born Lhamo Thondup on July 6, 1935 in Taktser, China. As Tibet's spiritual and political leader-in-exile, he has given lectures and conducted humanitarian workshops worldwide. In 1989, he was awarded the Nobel Peace Prize. Although his schedule has been significantly reduced, given his age, he continues to speak on matters of peace and spirituality.

RIGHTS

"We define a set of fairly simple catechisms, the first part of which is we are endowed by our Creator with certain inalienable rights. These rights include life, liberty, and the pursuit of happiness. Government exists to secure these rights, not to deliver happiness."

— George Will
American Political Commentator
Born 5/4/1941

Chase your dream, but understand that it is entirely up to you to catch it. You are entitled only to that which you are willing to earn.

———◇———

George Frederick Will is an American political commentator and pundit. He is best known for writing columns for *Newsweek* and the *Washington Post*, as a panelist on political talk shows, and for his love of baseball.

Will earned bachelor degrees from Trinity College and Oxford University, and received a PhD from Princeton University. He taught political science at Michigan State University and at the University of Toronto, before taking the reins as the Washington editor at *National Review* magazine. In 1977, he won a Pulitzer Prize for commentary.

Known as a free-market capitalist and a supporter of traditional religious and social conventions, Will was instrumental in preparing the Republican candidate, Ronald Reagan, for his debates with the sitting President, Jimmy Carter. Reagan's success in the debates, and his carefully crafted policy positions, won him the election in 1980.

An avid supporter of the Chicago Cubs, Will has written several books on his favorite pastime, including *Men at Work: The Craft of Baseball*. He also appeared in Ken Burns's 1994 documentary, *Baseball*.

DESTINY

"A person often meets his destiny on the road he took to avoid it."

- Jean de La Fontaine
French Fabulist, Poet
7/8/1621 – 4/13/1695

We often waste time and energy trying to circumvent the inevitable, and our stubbornness is seldom rewarded. The irony of these exercises in futility might even be amusing if weren't for our inability to learn from them.

Jean de La Fontaine was a poet and fabulist, and one of the most popular and widely read authors of the seventeenth century. Possessed of a ribald and licentious sense of humor, his *Tales and Novels in Verse* shocked the sensibilities of French society. However, he is best known for his toned-down *Fables*, which are considered masterpieces of French literature.

Although he did not invent fables — de La Fontaine borrowed from everyone from Aesop to Phaedrus — he did manage to enrich and elevate them from simple morality tales to humorous and poetic classics. He ended up with some 240 poems, which he published in twelve volumes, with "The Ant and the Grasshopper" and "The Fox and the Crow" being among those which are best remembered today.

De La Fontaine once said, "I use animals to teach men," and indeed his *Fables* were generally aimed at an adult audience; however, they were so highly regarded that they soon became required reading for French schoolchildren.

July 9th

THE MIND

"Distinction is the consequence, never the object, of a great mind."

— Washington Allston
American Painter, Poet
11/5/1779 – 7/9/1843

We don't set out to be wise or distinguished or admired; like most things, they are the after-effects of a lot of hard work, determination, and accomplishment.

———◆———

Washington Allston was a painter and poet from Waccamaw Parish, South Carolina. He is considered to be first among important American Romantic painters, known for his dramatic landscapes and bold use of light and atmospheric color. A Harvard graduate, he studied at the Royal Academy in London and visited many of the great museums of Europe. He counted among his friends the poet Samuel Taylor Coleridge and writer Washington Irving. Allston was celebrated for his experimental approach to painting, and his best-known works include *The Deluge, Elijah in the Desert*, and *Moonlit Landscape*.

JOY

"There is not one blade of grass, there is no color in this world
that is not intended to make us rejoice."

— John Calvin
French Theologian
7/10/1509 – 5/27/1564

Anyone who has ever watched a sunrise, climbed a tree, walked on a beach, or planted a garden knows that we are surrounded by astonishing beauty, if we would just take the time to notice it.

———————◇———————

John Calvin was a theologian and pastor, and Martin Luther's successor as leader of the Protestant Reformation. Quiet and reverential, Calvin's stony countenance burnished his reputation as a serious and (some might say) unsentimental taskmaster. However, it was this intellectual, unemotional approach to scripture that served to underpin the very foundations of Protestantism.

Calvin was a prolific writer, and his best-known work, the *Institutes of the Christian Religion*, was an early attempt to standardize Protestant theories. Published in 1536, this landmark work would become the single most important statement of Protestant belief for generations. He was also well known for his prodigious output of biblical commentaries, which constitute by far the largest portion of his literary canon. In these religious texts, Calvin outlines and emphasizes his belief in the absolute sovereignty of the scriptures and in divine predestination, the idea that all events are controlled through the will of God.

PREJUDICE

"Prejudice is a great time saver. You can form opinions
without having to get the facts."

— E. B. White
American Writer
7/11/1899 – 10/1/1985

Prejudicial thoughts and attitudes are often rooted in ignorance, and that's no way for a thinking person to operate, at any time.

Always be sure that you have the facts — *all* of the facts — before you pass judgement on a fellow human being. A good place to start is by giving absolutely everyone the benefit of the doubt. You would have them do no less for you, would you not?

Elwyn Brooks "Andy" White was a celebrated author, long-time contributor to *The New Yorker* magazine, and co-author of the English language style guide *The Elements of Style*, which has been considered the "Writer's Bible" for generations. He is probably best remembered for his children's books, including *Stuart Little* and *Charlotte's Web*. Mr. White had a farm in Maine, and he credited his animals there with providing the inspiration for the beloved classics.

In all, E.B. White published nearly twenty books of prose and poetry, and won many awards over the course of his career. In 1963, he received the Presidential Medal of Freedom. He was awarded the National Medal for Literature in 1971, and was elected to the American Academy of Arts and Letters in 1973. In 1978, he was awarded a Pulitzer Prize special citation. He passed away, at his farm, in 1985.

July 12th

OBLIGATIONS

"The only obligation which I have a right to assume is
to do at any time what I think right."

— Henry David Thoreau
American Essayist, Philosopher
7/12/1817 – 5/6/1862

Your chief obligation in life is to your Self — more specifically, to your conscience. After all, if you can't live with yourself, where will you go?

———◇———

Sometimes referred to as the "Father of Environmentalism," Henry David Thoreau was a poet, essayist, philosopher, and naturalist. His masterwork, *Walden*, is a series of eighteen essays in which he describes his two-year attempt to live as simply and self-sufficiently as possible, using only materials he could find or cultivate in nature. He did this near Walden Pond, on land owned by his friend and mentor, the poet Ralph Waldo Emerson. Both Thoreau and Emerson were founding members of the New England Transcendentalist movement, a school of thought that emphasized spiritual matters over physical comforts and emotional connectedness over simple reason.

A dedicated abolitionist, Thoreau was also an energetic advocate of civil liberties and the rights of the individual. He argued that each of us must act according to our conscience, instead of blindly acquiescing to government power.

BIAS

"Men in general are quick to believe that which they wish to be true."

— Julius Caesar
Roman Politician, General
7/13/100 BC – 3/15/44 BC

No matter how knowledgeable we are, no matter how experienced or conscientious, it is difficult to overcome our personal biases — difficult, but not impossible.

There is always going to be a battle between the unvarnished, objective truth and our own personal predilections and peccadillos; we want to believe what we want to believe. However, if you want to give your integrity a fighting chance, arm yourself with the facts.

Gaius Julius Caesar had a two-pronged approach to expanding both the influence of Rome and his own power. As a general, possessed of one of the greatest military minds in history, he expanded the Roman Republic through a series of battles played out across Europe. As a politician, he vanquished the morally bankrupt Roman nobility and turned the Roman Republic on its head, establishing himself as dictator for life and laying the foundation for the Roman Empire.

Caesar's rule lasted just one year. He died on the steps of the Senate, killed by political rivals who feared the vast power he had accumulated. Although Caesar is quoted in Shakespeare's eponymous play as saying, "Et tu, Brute?" ("And you, Brutus?"), his actual last recorded words would be translated as, "You, too, my child?"

Today, Julius Caesar (and his assassination) is associated with the Ides of March, but he is also remembered, in a way, every summer: the Roman month Quintilis, in which he was born, was renamed "July" in his honor.

July 14th

PATRIOTISM

"Patriotism is when love of your own people comes first; nationalism, when hate for people other than your own comes first."

— Charles de Gaulle
French President, General
11/22/1890 – 11/9/1970

There is a fine line between patriotism and nationalism, and many have difficulty making a distinction between the two. Call it what you want, but it seems it's always the other guy's love of country that we question, never our own.

———◇———

Charles André Joseph Marie de Gaulle was a soldier and statesman. Wounded three times in World War I, he led the Free French Resistance against Nazi Germany in World War II.

A supremely self-assured and skilled politician, de Gaulle served as President of France from 1958 to 1969. His terms as President were marked by an insistence that France project her power and prestige onto the world stage, and a firm conviction that France's interests always came first. To underscore these points, he made it clear that France's autonomy would always supersede her participation as a member of the North Atlantic Treaty Organization (NATO), and his foreign policies in general made it clear that France would only honor those alliances which benefited France first and foremost.

De Gaulle had a propensity for overreach, insult, and even subversion, but in spite of his prickly (some might say arrogant) nature, de Gaulle will always be considered one of France's greatest patriots.

LAW

"It is just that there be law, but law is not justice."

— Jacques Derrida
French Philosopher
7/15/1930 – 10/9/2004

It is the *application* of law that brings justice; it is the *acceptance* of justice that brings order.

———————◇———————

Jacques Derrida was a highly influential post-modern philosopher who liked to analyze the everyday assumptions we make in order to challenge the way we think about them. He wrote over seventy books and essays, had hundreds of others written about him, taught and lectured throughout the world, and achieved rock star status and international celebrity — yet he is probably best known for coining the term "deconstruction," an off-hand literary device he used in discussing the seemingly arbitrary values we assign (for example) to hierarchal word pairs, such as nature and culture, speech and writing, and law and order. In these instances, the first word of each pair is assumed to have greater significance simply due to its placement, even though they are both branches of the same tree.

ADVENTURE

"Adventure is just bad planning."

— Roald Amundsen
Norwegian Polar Explorer
7/16/1872 – 6/28/1928

Some of us like to plan out every detail. Our motto is "Failing to Plan is just Planning to Fail." Others like to just "wing it," take life as comes, and revel in whatever comes around the bend. While the former aren't immune to surprises, the latter are far more likely to experience them.

Which are you? And why?

Roald Engelbregt Gravning Amundsen was an explorer and is widely regarded as one of the greatest figures of the Heroic Age of Antarctic Exploration. He was the first person to reach the South Pole, the first to complete a voyage by ship through the Northwest Passage, and the first to cross the Arctic by air, flying a dirigible from Norway to Alaska. His books, *The South Pole* and *First Crossing of the Polar Sea*, chronicle his adventures.

During the Antarctic expedition of 1910–12, Amundsen was racing against not just time and the elements, but also against the English explorer Robert Falcon Scott. Amundsen prevailed, reaching the South Pole on December 14th, 1911. He and his team were able to return to their base at the Bay of Whales on January 25, 1912. Scott was able to reach the South Pole on January 17th, but all were lost on the journey back.

Amundsen died in 1928 while trying to rescue his friend, Umberto Nobile, after a dirigible crash near Spitsbergen, an island in the Svalbard archipelago in northern Norway. Amundsen's plane went down and he was never found.

IDEALISM

"Idealism is fine, but as it approaches reality the costs become prohibitive."

— William F. Buckley, Jr.
American Author, Commentator
11/24/1925 – 2/27/2008

It has been observed more than once that idealists find it very difficult to understand that this place we inhabit is Earth, not Heaven. God bless them, anyway; for although it seems their naiveté and misplaced enthusiasms conjure one unattainable dream after another, every so often it turns out that they are right.

———◇———

William Frank Buckley Jr. was an intellectual, a political pundit, a television commentator, the founder of the conservative journal *National Review*, and the author of forty books. His best-known book is his first one, *God and Man at Yale*, in which he denounced the faculty at his alma mater for their decidedly left-wing political agenda.

Buckley came from a wealthy Irish-Catholic family in New York City. He was studying at the University of Mexico when World War II erupted, and he served in the Army as a second lieutenant. When Franklin Roosevelt died, in April 1945, Buckley was a member of the president's honor guard.

After the war, Buckley went to Yale, where he was a champion debater and chairman of the *Yale Daily News*. In 1951, he was recruited to be a Political Action Officer by the Central Intelligence Agency. He began publishing *National Review* in 1955.

As a publicity stunt, Buckley ran for mayor of New York City on the Conservative Party ticket in 1965. He received only 13.4 percent of the vote, but the exposure led to a job as host of a televised weekly debate program, called *Firing Line*. It ran from 1966 until Buckley retired, in 1999.

AFFECTION

"A mixture of admiration and pity is one of the surest recipes for affection."

— Arthur Helps
English Writer, Dean of Privy Council
7/10/1813 – 3/7/1875

What is it about pity that draws out our affection? Feeling sorry for someone seems to increase rather than diminish our regard for them. Perhaps this is because, in examining the misfortunes of others, it allows us to better understand our own. Add to that a little pluck, a little pride, a little I'm-going-to-get-through-this-no-matter-what determination, and it becomes nearly impossible to not root for someone when they are down.

Sir Arthur Helps was a writer and political administrator who rose to become Dean of the Privy Council and advisor to Queen Victoria.

Educated at Eton and at Trinity College, Helps was highly regarded by his peers, who included Alfred Lord Tennyson. A lifelong writer, Helps' first book was a collection of aphorisms, published in 1835. He also wrote biographies, plays, essays, and historical accounts of exploration, but his most popular works (*Friends in Council*) used lively dialogues between imaginary characters named Milverton, Ellesmere, and Dunsford to discuss many of the social and political issues of the day.

In 1860, Helps was appointed Clerk of the Privy Council. His new role brought him into the orbit of Queen Victoria and Prince Albert, both of whom came to regard him as a valued advisor and friend. When poor business decisions ruined him financially and he was forced to sell his estate, the Queen offered to let him reside in a cottage, in Kew Gardens, where he lived for the rest of his life.

BOREDOM

"Every life is a mystery. There is nobody whose life is normal and boring."

— Frank McCourt
Irish-American Writer, Pulitzer Prize Winner
8/19/1930 – 7/19/2009

Do you ever imagine that the lives of others are more exciting than your own?

They aren't; they're just different. Imagine *that*.

———————◇———————

After retiring from teaching for thirty years in New York City, Francis McCourt sat down and wrote a book called *Angela's Ashes*. It won him the Pulitzer Prize for Biography in 1997.

Born in Brooklyn, McCourt was three years old when his family, struggling through the Great Depression, decided to return to Ireland. When his alcoholic father deserted them, the family suffered through unrelenting poverty and hardship. Nonetheless, McCourt worked a series of menial jobs and managed to save enough money to return to the US, in 1950. Soon after, he was drafted into the Army and sent to fight in Korea. After the war, he earned degrees from New York University and Brooklyn College, and got a job teaching high school English, which he did for the next three decades.

Angela's Ashes is a bittersweet memoir of McCourt's impoverished childhood in Limerick and the lessons he learned about family, friendship, love and his Catholic faith. In addition to the Pulitzer, McCourt's book also won the National Book Critics Circle Award, the Los Angeles Times Book Award, and the American Booksellers Book of the Year Award, known as the ABBY.

July 20th

SUSPICION

"Suspicion is the cancer of friendship."

— Petrarch
Italian Scholar, Poet
7/20/1304 – 7/20/1374

Suspicion and skepticism do have their place, but when they reside within a friendship, perhaps it is time to reexamine it. Unconditional trust underpins our most intimate connections, and when that confidence has eroded, for whatever reason, it's best to put those relationships behind you and move on.

Never waste your time with people whom you do not trust unreservedly.

———————◆———————

Francesco Petrarca, known as Petrarch, was a scholar and poet of the Italian Renaissance. Born in Arezzo, Tuscany, Petrarch moved with his family to Avignon, France, as a child. He briefly studied law, but was compelled to follow his passion: the classics of Ancient Greek and Roman literature. He was soon traveling all over Europe, seeking out scholars and poring over Classical manuscripts in monastic libraries. In Paris, he was given a copy of St. Augustine's *Confessions*, and in Liege he discovered copies of two speeches by Cicero. His translations of these and other documents gained Petrarch a reputation as the greatest scholar of his time. His inquiring mind and unquenchable thirst for knowledge would provide the spark that ignited the fourteenth-century Renaissance.

Petrarch's other great passion was writing, and he was widely admired in his lifetime. His poignant odes to an unrequited love, named Laura, were very well known, and his sonnets were considered to be so good that he is credited with popularizing the form. In 1341, he was crowned the poet laureate of Rome. It is said that his colloquial writing style is the foundation of the modern Italian language.

SUPERIORITY

"There is nothing noble in being superior to your fellow man;
true nobility is being superior to your former self."

— Ernest Hemingway
American Writer
Pulitzer and Nobel Prize Winner
7/21/1899 – 7/2/1961

A truly superior person has no need, nor any inclination, to boast or brag about their own excellence. Indeed, they go to great lengths to ignore or downplay the differences between themselves and others.

———————◇———————

Ernest Miller "Papa" Hemingway was an American novelist, short story writer, and journalist, known as much for his adventurous lifestyle as his sparse prose. Although he often favored run-on sentences that stretched into paragraphs, his otherwise economical and understated approach to writing had a strong influence on twentieth-century fiction.

When he wasn't writing, Hemingway could be found pursuing "manly" outdoor adventures, such as fishing for marlin in the Caribbean, hunting big game in Africa, and attending bullfights in Spain. All of this, and more, would eventually find its way into his novels and short stories.

Hemingway rubbed shoulders with many of the great writers of his time, including Gertrude Stein, F. Scott Fitzgerald, Ezra Pound, and James Joyce. Today, he is remembered as perhaps the best of the bunch, for novels like *The Sun Also Rises*, *A Farewell to Arms*, *For Whom the Bell Tolls*, and *The Old Man and the Sea*, which won him the Pulitzer Prize in 1953 and helped to win him the Nobel Prize in 1954.

In 1961, his eyesight failing and his physical condition deteriorating, an increasingly paranoid and confused Hemingway put a gun in his mouth and committed suicide, at his home in Ketchum, Idaho.

UNITY

"Humankind has not woven the web of life. We are but one thread within it. Whatever we do to the web, we do to our- selves. All things are bound together. All things connect."

— Chief Seattle
Native American Orator, Diplomat
1780 – 6/6/1866

Although we might like to think otherwise, everything that we do has a consequence. Sometimes the outcome is positive — if we do a good, we can see and feel the result of that good. It is the bad that we must be careful of, however, because at the very least, when we do bad, we do psychic harm to ourselves. Unless you're a sociopath, in which case . . . *never mind.*

Chief Seattle was a respected leader of the Suquamish and Duwamish tribes. He was highly regarded for his handling of the westward expansion in the United States, and for maintaining unity among the tribes during this time.

Seattle gained a reputation as an orator because of his articulate speeches that addressed some of the issues that arose between the Native Americans and the white settlers. While he pursued a path of accommodation, he strongly advocated for responsible stewardship of the land, while urging the "powers that be" to respect the land rights of the Native Americans.

French missionaries converted Seattle to Christianity, and he was given the baptismal name Noah. When he died in 1866, he was buried in the cemetery behind St. Peter's Catholic Church, located in the hamlet of Suquamish, on Washington's Kitsap Peninsula. His name lives on, through the city of Seattle, which was named after him.

REASON

"Reason is God's crowning gift to man."

— Sophocles
Greek Dramatist
c. 496 BC – c. 406 BC

If there is one overarching concept to take away from these pages, it is the importance of critical thinking. It is absolutely essential that you think for yourself; do not accept a life of headline-skimming and the simple-minded parroting of Media talking points in the mistaken assumption that you can then call yourself informed.

Seek out the Facts. Apply Reason. Follow the Logic.

———————————◇———————————

Sophocles of Colonus was one of the most famous and celebrated writers of Greek tragedies, part of the celebrated triumvirate that includes Aeschylus and Euripides. Together, these three dominated the Dionysian drama festivals of the mid fifth century BC, and Sophocles was the foremost talent among them. He took first place twenty times in thirty years.

Sophocles enjoyed making his audiences uncomfortable, with his plays often reflecting unflattering truths about many of the social and political mores of Greek life. His most famous play is *Oedipus Rex*, which Aristotle described as "the perfect tragedy." In addition to *Oedipus*, six other Sophoclean tragedies survive in their entirety: *Ajax, Antigone, Women of Trachis, Philoctetes, Oedipus at Colonus*, and *Electra*.

Sophocles was born into wealth but loved being a citizen of Athens and was active in his community. In addition to his artistic talents, he also served as a city treasurer and as an army officer under Pericles. He lived to be ninety years old, and it would not be wrong to say that his lifetime spanned Athens's most prosperous and glorious era.

GENERALIZATIONS

"All generalizations are dangerous, even this one."

— Alexandre Dumas
French Writer
7/24/1802 – 12/5/1870

Mind your assumptions. The difference between what you *believe* and what you *know* can be very vast, indeed.

Alexandre Dumas was a celebrated author, best known for his novels *The Three Musketeers* and *The Count of Monte Cristo*. *The Man in the Iron Mask* is another of his well-known stories. His Romantic style was often compared to that of his contemporary and rival, Victor Hugo. A prolific writer, Dumas also wrote numerous essays, short stories, plays, and travelogues.

Although his works were often referred to as historical novels, Dumas's adventurous tales were not particularly concerned about historical accuracy, per se, or even character development — his primary goal was to present an exciting story set against the colorful background of the recent past. His formula was extraordinarily effective: his works have been translated into nearly one hundred languages, and he is one of the most widely read French authors of all time.

Dumas was buried in the Panthéon in Paris, interred alongside other French literary greats, such as Émile Zola, Jean-Jacques Rousseau, and Victor Hugo.

ENTHUSIASM

"Enthusiasm moves the world."

— Arthur Balfour
British Prime Minister, 1st Earl of Balfour
7/25/1848 – 3/19/1930

All activities are the result of enthusiasm; it is merely a matter of degree (and polarity). The good news is, we control the level of enthusiasm we have for most things.

———————◇———————

Arthur James Balfour, 1st Earl of Balfour, was a statesman and diplomat who held various positions of power and influence within the British Conservative Party for over fifty years.

Balfour entered the House of Commons in 1874 as a Conservative MP for Hertford. He served in various capacities, including stints as Secretary for Scotland, Chief Secretary of Ireland, First Lord of the Treasury, and leader of the House of Commons. In 1902, Balfour was named Prime Minister, a position he held for three years, but he is perhaps best remembered for his support, as Foreign Minister, for the establishment of a Jewish homeland. His statement, known as the Balfour Declaration, pledged British aid for the Zionist movement and eventually led to the founding of the State of Israel.

HEROISM

"You cannot be a hero without being a coward."

— George Bernard Shaw
Irish Playwright, Critic
Nobel Prize Winner
7/26/1856 – 11/2/1950

Sometimes, just getting out of your comfort zone constitutes a heroic effort. It can be scary, but then, sometimes so is the status quo.

Take that chance. Be a hero — to yourself, and for yourself.

———————◇———————

George Bernard Shaw was a playwright, critic, and political activist. He is among the most successful and influential playwrights in the English language, and is best known for his plays *Saint Joan*, *Heartbreak House*, *Candida*, and *Pygmalion*.

In 1876, Shaw resolved to become a writer, and he moved to England. His early attempts at writing failed miserably, and his work was rejected by virtually every publishing house in London. However, he stuck with it, and as time went by, he began to find his voice.

By 1885, Shaw had found steady work as a journalist, primarily as a book reviewer and theater critic. He also began writing his own plays, and soon found critical and commercial success. His funniest and most popular play, by far, was *Pygmalion*. First staged in 1913, it was made into a motion picture in 1938 and won Shaw the Academy Award for Best Screenplay. It was later made into the musical *My Fair Lady*.

REVENGE

"While seeking revenge, dig two graves – one for yourself."

— Douglas Horton
American Clergyman
7/27/1891 – 8/21/1968

The best revenge is to move on, with few words, fewer thoughts, and zero reprisals. Live, learn, and leave them to their own conscience.

———◇———

Douglas Horton was a Protestant clergyman, academic leader, and fence-mender who strongly advocated that churches dismiss interfaith bickering for the sake of ecumenical unity. His efforts to encourage interfaith cooperation eventually led to a merger between the Protestant Congregational Christian Churches and the Presbyterian Evangelical and Reformed Church, resulting in the United Church of Christ.

FREEDOM

"The secret of freedom lies in educating people, whereas the secret of tyranny is in keeping them ignorant."

— Maximilien Robespierre
French Lawyer, Politician
5/16/1758 – 7/28/1794

The correlation is clear: The more educated you are, the more autonomy you tend to enjoy and the higher your chances for success in life.

Don't let anyone keep you in the dark. We live in an age that is teeming, nay, *overflowing* with information; if you can't find a teacher, teach yourself.

———◇———

Some people need but one name, and Robespierre is one of them. A French lawyer and politician, he is probably the best known of all the characters of the French Revolution and the Reign of Terror — after Louis XVI and Marie Antoinette.

A tenacious lawyer, Robespierre made a living representing the disenfranchised; he liked to make the comfortable uncomfortable, and to sow unease among the privileged classes. As a member of the Committee of Public Safety, the authority behind the Reign of Terror, he exonerated (if not extolled) mob violence and called for the execution of Louis XVI.

It is estimated that Robespierre was responsible for some sixteen thousand deaths during the Reign of Terror. As is often the case, however, the forces of the Revolution eventually turned against one of their own, and Robespierre was sent to the guillotine, on this day, in 1794.

July 29th

HISTORY

"History is a gallery of pictures in which there
are few originals and many copies."

— Alexis de Tocqueville
French Diplomat, Historian
7/29/1805 – 4/16/1859

It is often a difficult thing, to learn from the past. Indeed, at times it is a challenge to learn no matter what the lesson or by whom we are being taught. And so, we make the same mistakes, over and over; yet, somehow, we manage to find our way forward.

While it may seem that good examples are hard to come by, and even harder to follow, they are out there. Find one, or be one.

———————◇———————

Alexis Charles Henri Clérel de Tocqueville was a political scientist, diplomat, and historian. He came to America in 1831, with friend and fellow lawyer Gustave de Beaumont, to study its penal system. His observations on American life, taken during his travels around the country, resulted in his best-known work, *Democracy in America*.

A few things stuck out to Tocqueville. He noted that Americans enjoyed a pretty high standard of living, and that societies in general were relatively safe and stable (though he did find it odd that everyone got up so early to eat breakfast). He was also impressed by the relative equality of the average citizen, and by their ability to pursue opportunities. At the same time, however, he found it difficult to reconcile the overall abundance of freedoms with the country's embrace of slavery.

OBSTACLES

"Obstacles are those frightful things you see
when you take your eyes off your goal."

— Henry Ford
American Industrialist
7/30/1863 – 4/16/1947

Few things are easier than rationalizing why we cannot accomplish what we should. We often imagine a thing is too difficult, when in reality, our reticence is merely a measure of our own determination.

The simple truth is that our attitude is in charge. If we think we can, we can.

———————◇———————

Henry Ford, the founder of the Ford Motor Company, was a visionary, a business magnate, and America's preeminent industrialist.

Ford got his start working for Thomas Edison, as an engineer for the Detroit Edison Company. A natural tinkerer, Ford experimented with cars and motors in his spare time. By 1903, having developed several working models, Ford had investors lined up and he launched the Ford Motor Company.

Ford is probably best known for revolutionizing mass production by using an assembly line for producing his cars. By subdividing the various components of production, and streamlining the assembly process through the use of conveyors, Ford was able to capture huge gains in productivity, reducing the manufacturing cycle from twelve hours to ninety minutes. This efficiency allowed Ford to keep prices low, which in turn helped to capture the widest possible market. His strategy was an unmitigated success: In the nineteen years of the Model T's existence, Ford sold almost seventeen million of them.

July 31st

FEAR

"Where fear is present, wisdom cannot be."

— Lactantius
African-Roman Rhetorician, Advisor
c. 240 AD – c. 320 AD

Fear robs us of our judgment. The best way to address this problem is through situational awareness: You've thought about what *could* happen; give equal consideration to what you will do if it *does* happen.

Think ahead. Have a plan. Be prepared to implement it.

———————◇———————

Lucius Caecilius Firmianus Lactantius was an early Christian apologist and teacher who served two Roman emperors under decidedly different circumstances. He was appointed by the Roman emperor Diocletian to teach rhetoric in modern-day Turkey, but as the emperor stepped up his relentless persecution of Christians, Lactantius resigned his post and retired to North Africa. A dozen years later, he came out of retirement at the behest of Constantine, the first Christian emperor of Rome, to tutor his son Crispus. It is believed that Lactantius, who also served as an advisor to Constantine, helped to shape official religious policy in its earliest stages.

Lactantius is best remembered for the *Divine Precepts*, in which he refuted pagan beliefs while simultaneously asserting the rationality of the Christian belief in a single Supreme Being. The *Precepts* are considered the first methodical account of Christian thought written in Latin, and Lactantius took great care to explain Christianity in terms that would be palatable to those who were practicing other religions that were popular in the Empire at that time. For this, he would come to be known as the "Christian Cicero."

August 1st

BEHAVIOR

"Everybody experiences far more than he understands.
Yet it is experience, rather than understanding, that influences behavior."

— Marshall McLuhan
Canadian Professor, Philosopher
7/21/1911 – 12/31/1980

Intellectually, we know that facts trump feelings, yet we offer little to no resistance to the idea that a gut feeling is a suitable authority for setting facts aside when the mood strikes us — "I knew it would never work, but I had to try it anyway," we offer by way of explanation for a bad decision.

Although it seems counterintuitive, intellectually it sometimes really does make sense to go with our instincts, rather than what we think we know. It is that "sometimes" thing, though, that is the tricky part.

———————◇———————

Herbert Marshall McLuhan was a communications theorist, professor, and public intellectual. A popular lecturer, he spent over thirty years at the University of Toronto, as a professor and as director of the university's Centre for Culture and Technology.

McLuhan predicted the World Wide Web almost thirty years before it was invented and regarded the printed book as a fading construct that would soon disappear. He was the author or co-author of half a dozen books, including *The Gutenberg Galaxy: The Making of Typographic Man*; *Understanding Media: The Extensions of Man*; and *From Cliché to Archetype*. His dictum, "the medium is the message," underscored the power of media to influence all manner of thought — even in the face of contradictory facts, reason, and logic.

August 2nd

PRIVACY

"A memoir is an invitation into another person's privacy."

— Isabel Allende
Chilean-American Writer
Born 8/2/1942

Make no mistake: social media is the new and modern memoir; an open invitation to the world, to scrutinize and judge every facet of our lives. And we solicit this invasion on a daily — if not an hourly — basis.

———————◇———————

In 1973, when her godfather, Chilean President Salvador Allende, was deposed in a military coup led by Augusto Pinochet, Isabel Allende's life was forever altered. Her career as a journalist, in which she was gaining some prominence, was put on hold as she and her family fled the brutality of the Pinochet regime. They would live in exile, first in Venezuela and then in the United States, but Allende soon found a new avocation, as an internationally acclaimed author.

Allende is best known for her realistic-yet-mystical literary style, and for the remarkably open and honest semi-autobiographical depictions drawn from her own life. In addition to her many best-selling novels, she has also published several deeply personal memoirs, perhaps none more so than *Paula*, about the passing of her twenty-eight-year-old daughter, who succumbed to a rare disease.

In all, Allende's works have been translated into over thirty different languages and have sold nearly seventy million copies. She has won numerous awards for her work, including the Chilean National Prize for Literature and the PEN Center USA's Lifetime Achievement Award. In 2014, she was presented with the Presidential Medal of Freedom.

GRATIFICATION

"We cherish our friends not for their ability to amuse us,
but for ours to amuse them."

— Evelyn Waugh
English Writer, Reviewer
10/28/1903 – 4/10/1966

When we delight our friends, there is a mutual gratification at work: their amusement is in effect a small payment for our own cleverness — no matter how corny, contrived, or clichéd. It is but one of the many acts of connectivity that we deploy, again and again, to sustain our friendships.

Arthur Evelyn St. John Waugh was a novelist, biographer, and travel book writer who was also a prolific journalist and book reviewer. He is probably best remembered for the novel *Brideshead Revisited*, which is widely regarded as his master work and is a cornerstone of the British literary canon.

It could be said that writing was a family affair: Waugh's father, also named Arthur, was a managing director of a publishing house that once handled the work of writer Charles Dickens; his older brother, Alec, was also a well-known novelist.

Waugh was married twice: first (and briefly) to a woman named Evelyn Gardner, and then to one of her cousins, Laura Herbert, with whom he had seven children.

Waugh's popularity faded as he grew older, but he continued to write up to the day he died, of heart failure, on Easter Sunday, April 10, 1966.

August 4th

FELLOWSHIP

"The fellowship of true friends who can hear you out, share your joys,
help carry your burdens, and correctly counsel you is priceless."

— Ezra Taft Benson
American Farmer, Religious Leader
8/4/1899 – 5/30/1994

Who's in your tribe? Chances are, you have more than one. There's the
family tribe, the work tribe, the neighborhood tribe, the school tribe, the best
friends tribe. These are the people who relate to — and empathize with — the
various facets of your life, just as you do for them and theirs.

It doesn't take a lot of effort to be supportive of others. Often, it's just
a knowing glance or a simple smile that helps a cohort to make it through
another day, and sometimes, it's just about being there.

———————————◇———————————

Ezra Taft Benson was an American farmer, government official, and religious leader. Born on a farm in Whitney, Idaho, in 1899, he was the oldest of
eleven children. He earned a bachelor's degree from Brigham Young University
in 1926, and in 1927 he received a master's degree in agricultural economics
from Iowa State. He pursued a Doctorate at the University of California at
Berkeley, but he never finished it.

Benson was a lifelong supporter of the Boy Scouts of America, and a
member of the organization's National Executive Board. In the 1950s, he
served as the United States Secretary of Agriculture under President Dwight
D. Eisenhower, and in 1989, he received the Presidential Citizens Medal from
President George H. W. Bush. Late in life, Benson was selected as President of
The Church of Jesus Christ of Latter-day Saints. He served from 1985 until
his death in 1994.

DESPERATION

"In difficult and desperate cases, the boldest counsels are the safest."

— Livy
Roman Historian
c. 59 BC – c. 17 AD

In desperate times, the boldest choices are often the safest options precisely because they free you from expectations. It couldn't possibly work anyway, so where is the harm in trying something different, and unexpected?

Sometimes it pays to be daring, or audacious. Is that time *now*?

———◆———

Titus Livius Patavinus, known as Livy, was a Roman historian whose monumental history of Rome, *Ad Urbe Condita Libri*, spanned seven centuries, from its founding in 753 BC through the reign of Augustus in Livy's own lifetime.

Livy never held a public office, nor did he serve in the military. However, he would ultimately turn his relative inexperience to his advantage — had he been a political insider, with access to government texts, documents, and records, and been privy to the inner workings of the Senate, he might have focused on the salacious behind-the-scenes details of the Roman government. Instead, Livy's writing presents the history of Rome in terms of the principles and character of its leaders, from all walks of life, which is perhaps why his life's work became a classic in his own lifetime, and influenced historians for the next two millennia.

August 6th

CLARITY

"Clarity is the counterbalance of profound thoughts."

— Luc de Clapiers
French Writer
8/6/1715 – 5/28/1747

It doesn't matter how deep or meaningful your insights might be; in order to effectively share them with others, you must be able to explain them in a way that is both instantly recognizable and easily understood. This is a very challenging task, but it is also one of the most intensely satisfying.

———————◇———————

Luc de Clapiers, Marquis de Vauvenargues, was a French writer and moralist who had a knack for finding universal truths in everyday life. He believed that each of us has a great capacity for goodness, and that individual dignity and fulfillment are attained through conscious decisions to act on those things we are most passionate about.

De Clapiers is best remembered today for two works: *Introduction to an Understanding of the Human Mind* and *Reflections and Maxims*, the latter of which consisted of the title essay and some seven hundred maxims, aphorisms, and contemplations. His friend Voltaire proclaimed the *Maxims* as one of the best books ever written in the French language.

PRUDENCE

"Whereof one cannot speak, thereof one must be silent."

— Ludwig Wittgenstein
Austrian-British Philosopher
4/26/1889 – 4/29/1951

Sounds crazy, right? In this day and age, where everyone has an opinion and a pulpit and an eagerness to overshare *with absolutely everyone*, we should consider remaining quiet, thus hiding (or feigning) our ignorance?

Yes! Absolutely, positively, yes! The art of appearing to possess even a modicum of intelligence (and discretion) begins with the ability to remain silent. It is an excellent quality to cultivate, if you can.

———————◇———————

Ludwig Josef Johann Wittgenstein is widely regarded as one of the greatest philosophers of the twentieth century. Born into one the wealthiest and most respected families in Vienna, young Ludwig often found himself spending time among many of the elite artists and intellectuals in Hapsburg society — Gustav Klimt, Sigmund Freud, Johannes Brahms, and Gustav Mahler were regular visitors to the family home. Despite his privileged upbringing, when World War I came, Wittgenstein joined the fight.

It was during the war years that Wittgenstein wrote his first important work, the *Tractatus Logico-Philosophicus*. He was primarily interested in logic, and the *Tractatus* is essentially Wittgenstein's assertion that the world itself is comprised of facts, not objects. He also rejected all so-called "unified" or foundational philosophical theses, in which simple maxims could be used to explain the complexities of life. When asked "What is the task of philosophy?" Wittgenstein famously replied, "To show the fly the way out of the bottle."

August 8th

SUPERSTITION

"Conscience without judgment is superstition."

— Benjamin Whichcote
British Philosopher, Theologian
c. 1609 – c. 1683

We tend to be grounded in the ethical codes of our family, our society, our culture, or our religious beliefs. Not surprisingly, many of these conventions have been passed down from generation to generation, often for millennia, and we bear them forward unreservedly. The question is: Do they make sense? If we haven't truly examined our own dogma, how do we justify the conflicts that arise when it conflicts with the moral constructs of those who are just as adamant in their beliefs?

———————◇———————

Benjamin Whichcote was a theologian and Provost of King's College at Cambridge. In 1636, he was ordained, and was appointed Sunday afternoon lecturer at Trinity Church in Cambridge, a post he held for nearly twenty years. During a time of (sometimes violent) religious upheaval, Whichcote's views were often at odds with the rigid, Calvinistic doctrines of Church orthodoxy. His sermons, in which he appealed for liberality and acceptance, were published posthumously and constitute his most substantial work.

Central to Whichcote's moral and religious outlook were the ideas that faith is founded on reason — "the candle of the Lord" — and that religious tolerance was essential given the inability of reasonable people to adequately resolve their religious differences. He argued that it was the duty of every Christian to be sensitive to the views of others, no matter how mistaken one might believe them to be, and to acknowledge areas of agreement for the sake of cordiality.

CONSENT

"Let life happen to you. Believe me: Life is always right."

— Rainer Maria Rilke
Austro-German Novelist
12/4/1875 – 12/29/1926

Consent to life and the lessons it tries to teach you. It has been around a lot longer than you have, and it has seen *everything*.

———————◆———————

René Karl Wilhelm Johann Josef Maria Rilke is known as one of the most lyrically intense writers of both verse and prose. As a young boy he was enrolled in military schools, and as a young man he studied business administration, but Rilke had no interest in the mundane. He left his studies behind and moved to Munich, where he quickly immersed himself in the unstructured and spontaneous artistic culture of a major cosmopolitan city.

Determined to pursue a literary career, by 1894 Rilke had published his first volume of poetry. From Munich he traveled across Europe, to Russia, France, Spain, Austria, Switzerland, and Italy. As he matured, he quickly found his voice: a rhythmic, almost musical writing style that he used to explore existentialist themes of love, death, and God (often framed as a universal life force, or a shared consciousness).

Rilke attained international fame late in life. His *The Book of Hours* and the autobiographical *The Story of the Love and Death of Cornet Christoph Rilke* were his most acclaimed works during his lifetime, but he is probably best known today for his *Duino Elegies* and *Sonnets to Orpheus*. A frail and sensitive soul his entire life, Rilke succumbed to leukemia in Geneva, in 1926, at the very height of his popularity.

EXPERIENCE

"Experience is not what happens to you; it's what you do
with what happens to you."

— Aldous Huxley
English Novelist, Philosopher
7/26/1894 – 11/22/1963

The primary difference between a good experience and a bad experience is that a bad experience — a terrible experience, the worst experience — can teach us something that even the very best experience never could: resilience.

Aldous Leonard Huxley was a novelist, critic, and screenwriter whose works are notable for their intelligence, wit, and pessimism. His best-known novel, *Brave New World*, is a nightmarish vision of psychological conditioning by a Statist government and the abject acceptance of it by the populace. It is widely regarded as one of the greatest novels of the twentieth century, and a blueprint for much of the dystopian science fiction that has followed.

Born into a prominent intellectual family in Godalming, England, Huxley was educated at Eton. Upon graduation, he embarked on a life as a writer, and eventually settled in California, where he began writing screenplays. He took an interest in mysticism, and began experimenting with the hallucinogen mescaline. He wrote about these experiences in a 1954 collection of essays called *The Doors of Perception*, which would be the inspiration for the name of the rock band, The Doors.

Despite his tremendous literary stature, when Huxley died on November 22, 1963, his passing drew little media fanfare. He'd had the misfortune of dying on the same day that President John F. Kennedy was assassinated.

August 11th

DREAMS

"I dreamed I was a butterfly, then I awoke. Now I wonder: Am I a man who dreamt of being a butterfly, or am I a butterfly dreaming that I am a man?"

— Zhuangzi
Chinese Philosopher
c. 370 BC – c. 287 BC

Some prefer dreams to waking life, while others shun dreams in deference to reality. Which do you prefer? A better question might be: Does it really matter? As long as you dream, you get the best of both worlds.

———————◇———————

Zhuangzi, or "Master Zhuang," was a fourth-century philosopher who is considered a pivotal figure of Daoism (also known as Taoism). A compilation of his and others' writings, known as *The Zhuangzi*, is marked by humanist reflections on following "the path," a natural force that governs the universe and leads to harmony and inner peace. It is generally thought that the first seven chapters of *The Zhuangzi*, known as the "inner" books, were written by Zhuangzi himself, while the remaining chapters, called the "outer" books, were written by his later followers.

Except for anecdotes in *The Zhuangzi* itself, there are relatively few details about Zhuangzi's life. We know that he was a native of the state of Meng, that his personal name was Zhou, and that he was a minor official in his home state of Qiyuan. We also know that Zhuangzi was a contemporary of Mencius, an eminent Confucian scholar known as China's "Second Sage," and that his writings influenced Chan Buddhism, a philosophy that combined Daoism with Buddhism.

August 12th

FAITH

"Faith is not believing that God can. It is knowing that God will."

— Ben Stein
American Writer, Lawyer, Actor
Born 11/25/1944

There is a big difference between believing and knowing; after all, anyone can say they *believe* a thing to be true, but it takes a bit more to proclaim that one *knows* it to be true. That takes conviction.

If you've done your homework, you can be confident in your conclusions.

Benjamin Jeremy Stein is an American writer, lawyer, economist, commentator, and teacher, and an actor known for his droning, monotonous delivery. A graduate of Columbia University, Stein was the valedictorian of the Yale Law School Class of 1970. He crafted speeches for U.S. presidents Richard Nixon and Gerald Ford, and has been a columnist for *The Wall Street Journal*, *The Los Angeles Herald Examiner*, *New York Magazine*, *Los Angeles Magazine*, and *The American Spectator*. He also writes frequently for *The Washington Post*, and has written and published sixteen books.

Stein has worked in the entertainment field as an actor, comedian, and Emmy Award-winning host of the game show "Win Ben Stein's Money." His most iconic on-screen role is undoubtedly that of The Economics Teacher in 1986's *Ferris Bueller's Day Off* ("Bueller? Bueller?").

August 13th

DIVINITY

"The best theology is rather a divine life than a divine knowledge."

— Jeremy Taylor
English Cleric, Author
8/15/1613 – 8/13/1667

We can argue, fight, and kill over whose "understanding" is divine, or we can go about living our life trying to be the very best person that we can possibly be.

Choose to do good, and you will be good.

———◇———

Jeremy Taylor was a cleric in the Church of England who achieved fame as an author during the Protectorate of Oliver Cromwell (1653 – 1658). He has been referred to as the "Shakespeare of the Divines" for his poetic writing style and is considered one of the greatest prose writers in the English language.

Taylor graduated from the University of Cambridge and was ordained in 1633. He cultivated many important relationships and had numerous sponsors, not the least of whom was Charles I, who named him Doctor of Divinity by royal decree in 1643. By 1655, Taylor had written his two best-known works: *The Rule and Exercises of Holy Living* and *The Rule and Exercises of Holy Dying*. These devotional handbooks contained spiritual insights that appealed to members of all denominations for the next hundred years.

To this day, Taylor's unwavering plea for toleration among all believers is celebrated every August 13th by the Church of England, with a Lesser Festival on their Calendar of Saints.

PITY

"When Man evolved Pity, he did a queer thing—
deprived himself of the power of living life as it is without wishing it
to become something different."

— John Galsworthy
English Novelist, Playwright
8/14/1867 – 1/31/1933

There are actually a great many emotions that distract us from living life as it is, and being grateful for it. The remedy is quite simple: Remember that it could always be worse, and that, for good or ill, we generally tend to get what we have earned, not what we deserve.

John Galsworthy was a novelist and playwright who is best known for *The Forsyte Saga*, a multi-volume semi-autobiographical chronicle of a large, upper middle-class family at the turn of the century. It won the Nobel Prize in Literature in 1932.

Galsworthy was going to be a lawyer, with an eye toward specializing in maritime law. He booked a voyage around the world, where he met the writer Joseph Conrad, who was then working as a mate aboard a merchant ship. They struck up a friendship that would last their entire lives.

Galsworthy decided to forsake a career in law and soon took to writing. His first novel, *The Man of Property*, was a harsh criticism of the same upper middle-class to which he himself belonged. It was published in 1906, to wide acclaim.

Galsworthy was also a successful dramatist. A social activist, his plays are often focused on controversial ethical or social issues. His most famous play, *Justice*, was a portrayal of English prison life that so aroused and enraged the audiences that it led to reforms in the British penal system.

August 15th

LEGACY

"Glory is fleeting but obscurity is forever."

— Napoleon Bonaparte
French Military Leader, Emperor
8/15/1769 – 5/5/1821

There is no honor in ambiguity; no glory in anonymity. Opportunities abound. You control your destiny. You design your legacy. So, ask her to lunch. Lobby for that promotion. Explain why you should get that assignment. Speak. Act. *Live.*

Napoléon Bonaparte, also known as Napoleon I, was a French statesman and military leader who rose to prominence during the French Revolution and crowned himself emperor. A shrewd and ambitious strategist, Napoleon successfully used war to expand the French empire. He lost his throne not once, but twice, and was exiled both times. He died during his second exile, on the remote island of Saint Helena, and was buried there against his wishes. However, twenty-five years later, his remains were returned to France and he was entombed in a crypt at Les Invalides in Paris, alongside many of France's other famous military leaders.

Napoleon was a Big Personality, and a Man of Action. It seems he knew that history favors the bold, and he wasn't afraid to take chances. He also appreciated that sometimes there are unanticipated rewards for being in the right place at the right time — like his campaign in Egypt, in 1799, when one of his soldiers discovered the Rosetta Stone. The find would help crack the hieroglyphic code, unlocking the culture of Ancient Egypt through a language that had been lost for millennia.

August 16th

DEATH

"If some persons died, and others did not die,
death would be a terrible affliction."

— Jean de la Bruyere
French Philosopher, Satirist
8/16/1645 – 5/11/1696

While there is much that distinguishes us, one from another, there are also a great many things that unite us; that bring us together for the common good in spite of the unavoidable end that awaits us all. It is the shared touchstones of life which allow us to conjure great strengths from the depths of our weakness — for ourselves, and for others.

Jean de la Bruyere was a satiric moralist who is best known for a single work, *The Characters, or the Manners of the Age, with The Characters of Theophrastus*, in which he wrote in the manner of fourth-century BC writer Theophrastus, assigning specific characteristics to actual people and then critiquing their actions. It ruffled some gilded feathers in its time, but is widely regarded as one of the masterpieces of French literature.

As a young man, de la Bruyere became a tutor in the household of the Duke de Bourbon, which allowed him to gain an insider's view into the daily lives of the rich and powerful. His intimate and penetrating observations about their lives was as much a character study as it was a commentary on money, social customs, and ennui-driven idleness among the elites of seventeenth-century France. When *The Characters* first appeared in 1688, it made de la Bruyere a number of well-connected enemies, even though his motive for writing *The Characters* was not to irreparably sully the reputations of his wealthy countrymen, but to remind everyone of their moral duties.

August 17th

MALICE

"Malice can always find a mark to shoot at, and a pretence to fire."

— Charles Simmons
American Novelist, Editor
8/17/1924 – 6/1/2017

Why is it that sometimes we just don't like someone? And why is it that this unquantifiable dislike can stir in us a wish to see misfortune visited upon the subject of our unjustifiable ire?

More often than not, these kinds of feelings are the result of our own inner turmoil and our own personal problems; things aren't going our way, and suddenly we are a hammer in search of a nail. Once we realize what is happening, we can recalibrate, and redirect our energy where it belongs: on addressing the root cause of our malevolent attitude.

———◦———

Charles Paul Simmons was a long-time editor at *The New York Times Book Review*, and the author of *The Belle Lettres Papers*, a behind-the-scenes satire that mocked the very idea of being an editor for an institution such as *The New York Times Book Review*. He wrote four other books, including *Powdered Eggs*, which won the William Faulkner Foundation Award in 1965.

A World War II veteran, Simmons was a graduate of Regis High School in Manhattan, and Columbia University. He had an encyclopedic knowledge of Shakespeare's plays, and was a co-author, with Alexander Coleman, of *All There is to Know: Readings From the Illustrious Eleventh Edition of the Encyclopaedia Britannica*. Other books include *An Old Fashioned Darling*, *Wrinkles*, and *Salt Water*.

August 18th

FRATERNITY

"We are not primarily put on this earth to see through
one another, but to see one another through."

— Peter de Vries
American Editor, Novelist
2/27/1910 – 9/28/1993

All of us are passengers heading in the same direction. Some of us have stops that are nearby while others will travel on much farther, but we are all on board the same train. We may never see one another again, but that doesn't excuse us from being considerate. After all, being nice doesn't cost us anything, but it could gain us everything.

———————◇———————

The son of Dutch immigrants, de Vries was reared on Chicago's South Side. He served in the Marine Corps during World War II, attaining the rank of Captain, and briefly worked for the OSS, which was the predecessor to the CIA. After a stint as an editor for *Poetry* magazine in Chicago, de Vries joined the staff of *The New Yorker* magazine and moved to Westport, Connecticut, where he formed a lifelong friendship with author J. D. Salinger.

A prolific writer, de Vries was known for his imaginative wordplay and sardonic humor, and is credited with such witticisms as "Nostalgia ain't what it used to be" and "Deep down, he's shallow." He had a wide range of interests and wrote everything from short stories, novellas, and a play, to poetry, essays, and reviews. He also wrote twenty-three novels, including *The Tunnel of Love*, which was adapted both as a play and as a motion picture.

TRUTH

"If we all worked on the assumption that what is accepted as true
is really true, there would be little hope of advancement."

— Orville Wright
American Inventor, Aviator
8/19/1871 – 1/30/1948

As history teaches, a great many Truths are temporary. They exist, but like all things are subject to review, and to change. We know, for example, that the earth isn't flat and that the sun doesn't revolve around it; however, these "truths" were once thought to be self-evident.

Never allow the blind faith of others to convince you to abandon your own search for truth. Where would we be if Magellan hadn't challenged the accepted orthodoxy? If Galileo hadn't defied convention? If the Wright brothers hadn't dared to believe they could fly?

Orville Wright was an aviator, engineer, and inventor who, with his brother, Wilbur, is credited with building and flying the world's first successful airplane.

On December 17, 1903, Orville made the first controlled, sustained flight of a powered, heavier-than-air aircraft the brothers called The Flyer. Soon after that first flight, the brothers began filling contracts for airplanes in both Europe and the United States. Today, they are considered the fathers of modern aviation.

As young boys, the brothers were fascinated by the possibility of flight. As engineers, they became convinced that it was possible. After experimenting with a curved-wing design and a movable rudder, the brothers took their work to Kitty Hawk, North Carolina, where heavy winds were more conducive to flying. The rest, as they say, is history.

August 20th

QUITTING

"Some men give up their designs when they have almost reached the goal;
while others, on the contrary, obtain a victory by exerting, at the last
moment, more vigorous efforts than ever before."

— Heroditus
Greek Historian
c. 485 BC – c. 425 BC

It is often difficult to tell if and when you will find success. You plan, you work, you revise your plan, and you work some more; naturally, you run into obstacles along the way, and perhaps you begin to question the wisdom of your quest. That is fine; that is normal. Just don't give up, because you seldom know which of your exertions will ultimately lead to success.

Herodotus was a historian who spent his entire life working on a single, massive project: *The Histories*, a complete and unabridged account of the Greco-Persian Wars (499 – 479 BC). A contemporary of Thucydides, Socrates, and Euripides, Herodotus traveled throughout Asia Minor and the Middle East, collecting what he called "autopsies," which he used to explain how and why Greece and Persia engaged in brutal warfare for twenty years, "in order that the deeds of men not be erased by time."

Some have questioned the veracity of his work, since Heroditus had a tendency to include the occasional bit of gossip and hearsay, but in general he has been forgiven since the overall effect has been to turn the tedium of day-to-day history into great literature.

Sometime around 443 BC, Herodotus joined a group of Athenians to colonize Thurii, a city in southern Italy. He died there in 425 BC. The ruins of the city can be found near Sibari, in Calabria, Italy.

ANGER

"There was never an angry man that thought his anger unjust."

— Saint Francis de Sales
Swiss Bishop
8/21/1567 – 12/28/1622

. . . but there have been plenty of folks who have discovered, after their anger had subsided, that they had been unfair. Some were fortunate enough to have restrained themselves from action, but a great many have regretted the actions they took in anger; some, for the rest of their lives.

Stop, think, and remember that where there is anger, there is seldom good judgment.

———————◇———————

Francis de Sales was a Bishop of Geneva and is a saint in the Catholic Church. He is noted for his insistence that every Christian is called to holiness and sanctity, regardless of their station in life, and that the worst sin is to judge someone or to gossip about them.

De Sales's most successful work was called *Introduction to the Devout Life*, and was written with the lay person in mind. Published in 1608, the *Introduction* took a less serious approach to living one's faith, encouraging the readers to find humor in their day-to-day lives and to be as forgiving of themselves as they are of others. It quickly became wildly popular all over Europe.

HORIZONS

"I prefer a short life with width to a narrow one with length."

— Avicenna

Persian Polymath

8/22/980 – c. 6/1037

It is often the things that we didn't do that we lament the most. Since none of us ever know how much time we have been given on this earth, perhaps we should consider trying to get out of our comfort zones more often, for the expressed purpose of broadening our horizons.

Don't be paralyzed by mindless habits. Start here: Do one thing, do *some* thing, different, today!

———————◇———————

Abu Ali al-Husayn ibn Sina, better known in the Western world as Avicenna, was a Persian polymath who is regarded as one of the most famous and influential physicians, philosophers, and writers of the Islamic Golden Age.

A child prodigy, Avicenna is said to have read and memorized the entire Quran by age ten. He was also instructed in logic and Ancient Greek literature. By age sixteen, Avicenna began the study of medicine, a discipline he is said to have found relatively easy to master. It must have been: His book, *The Canon of Medicine*, would become one of the most famous and influential medical journals in the history of medicine, and was a primary reference in European medical schools for the next six hundred years.

August 23rd

ENVY

"They envy the distinction I have won; let them therefore envy my toils,
my honesty, and the methods by which I gained it."

— Sallust
Roman Historian, Politician
c. 86 BC – c. 35 BC

It seems we always covet the spoils, but not the toils. We want the good life! We just don't want to put in the time and effort needed to attain it.

The reality is, few things are beyond the reach of those who are willing to work for them. The question is: How badly do you want it?

Gaius Sallustius Crispus was a historian and politician who is best known for his five-volume account of Roman history, spanning the years 78 to 67 BC, called *The Histories*. Sallust focused largely on the politics of Rome, in particular the rivalries, the clashes of egos, and the inevitable corruption. Sallust had himself once been a senator, but he was expelled amid allegations of immoral behavior.

In spite of his own patrician heritage, Sallust supported Julius Caesar's opposition to Roman aristocracy and the re-establishment of the Roman Empire. His loyalty was rewarded with a governorship in North Africa (present-day Algeria), but he was soon facing accusations of extortion, and of using his position to steal the wealth of his province.

Sallust's questionable conduct stands in stark contrast to his disapproving, even hypercritical depictions of Roman political intrigue, but history does seem to provide an "out" for his apparent hypocrisy: it seems that some of his actions have been confused with those of his adopted son, Sallustius Crispus, who was apparently a man of great wealth and an appetite for the extravagant.

SACRIFICE

"Let others laugh when you sacrifice desire to duty, if they will.
You have time and eternity to rejoice in."

— Theodore Parker
American Minister, Abolitionist
8/24/1810 – 5/10/1860

Does it really matter what others think about how you spend your time? We get one life. Only one. And there is no end to the compromises and sacrifices inherent in the deal. It isn't always easy, but we do what we must; sometimes that means jettisoning the Negative Nellies in order to focus on the things that bring us joy, make us proud, or further our cause.

Never let the opinions of others determine what you do, who you see, or how you prioritize the values and virtues that are most important to you.

———————◦———————

Theodore Parker was a theologian, scholar, and abolitionist whose sermons inspired speeches by Abraham Lincoln and Martin Luther King, Jr. A pastor ordained in the Unitarian Church, Parker was a Transcendentalist in the sense that he ignored a lot of traditional Christian dogma in favor of the instinctive and intuitive spiritual awareness and knowledge of God that each of us derive from our own individual experiences.

Parker's liberal interpretation of official church doctrine was met with opposition and he was forced to resign his pastorate. However, he soon accepted a ministry in Boston, where he worked tirelessly as an abolitionist, making impassioned speeches, helping slaves to escape, and serving on a secret committee that supported the abolitionist John Brown.

August 25th

HOPE

"Hope is the pillar that holds up the world."

— Pliny the Elder
Roman Author, Philosopher
c. 23 AD – 8/25/79 AD

Hope is optimism in the face of near-certain defeat; a trust placed in the improbable; and a reaffirmation of the belief that miracles still exist, and still happen. We are let down more often than we aren't, but even during the most heart-wrenching crisis, hope helps to dampen our most crushing losses.

Where would we be without hope?

———◇———

Gaius Plinius Secundus, aka Pliny the Elder, was an author, a scientist, a philosopher, and a commander of both army and naval forces during the early Roman Empire. He was a friend of the emperor Vespasian, with whom Pliny had served in Germany.

Pliny's most enduring work is his *Natural History*, which he called, simply, "a study of the nature of things." Comprising thirty-seven books that encompassed everything from astronomy to zoology, *Natural History* was considered the authoritative text on scientific matters until well into the Middle Ages. Unfortunately, Pliny often mixed fact with fiction, fables, exaggerations, and superstitious beliefs, none of which were seriously challenged until the fifteenth century.

Pliny died when, as commander of the Misenum fleet in the Bay of Naples, he went ashore to investigate a strange cloud formation. The "cloud" was the result of a volcanic eruption from Mount Vesuvius, which had buried the cities of Pompeii and Herculaneum. The air was full of ash and toxic fumes, and Pliny succumbed to them on this day in 79 AD.

August 26th

DISTRACTIONS

"By prevailing over all obstacles and distractions,
one may unfailingly arrive at his chosen goal or destination."

— Christopher Columbus
Italian Explorer
c. 1450 – 5/20/1506

We all get distracted, from time to time. Even these words you are reading are, in their own way, a distraction (hopefully an enjoyable one). The good news is: If it is important to us, when we need to, we can overcome any distraction through focus, determination, and sheer force of will.

Speaking of distractions, here's another one for you: Michelangelo, Leonardo Da Vinci, Martin Luther, Niccolo Machiavelli, and Saint Ignatius were all living and working during Christopher Columbus's lifetime. I think it's safe to say that each of them had a certain focus and determination. Wouldn't you agree?

———◇———

Christopher Columbus was a master navigator and explorer who was determined to find a direct seagoing route to Asia, traveling west from Europe. Perhaps distracted by his quest for wealth and fame — the Spanish monarchy promised him 10 percent of all bounties he found, along with a noble title and the governorship of any new lands he discovered —Columbus was hamstrung from the very beginning by a fundamental flaw in his calculations: His estimation of the earth's circumference was off by a factor of nearly six.

He never did find a western route from Europe to Asia, but between 1492 and 1504, Columbus made a total of four voyages across the Atlantic Ocean to the Caribbean and the Americas, establishing a European presence that would lead to the exploration, conquest, and colonization of the New World.

GREATNESS

"Nothing great in the world has ever been accomplished without passion."

— Georg Wilhelm Friedrich Hegel
German Philosopher
8/27/1770 – 11/14/1831

Can you imagine how different the Sistine Chapel would look if Michelangelo hadn't been so obsessed with getting it just right? What if Shah Jahan had decided that a simple tomb was good enough for his beloved wife? What if Shakespeare had stuck to sonnets, or if Einstein had stayed in that Swiss patent office?

Follow your dream, and whatever you do, do it with all your heart, for without passion there is only the adequate, the passable, the "good enough." Do not settle for mediocrity; it is intolerable to living your best life.

———————◇———————

Georg Wilhelm Friedrich Hegel was a philosopher who is widely regarded as one of the most important figures of German idealism. He is best known for developing a philosophical construct that emphasized the study of human thought from its original thesis, to its antithesis, and to the eventual (and inevitable) synthesis into absolute knowledge. His first book, *The Phenomenology of Spirit*, was published in 1807 and expounds on this hypothesis.

Hegel also published three other works, which collectively define his legal, moral, social, and political philosophy. They are: *Science of Logic*, *Encyclopedia of the Philosophical Sciences*, and *Elements of the Philosophy of Right*.

TEACHING

"Correction does much, but encouragement does more."

— Johann Wolfgang von Goethe
German Writer, Statesman
8/28/1749 – 3/22/1832

Teaching imparts knowledge, and correction leads to competence, but encouragement provides something equally important: a desire to learn.

You have it in you to do what you were born to do. Seek out those mentors who can not only educate you, but who can and will motivate you, as well.

Johann Wolfgang von Goethe was a poet, playwright, novelist, statesman, and philosopher who is probably best known for his tragic play, *Faust*, which took him nearly sixty years to complete. In addition to poetry and plays, he wrote four novels, treatises on botany and anatomy, numerous criticisms, an autobiography, and his memoirs. An autodidact, he also studied physics, philosophy, geology, multiple foreign languages, and left behind nearly three thousand drawings.

Goethe was a practicing attorney by age twenty-two, but he attained worldwide fame at twenty-five when his novel, *The Sorrows of Young Werther*, became an instant cult classic. The Weimar Duke, Karl August (or Charles Augustus), invited Goethe to join his court, so that he could focus on his writing. Goethe accepted the offer and would spend most of the rest of his life in the residences provided by the Duke. He was eventually given title to a small house, where he died and which today is the site of the Goethe National Museum. He is widely regarded as the greatest German literary figure of the modern era.

August 29th

RULES

"The young man knows the rules, but the old man knows the exceptions."

— Oliver Wendell Holmes, Sr.
American Physician, Poet, Polymath
8/29/1809 – 10/7/1894

If wisdom comes with age — and let us pray that it does — then so, too, might we hope that within our youth there resides enough sense to seek the counsel of those who have gained it through experience.

———————◦———————

Oliver Wendell Holmes, Sr., was a physician by trade, but his lasting fame accrued through his poetry, and by his association with fellow poets William Cullen Bryant, Henry Wadsworth Longfellow, John Greenleaf Whittier, and James Russell Lowell. Collectively known as the Fireside Poets, they were the first American poets who were thought the equal of their British counterparts. Holmes was considered the best among them.

In 1833, Holmes began his medical studies in Paris, which was credited with having the most advanced medical system in the world. He continued his studies at Harvard, where he earned his M.D. degree, and then took a faculty position doing research and teaching Anatomy and Physiology at the school. His observations on the connection between sanitation and disease predated Louis Pasteur's Germ Theory of Disease by nearly twenty years. He is also credited with coining the term "anesthesia."

As a writer, Holmes had numerous critical and commercial successes; however, it was his poem "Old Ironsides" that would have the most enduring impact. An ode to the eighteenth-century frigate, the USS Constitution, which was destined for the scrap yard, Holmes's poem generated such a public outcry that the ship was saved. Today it is the world's oldest commissioned warship still afloat, and a national monument.

August 30th

JUSTIFICATION

"Justifying a fault doubles it."

— French proverb

Rationalizing a lapse in judgment instead of apologizing for it is the surest way to damage the reputation you are trying to salvage. Admit when you are wrong, or have done wrong, and both your character and integrity will be saved.

———◇———

French proverbs are known for their biting wit, observational wisdom, and bluntness.

August 31st

PATIENCE

"Patience has its limits. Take it too far and it's cowardice."

— Holbrook Jackson
British Writer, Publisher
12/31/1874 – 6/16/1948

Careful plans have their place, but at some point you simply have to put those plans into action.

Don't let a fear of failure hold you back: History is full of people who have succeeded with less — and they weren't nearly as brave as you.

———————◆———————

George Holbrook Jackson was a writer, publisher, and avid bibliophile whose devotion to the printed word led to improvements in the production standards of everyday books.

Born in Liverpool, Jackson worked as a clerk and a freelance writer. In 1907, with financing from George Bernard Shaw, he and business partner A. R. Orage bought *The New Age*, a struggling Christian Socialist weekly magazine. The following year, Jackson left the magazine and took Orage's wife with him (although she refused to divorce Orage).

Jackson would take other editorial positions, and in 1914 he bought a weekly newspaper and converted it to a literary magazine, called *To-Day*. He would publish his magazine until 1923, when it merged with another English literary journal, *Life and Letters*. Despite contributions from the likes of Max Beerbohm, Hilaire Belloc, E. M. Forster, Thomas Hardy, Evelyn Waugh, and Virginia Woolf, *Life and Letters* ceased publication in April 1935.

Jackson would continue writing for the rest of his life, mostly book reviews and essays about reading and collecting books. The sum of his obsession can be found in his 1931 book, *The Anatomy of Bibliomania*.

EFFORT

"In great attempts it is glorious even to fail."

— Cassius Longinus
Roman Senator
c. 87 BC – c. 42 BC

While trying to invent a commercially viable lightbulb, Thomas Edison failed countless times. He estimated that he tried over six thousand different materials to use as a filament before he finally found one that worked.

We all experience failure — countless times — and each time we do, we have an opportunity to do one of two things: quit, or go on. If we go on, we risk failure; yet there is also the tantalizing possibility of success. If we quit, however, we risk a lifetime of asking ourselves, "What if I had tried just one more time? Or tried just a little bit harder?"

Gaius Cassius Longinus was a Roman senator and one of the leaders of the plot to kill Julius Caesar. He was the brother-in-law of one of the co-conspirators, Marcus Junius Brutus, having married Brutus's half-sister, Junia Tertia.

In 44 BC, as an officer of Rome, Cassius was promised the governorship of Syria. However, he began to suspect that the appointment would never materialize, and he joined the conspiracy to assassinate Caesar. After the murder, Cassius was forced to leave Rome and he went to Syria, where he raised a large army and overthrew the governor of the province, Publius Cornelius Dolabella, who had been installed by the Senate. War followed, and in 42 BC, near Philippi, Greece, Cassius's forces were overrun by Mark Antony's. Believing the battle was lost, he killed himself. Meanwhile, Mark Antony had to retreat in order to aid Octavian's army, which had been captured by Brutus.

RELATIONSHIPS

"Truth is, everybody is going to hurt you;
you just gotta find the ones worth suffering for."

— Bob Marley
Jamaican Singer-Songwriter, Activist
2/6/1945 – 5/11/1981

We all have to choose who we allow into our lives, and who we allow to stay in our lives. It is wise to surround yourself with people who are worthy of your love and friendship, but wiser still to understand that all relationships exact an emotional toll. How much is too much? Only you can say.

———————◇———————

Robert Nesta Marley was a singer-songwriter who became an international musical and cultural icon while advocating for social change. Best known for hits such as *Three Little Birds, One Love, No Woman No Cry, Jamming, Buffalo Soldier, Is this Love?*, and *Stir It Up*, Marley sang about politics and social revolutions while simultaneously getting his listeners to get up and dance. His distinctive songwriting and vocal style resonated with audiences all over the world, and it is estimated that he and his band, The Wailers, have sold over 100 million records.

Born in St. Ann Parish, Jamaica, Marley became a worldwide ambassador for reggae music, for peace, for love, for tolerance, and for human rights. He was awarded the Medal of Peace from the United Nations in 1980, and the Jamaican Order of Merit in 1981. In 1994, he was inducted, posthumously, into the Rock and Roll Hall of Fame.

JEALOUSY

"There is never jealousy where there is not strong regard."

— Washington Irving
American Writer, Essayist
4/3/1783 – 11/28/1859

Jealousy is a negative emotion that carries some creepy connotations, but it's also a back-handed compliment (of sorts): There is something about you or your situation that the jealous person finds highly desirable.

If you notice that someone is envious of you, perhaps it will remind you of how truly lucky you are — and how grateful you ought to be for what you have.

———————◇———————

Washington Irving was a short story writer, essayist, biographer, historian, and diplomat of the early nineteenth century. He achieved international fame in 1819 with the publication of *The Sketch Book of Geoffrey Crayon, Gent.*, in particular for two short stories contained therein: *Rip Van Winkle* and *The Legend of Sleepy Hollow*. The book itself is an eclectic collection of humorous tales that mix fantasy with reality, and fact with fiction. As it turns out, both *Rip Van Winkle* and *The Legend of Sleepy Hollow* are Americanized versions of old German folktales.

The tremendous success of *The Sketch Book*, both in the United States and England, provided Irving with financial security and the freedom to pursue his literary dreams. He would publish eighteen books in all, encompassing biographies, travelogues, history, and of course, more short stories.

SCHADENFREUDE

"People respect unhappiness and find it especially hard to forgive success."

— Francoise Sagan

French Playwright, Novelist

6/21/1935 – 9/24/2004

Hopefully, you don't engage in schadenfreude — the taking of malicious pleasure in someone else's misfortune — but if you do, hopefully you aren't a big believer in Karma, as well. Just as positivity begets positivity, negativity has a knack for attracting negativity.

———————◇———————

Francoise Sagan — the pen name of Francoise Quoirez — was a French playwright, novelist, and screenwriter. Her best-known work is *Bonjour Tristesse* (Hello, Sadness), a best-selling novel she wrote in six weeks while a student at the Sorbonne. The tragic story of a jealous, meddling teenage girl who interferes with her father's remarriage, *Bonjour* was translated into fifteen languages and sold over two million copies. Published in 1954, the novel won the Prix des Critiques later that year. In 1984, Sagan was awarded the Prix de Monaco in recognition of her body of work.

CREATIVITY

"Creativity is the defeat of habit by originality."

— Arthur Koestler
Hungarian-British Author, Journalist
9/5/1905 – 3/1/1983

Habits can become chains, tethering us to the prisons of practices that we no longer give a second thought to; we just do this thing, then that thing, then the next thing. Take a moment. Reflect on your routines. Are they still pertinent? Are they still necessary? Is there some other way, or some other thing, to do instead?

Arthur Koestler was an author and journalist whose experiences as a war correspondent led him from arch-Communist to devout anti-totalitarian and worldwide fame. He is best known for his novel *Darkness at Noon*, a 1940 work of fiction that examined the inner demons of a man imprisoned — as Koestler was — by a regime possessed of absolute power over his every waking thought. It was translated into thirty languages and was an international best-seller.

Other works include *The Gladiators, Spanish Testament,* and *The Act of Creation*, in which Koestler examines the connection between creativity, art, and science. He was awarded the Sonning Prize for Outstanding Contribution to European Culture in 1968, and in 1972, he was made a Commander of the Order of the British Empire (CBE).

In his later years, suffering from Parkinson's disease and leukemia, Koestler made the decision to take his own life. His wife, Cynthia, decided to join him in suicide, and they took their lives, together, at their home in London.

September 6th

WIT

"Wit lies in recognizing the resemblance among things which differ and the difference between things which are alike."

— Madame de Stael
French Author, Scholar, Intellectual
4/22/1766 – 7/14/1817

What makes wit so clever is that it could not exist without irony. It is fortunate for us, then, that life is full of irony. The trick is to appreciate it when you recognize it.

———— ◆ ————

Anne Louise Germaine de Staël-Holstein, known as Madame de Staël, was a gregarious yet cerebral woman who turned a critical eye on the people and events of her time, which included both the French Revolution and the Napoleonic era.

Her father was a wealthy banker who served as a financial advisor to King Louis XVI, and her mother liked to host salons for their guests while in Paris. De Stael attended these gatherings, rubbing shoulders with the likes of Voltaire, Rousseau, and Châteaubriand, and quickly gained a reputation for her quick wit.

De Stael's outspoken political views earned the enmity of Napoleon Bonaparte, who suspected she was part of a conspiracy against him. When he branded her an enemy of the state and banned her from Paris, De Stael became one of the most famous people in Europe. She retreated to the family residence in Coppet, Switzerland, where she hosted salons that drew many of the continents' leading intellectuals for the next ten years.

INTELLECT

"All generous minds have a horror of what are commonly called 'Facts.' They are the brute beasts of the intellectual domain."

— Thomas Hobbes
English Philosopher
4/5/1588 – 12/4/1679

There are some who confuse intellect with intelligence, and those who do are usually the ones who resort to playing word games or name-calling when the facts prove 'stubborn.' The so-called "intellectual" is someone who would rather joust disingenuously than admit that their opinion is at odds with a known truth. They spar, they offend, they bully — even when they know they are wrong. Do not engage with them, for there are a great many other things, fruitful things, on which to spend your precious time.

———————◇———————

Thomas Hobbes is considered one of the founders of modern political philosophy. He is best known for his 1651 work, *Leviathan*, in which he proposed the social contract theory, whereby some individual or "natural" rights are willingly subsumed in order to secure peace — and the prospect of prosperity — among fellow citizens. In its simplest form, the social contract theory can be reduced to the essence of the so-called Golden Rule: Do unto others as you would have them do unto you. While human beings are naturally self-centered and competitive, the idea that certain self-imposed restraints can and do result in numerous benefits to the collective is well established, and it is one of the pillars of modern Western societies.

September 8th

THINKING

"Clear thinking requires courage rather than intelligence."

— Thomas Szasz
Hungarian Academic, Psychoanalyst
4/15/1920 – 9/8/2012

You have to embrace the facts — no matter their source — and accept the reality — no matter how troublesome. To do otherwise is to purposely deceive yourself.

———————◇———————

Dr. Thomas Stephen Szasz was an academic, psychiatrist and psychoanalyst. His 1961 book, *The Myth of Mental Illness*, questioned the legitimacy of psychiatry's purported moral and scientific foundations, likening much of the (then) current practices to alchemy or astrology. He also argued that, barring a genuine brain disease, there is no such thing as mental illness, and that for most patients, their problems could be attributed to generalized difficulties in living.

Although his views angered many of his fellow doctors, Szasz's criticisms did force the industry to look inward and address many of the concerns (misdiagnoses, over-medication, and a rush toward institutionalization) that had been brought forward by patient advocacy groups.

September 9th

CHANGE

"Everyone thinks of changing the world,
but no one thinks of changing himself."

— Leo Tolstoy
Russian Writer
9/9/1828 – 11/20/1910

It has been said that the only constant in life is change, and change can be incredibly difficult — particularly when the aim is make a change within ourselves. Too often we wear blinders where our own attitudes and behaviors are concerned, and most of those times we've put them on ourselves.

Count Lyov Nikolayevich Tolstoy is widely regarded as one of the greatest writers of all time. He is best known for his novels *War and Peace, Anna Karenina*, and *The Death of Ivan Ilyich*, but he also wrote short stories, plays, and essays — and played an important role in helping India to become an independent nation.

In 1908, Tolstoy received two letters from Taraknath Das, a Bengali scholar and revolutionary who was seeking advice and support for Indian independence from British colonial rule. In his reply, Tolstoy recommended peaceful, non-violent protests as a means for India to achieve its freedom. The letter was published in the Indian newspaper *Free Hindustan*, and it was seen by a young activist named Mohandas Gandhi. Gandhi reached out to Tolstoy — the two exchanged letters over the next year — and he soon embraced the idea that widespread strikes, demonstrations, and other forms of peaceful resistance, not violent revolution, were the surest ways to foment change on the sub-continent. It worked: In 1947, India gained its independence from Great Britain.

September 10th

ETHICS

"Ethics is knowing the difference between what you have a right
to do and what is right to do."

— Potter Stewart
American Supreme Court Justice
1/23/1915 – 12/7/1985

Just because you can, doesn't mean that you should. Give someone a break today, if you can.

Potter Stewart was an Associate Justice of the United States Supreme Court. Nominated by President Dwight D. Eisenhower, he served from 1958 to 1981.

Considered a "centrist," Stewart was by nature a moderate justice, holding to common sense and pragmatic positions that found the truth of a thing somewhere in the middle. He is best known for the phrase "I know it when I see it," which he uttered in reference to his opinion about what may or may not be considered obscene, in *Jacobellis v. Ohio*. Stewart joined the majority in saying that the French film, *The Lovers*, was not obscene. Two years later, in *Ginzburg v. United States*, he remarked that "Censorship…is a hallmark of an authoritarian regime."

Stewart retired in 1981 and was succeeded by Sandra Day O'Connor, who was the first woman to serve on the Supreme Court. He died in 1985, and is buried in Arlington National Cemetery.

REGRET

"I want to live my life so that my nights are not filled with regrets."

— D. H. Lawrence
English Novelist, Poet, Playwright
9/11/1885 – 3/2/1930

We all make mistakes that we rue, deep in our soul, and anyone who says otherwise is either a fool or a liar. The difficulty, of course, lies in recognizing those gut-wrenching moments when we must choose between ego and character. Hint: You will never regret doing the right thing.

———————◇———————

David Herbert Lawrence was a writer and poet, a man of letters, and the author of novels, short stories, poems, plays, travelogues, and essays. His novels *Sons and Lovers*, *The Rainbow*, and *Women in Love* brought him critical and commercial success, and established him in the Parthenon of English literature, but his name is undoubtedly best remembered for the controversy surrounding a novel that was published nearly thirty years after his death: *Lady Chatterly's Lover*.

Lawrence wrote in vivid prose, and he was not afraid to explore human sexuality in frank and colorful terms. Although *Chatterly* had been privately published elsewhere (as a limited edition), it had been banned in England and the United States. In 1959, when Penguin Books sought to publish it for widespread public consumption, they were prosecuted under the British Obscene Publications Act. At issue was Lawrence's explicit and repeated descriptions of sexual intercourse, using terms that, at the time, were considered indecent and vulgar. During the trial, many prominent writers appeared as witnesses for the defense, and Penguin was eventually exonerated. Unexpurgated editions were released in 1960.

September 12th

JUSTICE

"Injustice is relatively easy to bear; what stings is justice."

— H. L. Mencken
American Journalist, Satirist
9/12/1880 – 1/29/1956

Life is rarely fair when it counts: you will be denied the credit due to you; you will be blamed when you are blameless; and you will get kicked when you are down. But if you think that's bad, know that what really hurts is when we get what we deserve. Somehow, knowing that we have earned a particularly brutish bit of Karma intensifies the impact — and amplifies the lesson.

--------◇--------

Known as the "Sage of Baltimore," Henry Louis Mencken was a journalist, satirist, social critic, and chronicler of American linguistics. He was a reporter for two Baltimore newspapers, worked as an editor for the influential magazine *The Smart Set*, and was the founder and editor of *American Mercury*, a literary magazine known for its critical examination of American culture, politics, and customs.

Besides his caustic wit and fearless critiques of uncomfortable realities, Mencken is perhaps best remembered for his book, *The American Language*, a substantial collection of popular American expressions and idioms. Revised and updated through the years, *The American Language* stamped Mencken as the country's leading authority on etymology, philology, and semantics.

MATURITY

"In youth we learn; in age we understand."

— Marie von Ebner-Eschenbach
Austrian Writer
9/13/1830 – 3/12/1916

It is one thing to grasp the rudimentary outlines of a hypothesis, or the broad strokes of a theory or concept; however, it is quite impossible to fully and precisely comprehend an issue without seeing, doing, or living it.

Known for her psychological novels, Baroness Marie von Ebner-Eschenbach is considered one of the most important German-language writers of the nineteenth century, and remains a respected member of Austria's literary elite.

Born a countess, she began writing as a child. Despite the disapproval of her noble family, who considered it an unsuitable and unseemly occupation for a noblewoman, Eschenbach was obsessed with exploring the daily dramas of the lower class and the sharp differences between the haves and the have-nots. To make matters worse, she tended to blame her own noble class for the poverty of the peasant farmers.

A prolific writer, Eschenbach's works included many insights into her own life, particularly her experiences as a child and the complex relationship between castle life and village life. Works such as *Das Gemeindekind* and *Zwei Comtessen* explore the give-and-take of Austrian life, both in town and country.

In spite of her pointed criticisms, she also took great care to demonstrate that kindness could be found in members of every social class. When she died, in 1916, she bequeathed the money she had earned from her writing career to aid struggling writers in their creative efforts.

PLEASURE

"The rule of my life is to make business a pleasure,
and pleasure my business."

— Aaron Burr
American Vice President, Lawyer
2/6/1756 – 9/14/1836

They are luckiest who do what they love and love what they do. For them, the usual words don't apply: work isn't toil; nor is it drudgery. It barely qualifies as labor.

History records Aaron Burr as a scoundrel and a villain; a former Vice President of the United States whose political career effectively ended when he killed a political and social rival in a duel.

When the American Revolution began, Burr served under Benedict Arnold before joining the staff of General George Washington. There he undoubtedly crossed paths with another brave and ambitious young officer, Alexander Hamilton, whom Washington loved like a son.

After the war, Burr and Hamilton repeatedly found themselves at odds. In 1791, Burr defeated Hamilton's father-in-law, Philip Schuyler, in an election for the U.S. Senate. In 1800, when Burr tied Jefferson with an equal number of electoral votes for the presidency, it was Hamilton's determined opposition to Burr that swung the election to Jefferson. In 1804, when Burr was nominated for the governorship of New York, Hamilton once again thwarted Burr's aspirations by disseminating derogatory comments about him. When Burr challenged Hamilton to a duel, he accepted. On July 11th, 1804, Burr shot and killed Hamilton.

Burr lived the rest of his life under a cloud of suspicion and distrust. He died, broke and in debt, on this day in 1836.

PRIDE

"Pride does not wish to owe and vanity does not wish to pay."

— Francois de La Rochefoucauld
French Author
9/15/1613 – 3/17/1680

Our wishes notwithstanding — and whether we like to admit it or not —we are all going to need some help, at some time. The thing is, there is tremendous power in asking for help, as well as responding with help: Whether you are freely giving aid or gladly receiving comfort, whether it's a little or a lot, you are binding yourself to another human being — sometimes for a moment, sometimes for a lifetime.

———————◇———————

François VI, Duc de La Rochefoucauld, Prince de Marcillac, was a nobleman, an intellectual, a rebel, and a writer best known for his ability to condense universal truths into as few words as possible. His *Maximes*, first published in 1665, contains hundreds of pithy observations on the intersection between human values, foibles, and weaknesses. With clear-eyed succinctness, Rochefoucauld used wit and irony to show that we all have our motives, and that it isn't always the virtuous who succeed.

WORK

"Thunder is good, thunder is impressive;
but it is lightning that does the work."

— Mark Twain
American Writer, Humorist
11/30/1835 – 4/21/1910

Anyone can talk about what they are going to do, but it takes a certain amount of character to actually see things through to the end.

Be the person who does, not the one who talks about doing.

Samuel Langhorne Clemens, better known by his pen name, Mark Twain, was a writer, humorist, adventurer, and international lecturer. His novels, *The Adventures of Tom Sawyer* and *Adventures of Huckleberry Finn*, are universally regarded as literary classics.

When his father died unexpectedly, twelve-year old Twain found part-time work as an apprentice printer at the local newspaper; by fifteen, he was submitting articles for publication. At twenty-four, Twain was a licensed steamboat pilot on the Mississippi river. When that career was cut short by the Civil War, he headed west to prospect for gold, but soon found himself broke. He managed to find work as a reporter in Virginia City, Nevada, where he first began writing under the name Mark Twain, which is riverboat slang for twelve feet of water.

Twain began to write fiction, honing an irreverent narrative style that combined observational humor with homespun common sense. His stories began to appear in newspapers and magazines all over the country, and his books became best-sellers. Twain would continue to regale his readers for the next forty years, churning out hit after hit, including *The Prince and the Pauper, A Connecticut Yankee in King Arthur's Court, A Ghost Story*, and numerous other novels, short stories, and essays, as well as an autobiography. He is considered an American national treasure.

KNOWLEDGE

"Our knowledge can only be finite,
while our ignorance must necessarily be infinite."

— Karl Popper
Austrian-British Philosopher, Professor
7/28/1902 – 9/17/1994

We must never allow our ignorance to deter us from our pursuit of knowledge. Knowing or not knowing isn't the most important thing; the most important thing is to understand that the knowledge we seek can always be found, if we really need or want to know.

While our ignorance may be infinite, it does not have to be permanent.

———◦———

Sir Karl Raimund Popper was a highly influential professor and philosopher of natural and social science. He is most noted for contributions on quantum mechanics and the nature of probability, and for differentiating between science and non-science, holding that true scientific practice is characterized by clearly defined scientific methodology, not untestable ad hoc hypotheses. In general, Popper rejected the rote empiricism of "universal" knowledge, insisting that such laws were actually a reflection of the situational logic inherent to their individual time, not the whole of human history.

September 18th

KINDNESS

"Kindness is in our power, even when fondness is not."

— Samuel Johnson
English Writer, Poet, Essayist
9/18/1709 – 12/13/1784

The world is full of petulant, insufferable people, but the way we treat the intolerable will always say far more about us than it does about them.

Inner peace and tranquility lie in being kind when you don't have to be.

Samuel Johnson was a writer who made many lasting contributions to English literature as a poet, essayist, biographer, literary critic, and editor. Among his many achievements was the translation of Alexander Pope's "Messiah" into Latin; a ten-volume edition of the complete works of William Shakespeare; and his monumental *A Dictionary of the English Language*, which took nine years to complete and was the pre-eminent British dictionary for 150 years.

Like Rochefoucauld, Johnson possessed the ability to condense "the great rules of life into short sentences," and he is well-remembered for his aphorisms. Among his more famous sayings are the assertions that "Patriotism is the last refuge of a scoundrel" and "Marriage has many pains, but celibacy has no pleasures."

Johnson had numerous health issues, including depression, deafness in one ear, and blindness in one eye, and it is believed that he may have had Tourette's syndrome. However, in spite of his difficulties, Johnson's legacy is one of hard work, literary genius, and generous philanthropy.

GREED

"Do not spoil what you have by desiring what you have not; remember that what you now have was once among the things you only hoped for."

— Epicurus
Greek Philosopher
c. 341 BC – c. 270 BC

Material things may bring some measure of happiness, but it is almost always fleeting. In the end, the best antidote for greed is gratitude: Better to cultivate an appreciation for the things you already have than to lust tirelessly for the things that you do not, cannot, or should not have.

Epicurus was an Ancient Greek philosopher and the author of an ethical philosophy focused on simple pleasures, friendship, and a rejection of the busy life. He believed that pleasure, in and of itself, was the greatest good, but that the way to attain it was to live within one's means, to learn to be content with what one has by limiting one's desires, and to seek knowledge about the world around you. He is the founder of the eponymous school of philosophy known as Epicureanism.

Not many of Epicurus's personal writings have survived, although his popularity in Ancient Rome was noted by several of her famous denizens. Diogenes Laertius described Epicurus as a prolific writer and preserved three of his letters as well as his Principal Doctrines, a set of forty aphoristic statements that outline his overall philosophy. The poet-philosopher Lucretius was both enthralled and inspired by Epicurus, and the statesman Cicero made references to his teachings. The biographer Plutarch also mentioned Epicurus, through an anecdote about how Brutus was soothed by Cassius quoting Epicurus.

COVETOUSNESS

"He who is not contented with what he has,
would not be contented with what he would like to have."

— Socrates

Greek Philosopher

c. 470 BC – c. 399 BC

For some, it appears that all they want is to want. There is no pleasing them — their motto is "More, more, more," enough is never enough, and if you've got it, they simply have to have it, too.

Those who covet will never be content, for their appetite will never be sated. There will always be something to chase; always something to shovel into the abyss of their desire.

———————◇———————

Socrates was a classical Greek philosopher and is widely credited as one of the founders of Western philosophy. His style of teaching — known today as the Socratic Method — involved a series of probing questions that forced a student to continually clarify their own understanding of an issue while also exposing the underlying assumptions of that "understanding."

It seems that Socrates wrote down nothing himself, and we have no first-person accounts of his life. What we do know comes primarily from Plato, his devoted student. We know that Socrates was born and lived nearly his entire life in Athens; that he worked as a mason for several years; and that he fought, bravely, in the Peloponnesian War.

We also know that Socrates rubbed many Athenians the wrong way, and that a jury found him guilty of impiety and sentenced him to death by poison. Socrates accepted his fate, and spent his final days in the company of friends. According to Plato, when the executioner presented him with a cup of poisonous hemlock, Socrates drank it without hesitation.

INDIGNATION

"Moral indignation is jealousy with a halo."

— H. G. Wells
English Writer
9/21/1866 – 8/13/1946

Have you ever witnessed someone's faux "outrage" and got the distinct impression that it wasn't so much an actual protest against a particular deed, but rather a lamentation that they hadn't thought of it first?

Indignation is a tricky thing. Judge not, lest ye be judged.

———◇———

Herbert George Wells was a prolific author who engaged in many different genres, writing novels, short stories, historical biographies, satire, and social commentary. He is best known for his science fiction novels *The Time Machine*, *The Island of Doctor Moreau*, *The Invisible Man*, and *The War of the Worlds*.

A former science teacher, Wells seemed to have a knack for predicting the ways in which new technologies — and those not yet invented — would be used in the future. His works highlighted the possibilities of DNA sequencing, military aircraft, and space travel long before they would become a reality. He was also deeply concerned about the impact of technology upon mankind, and his stories were imbued with a deep and abiding sympathy for the struggles that society would face in the future he envisioned.

September 22nd

EGO

"He makes people pleased with him by making them
first pleased with themselves."

— Philip Stanhope
British Statesman, 4th Earl of Chesterfield
9/22/1694 – 3/24/1773

Have you ever noticed how the most popular people also tend to be the most congratulatory and upbeat people? It's true: People like spending time around those who make them feel good about themselves. So smile! And try to be a positive influence in the lives of those around you. It's good for them, and it's good for you.

———————◇———————

Philip Dormer Stanhope, the 4th Earl of Chesterfield, was a statesman, diplomat, and author. He was praised by his contemporaries for his impeccable manners, quick wit, and supreme oratory skills. He counted among his friends Alexander Pope, John Gay, and Voltaire.

As an ambassador, Stanhope earned an excellent reputation for the wise and tactful manner in which he handled political affairs. He was instrumental in the negotiation of the Treaty of Vienna in 1731, which created an alliance with Austria, and in 1745 he persuaded the Dutch to join the War of Austrian Succession. He was also largely responsible for Britain's decision to adopt the Gregorian calendar in 1752.

Stanhope is chiefly remembered as the author of *Letters to His Son* and *Letters to His Godson*, which contain observations and guidance on proper etiquette, getting along with others, and the pursuit of an honest and dignified life. Both collections are considered brilliant pieces of literature, but Stanhope thought of them as merely private correspondence, and as practical paternal advice. They were published posthumously, to wide acclaim.

September 23rd

INFLUENCE

"The art of being a slave is to rule one's master."

— Diogenes
Greek Founder of Cynic Philosophy
c. 412 BC – c. 323 BC

The trick to "managing upward" is to establish a reputation for making your boss look good. This establishes trust, and gives you some small degree of influence — if not leverage — and a voice in how things ought to be done.

A good leader can take orders as well as give them; a great leader knows when to do each.

Diogenes of Sinope, also known as Diogenes the Cynic, was a philosopher and one of the founders of Cynic philosophy. The Cynics were advocates of stoic self-sufficiency, a strict moral code, and the belief that each of us possess, within ourselves, all that is needed for happiness. He is probably best remembered today as an agitator, a contrarian, and the man who searched Athens for an honest man, carrying a blazing lantern in broad daylight.

Diogenes rejected most conventional standards and intentionally lived a life of poverty. His goal was to demonstrate that independence and contentment were attainable even under the harshest of circumstances. As a former slave, he knew of what he spoke. He had been captured by pirates and sold into slavery, but soon found himself teaching his master's children. Diogenes's influence would eventually lead to the establishment of Stoicism.

TRAGEDY

"This world is a comedy to those that think, a tragedy to those who feel."

— Horace Walpole
English Writer, Historian, Politician
9/24/1717 – 3/2/1797

There are numerous differences between Thinkers and Feelers, and it should come as no great surprise (and studies have shown) that, in life, one is generally happier when engaged in more of the former and less of the latter.

———◇———

Horatio Walpole, also known as Horace Walpole, was a writer, art historian, and a member of the British Parliament. He gained fame for his medieval horror tale *The Castle of Otranto*, which is generally regarded as the first gothic novel, and — lucky for us — he is said to have coined the term "serendipity."

In addition to novels, Walpole also wrote a historical speculation about King Richard III and a critically-acclaimed four-volume history of English paintings. Over the course of his lifetime, he exchanged over four thousand letters with numerous friends, acquaintances, and admirers. These private correspondences were published, posthumously, in forty-eight volumes.

Walpole was the 4th Earl of Orford, but since he died unmarried and without an heir, the earldom became extinct upon his death in 1797.

September 25th

FORTITUDE

"Gird your hearts with silent fortitude, suffering yet hoping all things."

— Felicia Hemans
English Poet
9/25/1793 – 5/16/1835

The Stoic philosophy urges us to prepare ourselves for all manner of challenges. Some we can control, others we cannot, but the idea is that simply having considered the possibilities helps us to guard against their impact. This is a positive construct that we can employ against the whims of fortune as they are inevitably thrust upon us, giving us the courage to face those things that are beyond our control.

Felicia Dorothea Hemans was a Romantic poet. Influenced by William Wordsworth and Lord Byron, she was known for her highly lyrical compositions. Her best-known poems are probably the solemn "Casabianca" ("The boy stood on the burning deck") and the patriotic "The Homes of England" ("The stately homes of England").

Although her popularity has declined, in her day, Hemans was able to earn a living with her poetry — she raised five sons alone after she and her husband separated — and she was highly-regarded among her contemporaries. When she died of dropsy, in 1835, Wordsworth wrote a memorial verse in her honor.

September 26th

ANXIETY

"Anxiety is the hand maiden of creativity."

— T. S. Eliot
British Poet, Essayist
9/26/1888 – 1/4/1965

Isn't it amazing how a bit of duress sharpens the senses and focuses the mind? At the same time, it also introduces an element of fear. Just ask any student who has put off a major project until the last possible moment . . .

Thomas Stearns "T.S." Eliot was a playwright, an essayist, a publisher, and a critic, and is widely regarded as one of the most important poets of the twentieth century.

Born and raised in St. Louis, Missouri, Eliot earned a master's degree from Harvard and studied at the Sorbonne, in Paris. He settled in England in 1914, where he was befriended by Ezra Pound, who immediately recognized Eliot's talent and was instrumental in getting him published. His first book of poetry, *Prufrock and Other Observations*, came out in 1917. In 1922, *The Waste Land* was published and received international acclaim. Even today, it is recognized as one of the most influential poetic works of this or any age.

Eliot married in England, and at the age of thirty-nine he surrendered his American citizenship and became a British subject. In 1948, Eliot received the Order of Merit and was awarded the Nobel Prize for Literature. He died in London in 1965, and is commemorated in the Poet's Corner of Westminster Abbey.

FEELINGS

"Mankind are governed more by their feelings than by reason."

— Samuel Adams
American Statesman, Philosopher
9/27/1722 – 10/2/1803

According to personality studies conducted by Karl Jung, Myers & Briggs, and others, about 75 percent of us are considered Feelers, while just 25% of us are characterized as Thinkers. If you are a Thinker, the idea that you are surrounded — three to one! — by people who make decisions based largely on what they *believe*, not on what they actually *know*, must be positively exasperating. It makes one wonder what all those Feelers think about that . . .

———————◇———————

Samuel Adams was a statesman and political philosopher, and one of the Founding Fathers of the United States. He played a vital role in convincing the colonies to break from Great Britain during the American Revolution, insisting that free men have no obligation to follow unjust laws that run counter to their own interests. He is a second cousin to fellow Founding Father, John Adams, who was the second President. Both are signatories to the Declaration of Independence.

As relations deteriorated, Adams was among the first to openly call for independence. Toward that end, he began to unite and organize resistance leaders throughout the colonies. His persistent opposition and agitation made him a marked man. It has been suggested that the Revolutionary War began when British soldiers, who were trying to capture and arrest Adams in Lexington, Massachusetts, ran into one of the militias that Adams was arming. The ensuing scuffle, and the "shot heard 'round the world," marked the beginning of hostilities.

GOALS

"When it is obvious that the goals cannot be reached,
don't adjust the goals, adjust the action steps."

— Confucius
Chinese Teacher, Philosopher
9/28/551 BC – c. 479 BC

Sure, it's difficult. But is it really impossible? Or is it that it is only impossible doing it the way you have been doing it?

———————◇———————

Confucius was an educator, a political theorist, and the founder of the Ru School of Chinese thought. He is best known for his teachings, as preserved in the *Analects*, a collection of sayings and ideas attributed to him by his disciples and followers. Compiled during the centuries following his death, the central theme of the *Analects* is to focus on behaving morally and doing the right thing regardless of consequence.

Confucius's influence in the East may be compared to that of Socrates in the West. The timeless traditions he instituted remain central to the Chinese social code and moral values to this day.

DISCIPLINE

"It is one thing to praise discipline, and another to submit to it."

— Miguel de Cervantes
Spanish Writer, Playwright, Poet
9/29/1547 – 4/22/1616

Discipline is one of those things that we admire in others but don't necessarily demand of ourselves. This is a shame, because without discipline, all of life is aimless, disordered, and without purpose.

———◇———

Miguel de Cervantes Saavedra is credited with writing the first modern novel, *Don Quixote*, which became the world's first best-seller. It was eventually translated into more than sixty different languages, and Cervantes is considered the most important and celebrated figure in Spanish literature.

Born near Madrid, Cervantes was the fourth of seven children. He was an avid reader but his education was elementary. As a young man, he became a soldier and gained a reputation for bravery. His actions during the Battle of Lepanto, in 1571, attest to his courage: Sick with fever, he refused to stay in bed and joined the fighting. He was shot twice in the chest, and a third bullet ripped through his left hand, rendering it useless forever after. In 1575, en route to Spain, his ship was attacked by pirates and he was captured and sold into slavery. He would remain in captivity for five years, before a ransom was paid and he was released.

Cervantes's adventures would color several of his poems, plays, and novels, including *Don Quixote*, a story about an old man who believes he is a brave knight. Although it is not autobiographical, strictly speaking, his masterpiece is highly allegorical. Published in two parts, the second part was released in 1615, the year before Cervantes's death.

September 30th

PROSPERITY

"The key point to understand is that prosperity is an internal experience, not an external state, and it is an experience that is not tied to a certain amount of money."

— Shakti Gawain
American Author, Speaker
9/30/1948 – 11/11/2018

We are truly prosperous when we have all that we need, or have learned to be content with all that we possess.

Shakti Gawain, born Carol Louisa Gawain, was a New Age and personal development author and teacher of consciousness. Through her writing, Gawain sought to bring greater awareness, wholeness, and balance to the lives of her readers. Her books have been translated into over thirty languages and have sold over ten million copies. Best-selling titles include *Creative Visualization*, *Living in the Light*, *The Path of Transformation*, *Four Levels of Healing*, *Creating True Prosperity*, and *Developing Intuition*. Reportedly, *Creative Visualization* was the inspiration behind British pop star Des'ree's 1994 hit song, "You Gotta Be."

FRUGALITY

"By desiring little, a poor man makes himself rich."

— Democritus
Greek Philosopher
c. 460 BC – c. 370 BC

We don't always realize how much the little things add up: the morning stop for coffee, the take-out lunches, memberships and subscriptions. How easy it is to ignore the aggregate costs of these so-called "simple pleasures" — until we find ourselves struggling to purchase bigger-ticket items.

Evaluate your spending habits. You'll be all the richer for it.

Democritus was a pre-Socratic philosopher whose many hypotheses and deductions were eerily prescient, his most famous being an atomic theory of the universe in which all things are comprised of tiny particles that are in constant motion, interacting and colliding with each other.

Unlike most of his peers, Democritus understood the universe to be governed entirely by natural and systematic laws, rather than gods. He speculated that the universe contains a multitude of worlds, some of which are assuredly inhabited, and deduced that the light of stars makes it possible to see the Milky Way.

Democritus wasn't an overly serious, all-work-and-no-play man. History records that he was fun-loving and quick to laugh, and valued cheerfulness. He believed that the main goal of life should be to attain happiness, and that happiness itself may be achieved by mimicking good behavior and avoiding over-indulgence.

October 2nd

PREPARATION

"Live as if you were to die tomorrow. Learn as if you were to live forever."

— Mahatma Gandhi
Indian Activist
10/2/1869 – 1/30/1948

Life, as amazing and wonderful as it is, can be made even better through knowledge and wisdom. The more you know, the more interesting life is and the more effectively you can manage it. The trick is to recognize and value that correlation, and constantly seek out opportunities to learn.

———————◇———————

Mohandas Karamchand Gandhi was a lawyer, politician, writer, social activist, and tireless leader of the Indian independence movement against British rule. A great mediator and reconciler, Gandhi united the many different factions within India in order to address the conflicts that existed between India and Great Britain. His use of nonviolent civil disobedience — and boycotting all British products and services — eventually led India to independence and inspired civil rights movements in their struggles for freedom around the world.

To his fellow Indians, Gandhi was the Mahatma, or "Great Soul," and today he is remembered as the father of his country.

October 3rd

FORGIVENESS

"It is in pardoning that we are pardoned."

— Francis of Assisi
Italian Friar, Deacon, Preacher
c. 1182 – 10/3/1226

When we accept an apology, it isn't only the transgressor who is absolved. We also free ourselves from the psychic burden of an unresolved conflict.

Never carry the weight of a disagreement any longer than you have to. Moving on, with or without an apology, provides its own sort of closure.

Giovanni di Pietro di Bernardone was a Catholic friar, deacon, and preacher. Born to a wealthy family in the Italian region of Umbria, he renounced all of his worldly goods when God told him to resurrect the Church and to live a life of poverty. He went on to establish the men's Order of Friars Minor, the women's Order of Saint Clare, and the Third Order, a lay community of religious-minded married men and women. Known as St. Francis, he is the patron saint of merchants, animals, and the environment, and is one of the most revered and venerated religious figures in history.

October 4th

CONSCIENCE

"Conscience is the authentic voice of God to you."

— Rutherford B. Hayes
American President
10/4/1822 – 1/17/1893

If you have received any sort of moral, religious, or ethical training, it is likely that you have developed a certain set of values: guiding principles that reside in your conscience and help to define your personal level of integrity. We probably agree that it is difficult to be virtuous 100 percent of the time, so where are your lines drawn?

———◇———

Rutherford Birchard Hayes was a lawyer, a congressman, the governor of Ohio, and the 19th President of the United States.

A staunch abolitionist who defended runaway slaves in court proceedings, Hayes was an active member of the newly formed Republican Party, which was formed for the expressed purpose of opposing slavery. When the Civil War began, he joined the Union Army, and in 1862, while fighting in Maryland, he was seriously wounded during the Battle of South Mountain.

In 1864, the Republican Party of Cincinnati wanted to run Hayes as their candidate for Congress, but he refused to leave the battlefield to campaign for the office. He was elected anyway, and re-elected in 1866, but he resigned soon after to run for Governor, a post he would hold for three terms.

In 1876, Hayes's reputation as an honest and loyal man of integrity made him the Republican candidate for President. He won, and served a single term, just as he had promised in his inaugural address. His presidency is noted for the end of Reconstruction in the South, and for the Act to Relieve Certain Legal Disabilities of Women, which gave female attorneys the right to argue cases in the U.S. federal court system.

October 5th

LIES

"Lying can never save us from another lie."

— Václav Havel
Czech Playwright, Statesman
10/5/1936 – 12/18/2011

Once you resolve to never tell another lie, and to always be truthful, it changes your behavior. Not only that, it changes your life: One lie usually leads to another, and another, and who wants to keep up with all of that drama?

———————◇———————

Václav Havel was a playwright and dissident who became President of the Czech Republic. Outside of politics, he is known for his plays, essays, and memoirs.

Havel was first exposed to theater when he found work as a stagehand at the Theatre of the Balustrade, in 1959. He was soon writing plays, and by 1968 he was the resident playwright of the company. 1968 was also the year of a Soviet clampdown in Czechoslovakia. Known as the Prague Spring, tanks were in the streets — and so was Havel. He was repeatedly arrested for his involvement in anti-communist protests, spent several years in prison, and lived under constant surveillance by the secret police.

Havel continued to write plays, usually examining the lies and moral compromises inherent in life under a totalitarian regime. He also became the face of democratic reform, and in 1989, having negotiated the peaceful transfer of power, he was elected President of Czechoslovakia, the first non-communist to lead the country in over fifty years.

The Czechoslovakian union dissolved in 1992 but was reconstituted as the Czech Republic the following year. Havel was re-elected President in 1993, and in 1999 his dream of seeing his country granted membership in the North Atlantic Treaty Organization (NATO) was realized.

MORALITY

"The rules of morality are not the conclusion of our reason."

— David Hume
Scottish Philosopher, Historian, Essayist
5/7/1711 – 8/25/1776

Reason alone should be enough to convince us to adapt and to live within a set of shared moral guidelines; but, as history shows, ignoble Man has often made a point of flaunting the very idea of sharing anything, much less a moral code.

Ignoble Man was wrong.

We reap a multitude of benefits by living within certain shared moral guidelines — no killing, no thieving, no raping and pillaging — but perhaps most importantly, a mutual respect for life and property allows us to redirect our energies toward next-level goals, like building economies, feeding the world, and exploring our universe.

Life can be hard, and it is even harder when surrounded by the schemes and machinations of those who wish to wreak havoc. Know your circle. Surround yourself with decent, ethical people who share your values, so that you can focus on the future. Who knows what you can accomplish?

David Hume was a philosopher, historian, economist, and writer. Among his best-known works is *An Enquiry Concerning the Principles of Morals*, in which he argues that passion and sentiment, rather than reason, govern human behavior.

Hume considered himself to be chiefly a moralist, and defined morality as the qualities that are accepted and approved by virtually everyone, regardless of any single, dominant cultural influence. Because so many of our experiences are similar, Hume held that so, too, are our definitions of what is right and wrong; of what is decent, and what is depraved.

October 7th

FAMILY

"You don't choose your family. They are God's gift to you,
as you are to them."

— Desmond Tutu
South African Cleric, Nobel Laureate
Born 10/7/1931

There is something about sharing a gene pool that both endears and appalls, irritates and enthralls. While it is true that we do not choose our family, there are few people on the planet whom you know more intimately — and who know you more intimately — than the members of your family. Yes, we might have a friend or two whom we consider to be "like family," but the reality is, there is nothing quite like *family*.

Desmond Mpilo Tutu is a renowned Anglican cleric and theologian whose work as a staunch opponent of South Africa's apartheid policies changed the course of his country. In 1984, he received the Nobel Peace Prize for his leadership of the South African Council of Churches, whose "work for human dignity, fraternity, and democracy incite the admiration of the world."

In addition to the Nobel Prize, Tutu has received numerous international awards, including the Presidential Medal of Freedom in 2009, and the prestigious Templeton Prize, which he won in 2013. Although he has largely withdrawn from public life, Tutu continues to write: his most recent book is *The Book of Joy: Lasting Happiness in a Changing World*, which he co-authored with the Dalai Lama.

GUILT

"Guilt is the price we pay willingly for doing
what we are going to do anyway."

— Isabelle Holland
American Writer
6/16/1920 – 2/9/2002

We almost always see guilt coming, because it rarely sneaks up on us; it nags at us beforehand and lies heavily on us ever after.

———————◇———————

Isabelle Christian Holland was a prolific author who wrote fictional books for both children and adults, specializing in gothic novels, mysteries, and thrillers.

Born in Basel, Switzerland, Holland moved to America in 1940 due to World War II. She did not begin writing until she was well into her forties, but she had over fifty novels published during her lifetime and was still writing when she died, in her eighties. Among her most well-known works are *Bump in the Night* and *The Man Without a Face*, both of which were made into movies.

October 9th

INTROSPECTION

"The first recipe for happiness is to avoid
too lengthy meditation on the past."

— Andre Maurois
French Author
7/26/1885 – 10/9/1967

It's done. It's over. It's in the past. Hopefully you learned something about yourself, and grew from the experience, but even if you did not, do not allow it to own you or define who you are. The same goes double if it was the best day of your life.

———————◇———————

Emile Salomon Wilhelm Herzog was a historian and author who wrote novels, essays, children's books, science fiction stories, and page-turning biographies that read like novels. Among his many subjects were Lord Byron, Victor Hugo, Percy Bysshe Shelley, George Sand, Honore de Balzac, and Marcel Proust. In addition, he was a noted academic who wrote histories of both England and the United States. In 1947 he had his name legally changed to Andre Maurois, which had been his pen name for decades.

PAIN

"The pleasure of those who injure you lies in your pain. Therefore they will
suffer if you take away their pleasure by not feeling pain."

— Tertullian
Tunisian Theologian, Author
c. 160 AD – c. 220 AD

Sometimes we can't help but cry out in anguish – a sudden sting brings
unexpected agony and we react, instinctively and emotionally – but quite
often, we can control not only *how* we react to painful scenarios, but *when*.

Don't give those who hurt you the satisfaction of seeing your pain; it
is yours, and you get to choose with whom it is shared, if it is shared at all.

———————◇———————

Quintus Septimius Florens Tertullianus was a prolific early Christian
author and apologist who was instrumental in establishing the terminology
and practices of Western Christianity.

Born in Carthage, a Roman province in North Africa, Tertullian was
exposed to the ever-expanding Christian faith as a young man. Impressed with
the devotion exhibited by the faithful, particularly the courage and determination of martyrs and their uncompromising belief in one God, he converted
to the Christian faith near the end of the second century.

A productive and creative writer, Tertullian committed himself to addressing a variety of pressing moral and practical problems facing Christians, including persecution, service in the Roman military, dressing appropriately, and
marriage and divorce. His works are notable for their use of clever aphorisms
and memorable phrases, and their abundance of puns, wit, and even sarcasm
— especially when it came to "correcting" those who were opposed to the
Christian faith.

October 11th

RESPONSIBILITY

"One's philosophy is not best expressed in words;
it is expressed in the choices one makes…and the choices we make
are ultimately our responsibility."

— Eleanor Roosevelt
American Politician, Diplomat, Activist
10/11/1884 – 11/7/1962

Once you decide to take responsibility for your own choices, and to own the repercussions that follow as a result of those choices, you will discover a newfound respect for contemplating those choices — and their consequences — in the first place.

———————◇———————

It is interesting to ponder Eleanor Roosevelt's wedding day: She was escorted down the aisle by her uncle, Theodore Roosevelt, who was the sitting President of the United States, to her soon-to-be husband, who would one day also become President of the United States.

Born Anna Eleanor Roosevelt, Eleanor is best known for serving as First Lady during her husband President Franklin D. Roosevelt's four terms in office. She was also a significant political figure in her own right.

A tireless advocate for racial, social, and gender equality, Eleanor was an active member of the Women's Union Trade League, the League of Women Voters, and the National Consumers' League, which sought to improve working conditions and labor practices for all working men and women. After President Roosevelt's death, she served as a delegate to the United Nations, and was a board member of the NAACP and the Peace Corps. She also published twenty-seven books and wrote a syndicated newspaper column, called "My Day," that ran for nearly thirty years.

October 12th

LIABILITY

"Man is fully responsible for his nature and his choices."

— Jean-Paul Sartre
French Philosopher, Novelist, Playwright
6/21/1905 – 4/15/1980

Clearly, we are responsible for our own choices, but our nature? Indeed we are, because we know who we are, what makes us tick, and what ticks us off. In other words, we *know* our own nature.

There is no one else to blame for the choices we make, or how we react to the consequences of those choices; we put ourselves on those paths, and we are liable precisely because we chose to follow them.

———————◦———————

Jean-Paul Charles Aymard Sartre was a philosopher, playwright, novelist, intellectual, and left-wing political activist. He is probably best known as a proponent of existentialism — the idea that life is a search for our true self, and that one person's truth is no more valid than any other person's truth. His highly influential book, *Being and Nothingness*, explores existentialism through the lens of free will and sexual desire.

Considered one of the central figures of twentieth-century French philosophy, Sartre's philosophical theses may be condensed to an examination of the roots (and anguish) associated with freedom. While freedom is empowering, it also comes with great responsibility. The origins of this particular line of philosophical examination are surely connected to the time Sartre spent as a prisoner of war, during World War II.

In 1964, Sartre was awarded the Nobel Prize in Literature, but he rejected both the medal and the substantial monetary reward that came with it. He declined the prize because he had consistently eschewed all official public honors. The Nobel Institute, however, still regards him as the winner for 1964.

October 13th

INDECISION

"Standing in the middle of the road is dangerous;
you get knocked down by the traffic from both sides."

— Margaret Thatcher
British Prime Minister
10/13/1925 – 4/8/2013

Most of us like to believe we are reasonable people, that we can see both sides of an issue. But if we're honest, we have to admit that there are certain instances where emotions cloud our judgment, where we waver because we worry about appearances, and our social standing.

Never be afraid to stand on the side of fact, reason, and logic. When you choose credibility over popularity, you ensure that, in the long run, you will have both.

———————————◇———————————

Margaret Hilda Thatcher served as Prime Minister of the United Kingdom from 1979 to 1990. She was the longest-serving British prime minister of the twentieth century and Europe's first female prime minister.

As Prime Minister, Thatcher steered the nation away from Statism, unleashing a decidedly conservative agenda that advocated for reduced government interference in the economy; for privatization of certain government-run industries; for more freedom and responsibility for the individual citizen; and to diminish the outsized power of trade unions.

Thatcher's drive and determination earned her the nickname "the Iron Lady," and made her many enemies. In 1984 she was nearly killed when the Irish Republican Army set off bombs at a conference in Brighton. Still, she persisted. A strong anti-communist, she joined forces with President Ronald Reagan to drive the Soviets to the bargaining table, to reform, and eventually to the end of the Cold War.

PLANNING

"Plans are nothing; planning is everything."

— Dwight D. Eisenhower
American President, General
10/14/1890 – 3/28/1969

Everybody has plans; we're all going to do something, someday. Or so we say.

What about you? Are you "meaning to," or "going to"?

Dwight David "Ike" Eisenhower was a five-star general and the Supreme Commander of all Allied forces in Europe during World War II. He also served two terms as the 34th President of the United States.

Born in Texas, Eisenhower was raised in Abilene, Kansas, the third of seven sons. Upon graduation from West Point, he was stationed in San Antonio, where he met his future wife, Mamie Dowd.

World War I ended just before Eisenhower was scheduled to deploy to Europe, and he was redirected to the Command and General Staff College at Fort Leavenworth, Kansas, where he graduated first in his class. He would serve as a military aide to Generals Jack J. Pershing and Douglas MacArthur, honing the leadership skills that would serve him well in World War II.

In 1952, the Republican Party persuaded Eisenhower to run for president. He won the Party's nomination on the first ballot, and defeated Adlai Stevenson in the general election to win the presidency. As President, Eisenhower is best remembered for ending the war in Korea, creating the Department of Health, Education and Welfare, shoring up Social Security, and building the Interstate Highway System, which would link the entire country through 41,000 miles of paved roadways. It remains the single largest public works program in U.S. history.

CONFIDENCE

"They are able because they think they are able."

— Virgil
Roman Poet
10/15/70 BC – 9/21/19 BC

Confidence is a powerful motivator: it amplifies purpose, incites boldness, and intensifies effort. If you have it, you are a formidable force. Without it, you will struggle.

Attitude is everything. Believe in yourself.

———————◇———————

The ancient Romans regarded Publius Vergilius Maro as their greatest poet, and his esteem has abated little over the last two thousand years.

Virgil wrote some of the most famous poems in Latin literature, none more so than his masterpiece, *Aeneid*. The *Aeneid* is a chronicle of the heroic journey undertaken by Aeneas, a Trojan whose descendants, Romulus and Remus, are destined to found the city of Rome and enlighten the world.

Virgil's influence cannot be overstated. His poetry continues to be read, particularly as part of Latin studies, and he has been imitated by writers from Ovid to Milton to Tennyson. Dante was so inspired by Virgil that he honored him by casting him as his guide through Hell and Purgatory in his epic, *The Divine Comedy*. Christianity's embrace of allegory may also be traced to Virgil, whose fourth eclogue is believed to have prophesied the birth of Christ. It was one of his earliest poems, written around 42 BC.

October 16th

FAIRNESS

"Life is never fair, and perhaps it is a good thing
for most of us that it is not."

— Oscar Wilde
Irish Poet, Playwright
10/16/1854 – 11/30/1900

We have a tendency to praise "fairness" when we find it favorably applied to our accounts, but not so much when it arrives on our doorstep in the form of karmic retribution.

Is it fair that fairness is not always distributed fairly? Let us be thankful that it finds us when it does — and equally so when it does not.

———◦———

Oscar Fingal O'Flahertie Wills Wilde was an Irish poet who found fame as a playwright in 1890's London. Wilde was a bit of a *poseur*, and was as well-known for his flamboyance and dandified dress as for his arrogance and razor-sharp wit. Upon his arrival in America for a speaking tour, a customs officer asked if he had anything to declare. Wilde replied that he had "nothing to declare but my genius."

Wilde is best remembered for his first (and only) novel, *The Picture of Dorian Gray*, and for his comedic play, *The Importance of Being Earnest*. He is also known for being put on trial and serving time in jail for committing homosexual acts. One of his last works was a poem he wrote about his prison experience, "The Ballad of Reading Gaol."

Wilde died rather suddenly of acute meningitis brought on by an ear infection. He joined the Catholic Church on his deathbed.

October 17th

WISDOM

"Wise men, though all laws were abolished, would lead the same lives."

— Aristophanes
Greek Playwright
c. 446 BC – c. 386 BC

You do not have to know, with absolute certainty, that a thing is wrong to avoid doing it. Nor must you know, with equal certitude, that a principle is true, and right, and just, in order to adhere to it.

Wisdom isn't just what we know; it is the sum of our experiences — and those of our ancestors, who have passed on to us what has worked, and warned us about what does not.

———————◇———————

Aristophanes was a comic playwright of ancient Athens, known for his witty dialogue, biting satire, ruthless caricatures, and bawdy parodies. His propensity for heaping ridicule onto some of the foibles and icons of Athens sometimes caused minor controversies but, undaunted, he not only carried on, he redoubled his efforts to make good-natured fun of the city and people he loved. Many of the forty-odd plays written by Aristophanes survive to this day, as does his reputation as the Father of Comedy.

SOUL

"Choose rather to be strong of soul than strong of body."

— Pythagoras
Greek Philosopher, Mathematician
c. 570 BC – c. 490 BC

In the grand scheme of time, and the cosmos, the human body is a mere earthly raiment; a temporary and ephemeral thing. Our days are numbered and the time we spend on this planet is most assuredly finite; however, according to virtually every belief system in the world, our souls are boundless and our consciousness is limitless. As such, doesn't it make sense to cultivate and maintain a generous and honorable spirit?

Forever is a long time to be an outcast. Be an agent of good.

———————◇———————

Pythagoras of Samos was a philosopher, mathematician, and founder of the Pythagoreanism movement, a religious brotherhood that influenced the philosophies developed by Plato and Aristotle. As a result, much of Western rational philosophy can be traced to Pythagoras's political and religious teachings, which emphasized the immortality of the soul and the importance of virtuous behavior toward all living creatures.

Nonetheless, Pythagoras is probably best known for his mathematical formulations, in particular his theory regarding the geometric relationship between the three sides of a right triangle: $A^2 + B^2 = C^2$. Because none of his writings survive, there are suspicions that some of the so-called "Pythagoras doctrines" were, in fact, discovered by his disciples, who honored Pythagoras by attributing them to him.

BETRAYAL

"Love is whatever you can still betray. Betrayal can only happen if you love."

— John le Carré (David J. M. Cornwell)
British Author
Born 10/19/1931

Disloyalty brings a singular kind of pain because it is especially agonizing when we are betrayed by someone whose fealty we believe has been rightly — and often intimately — earned. Knowing that we don't put nearly as much thought or effort into harming strangers as we do those we love makes betrayal doubly painful.

———————◇———————

John le Carré is the pen name of David John Moore Cornwell, a former intelligence officer who became an international best-selling author of espionage novels. Considered one of the very best writers of the genre, Le Carré is probably best known for *The Spy Who Came in from the Cold*, *Tinker Tailor Soldier Spy*, and *Smiley's People*. Many of his novels have been made into major motion pictures, and he counted venerated director Stanley Kubrick as a close friend.

Le Carré has been the recipient of numerous international awards and honorary degrees, and in 2011 he was awarded the Goethe Medal. He resides in St. Buryan, Cornwall, near Land's End, at the southwestern tip of England. He has lived there, surrounded by the sea, for more than forty years.

SKEPTICISM

"Skepticism: the mark and even the pose of the educated mind."

— John Dewey
American Philosopher, Psychologist
10/20/1859 – 6/1/1952

Do you believe everything you are told? Do you rely on cues from others to form your opinions? Do you react based on what *seems* true, on what *feels* right, when you don't really know all of the facts? Even worse: Do you parrot propaganda, willfully repeating hearsay and contributing to the ignorance of others?

The good news is, being un- or ill-informed is a reversible condition; treatment is available.

Question every assumption. Seek out the facts — not some of the time, but every time. You will be surprised by how much you think you know that simply isn't true.

———————◇———————

John Dewey was an influential philosopher and psychologist whose ideas were instrumental in education and social reform. He is one of the primary figures (along with William James) associated with the philosophy of pragmatism, which is based on the idea that the merits of an idea, proposal, or policy are rooted in their usefulness and practicality. He is also considered one of the fathers of functional psychology, a school of thought that asserts that our conscious behavior is a direct result of our adaptation to the challenges and opportunities present in the environment in which we live or work. A renowned public intellectual, Dewey was considered one of America's foremost scholars and remains one of the most cited psychologists of the twentieth century.

TREPIDATION

"Most of us experience a life full of wonderful moments
and difficult moments. But for many of us, even when we are
most joyful, there is fear behind our joy."

— Thich Nhat Hanh
Vietnamese Buddhist Monk, Peace Activist
Born 10/11/1926

The unease and disquiet that sometimes creeps into our mind — even during our most jubilant occasions — is due to the fact that, deep down, we know how quickly things can change. Such is life.

Always remember that our joys and our sorrows are equally transient, and equally fleeting. While there are no guarantees that good times will last, rest assured that the bad times won't be around forever, either.

———————◇———————

Thich Nhat Hanh is a Zen Master and peace activist, revered through-out the world for his powerful teachings and best-selling books on mindfulness and harmony. Called "an apostle of peace and nonviolence" by Martin Luther King, Jr., Hanh has been a pioneer in bringing Buddhism to the West, founding six monasteries and dozens of practice centers throughout America and Europe, including the Plum Village Monastery in southwestern France.

A prolific writer, Hanh has published over a hundred books, including manuals on meditation and mindfulness, commentaries on ancient Buddhist texts, poetry, and children's books. Some of his best-known works include *Being Peace, Peace Is Every Step, The Miracle of Mindfulness, The Art of Power*, and *True Love and Anger.*

Hanh's fundamental teaching is that only by living mindfully can we attain inner peace and learn to be content in the present moment.

October 22nd

PRODUCTIVITY

"What is it to enjoy life? Sit at the beach? No. What it is is that you have to do something, you have to be productive, make a contribution to the society, to the family, to yourself."

— Frank Lowy
Australian-Israeli Businessman
Born 10/22/1930

We all need down time. We all need time to recharge our batteries, and there is nothing wrong with taking a well-deserved rest, but note carefully that term, "well-deserved." Compare how you feel at the end of a lazy day, in which you did virtually nothing, with how you feel at the end of a busy and fruitful day. Why do we tend to associate guilt with doing nothing?

We derive no small part of our self-esteem from how we view our usefulness; how we rate our impact on (and standing within) our community; and our influence amongst co-workers, family, and friends. Our perception of our social rank is part of our internal barometer, and we feel better about ourselves when we are productive.

Do yourself some good by getting something done today.

———————◆———————

Sir Frank P. Lowy is a Czechoslovakian-born, Australian-Israeli businessman, who was knighted in 2017 by Queen Elizabeth of the United Kingdom. As the long-time Chairman of Westfield Corporation, a global shopping center company, Lowy is known for his philanthropy and service to Australia, and for his committed support of a wide range of social and cultural endeavors around the world. Perennially on the "richest people in Australia" list, with a net worth estimated to be over $8 billion, Lowy retired in 2010, at age eighty, and has since moved to Israel.

HEAVEN

"We shall one day find in Heaven as much rest and joy
as we ourselves have dispensed in this life."

— Saint Ignatius
Spanish Theologian
10/23/1491 – 7/31/1556

Life can be difficult; don't make it more so by inviting others to align against you. Be kind. Be friendly. Do what you can to lighten the load being carried by others. Some of them will surely do the same for you. Some of them won't, but it is not your place to keep score.

Born Inigo Lopez de Loyola in 1491, Saint Ignatius was the youngest of thirteen children. His mother died when he was seven, and he was taken in by Maria de Garin, the wife of a local blacksmith.

As a young man, Ignatius became a soldier. He participated in many battles but was always able to escape injury. However, in 1521, while defending the town of Pamplona against a French incursion, he was struck in the legs by a cannon ball. He underwent several painful surgeries, but the doctors were able to save only one of his legs.

During his recovery, Ignatius began to read whatever books he could find. The stories of the Saints, and the life of Jesus, had a profound influence upon him, and Ignatius decided to devote his life to Christ, in particular to converting non-believers to Christianity. Ignatius would go on to establish the Society of Jesus, whose followers were referred to as Jesuits. The organization would become known for their educational efforts, and for combating heresy around the world.

Ignatius was beatified in 1609, and was named a Saint on March 12th, 1622. He is considered the patron saint of soldiers.

LEADERSHIP

"Leadership is a choice, not a position."

— Stephen Covey
American Educator, Author, Orator
10/24/1932 – 7/16/2012

Not everyone is cut out to lead, but everyone is affected by those they must follow. There will be times when you must decide whether it is better to follow a bad leader or take a chance and become a leader yourself. It's okay to have doubts; in fact, doubt is an asset. The ones you have to worry about are those who want to lead too much, who covet the title, the salary, the prestige — everything but the opportunity to actually lead. They are seldom capable, or successful.

Stephen Richards Covey was an educator, businessman, and a popular keynote speaker who once won the Golden Gavel award from Toastmasters International. The best-selling author of over a dozen books, Covey's most popular book is *The 7 Habits of Highly Effective People*. He was also known for the Franklin Covey time management training. A spiritual man, Covey was a devoted Mormon and a member of The Church of Jesus Christ of Latter-day Saints.

Covey received numerous honors and awards, including the Thomas More College Medallion for continuing service to humanity, the Sikh's International Man of Peace Award, and the Maharishi Award from Maharishi University of Management. In addition to his MBA from Harvard and his PhD from Brigham Young, Covey was also granted ten honorary doctorates from various universities. In 1996, he was named one of *Time* magazine's 25 Most Influential Americans.

October 25th

FORBIDDEN

"Forbid us something, and that thing we desire."

— Geoffrey Chaucer
English Poet
c. 1342 – 10/25/1400

What is it about our passion for forbidden fruit? Why is it that we want what we cannot, or should not have? Is our struggle against authority, or our own (sometimes unhealthy) desires?

History (and human nature) tends to indicate that, depending on the circumstance, we are vulnerable to a little bit of both. Perhaps these are the truest tests of our free will. We must choose wisely — when we can.

Geoffrey Chaucer was a poet and author. He is widely regarded as the greatest English poet of the Middle Ages, and is considered the "Father of English literature."

Chaucer's best-known work is *The Canterbury Tales*, in which travelers from all walks of life participate in a story-telling contest. A mix of poetry and prose, the *Tales* embrace a variety of genres — from allegory to fable, legend to romance — and the reader hears from a variety of pilgrims whose stories are presented in brief but vivid sketches. Although it appears to be incomplete, *The Canterbury Tales* is considered to be a masterpiece, and it is revered as one of the foremost works in all of English literature.

Chaucer is buried in Westminster Abbey. He was the first writer to be buried in Poet's Corner.

October 26th

DESIRE

"The starting point of all achievement is desire."

— Napoleon Hill
American Author
10/26/1883 – 11/8/1970

It seems like a crazy idea: Me? A doctor? A singer? An engineer?
Only . . . it isn't crazy.
It is completely, positively, unquestionably possible.
Will it be easy? Probably not, but there is no doubt that you can do it.
The real question is: Are you willing to put in the effort?

———◇———

Oliver Napoleon Hill was an attorney, journalist, and author, and is considered the founder of the Self-Help industry. His best-known book, *Think and Grow Rich*, is one of the top ten best-selling self-help books of all time, with over fifteen million copies sold.

Hill insisted that our thoughts could bend the universe to our will, that our expectations are the key to improving all facets of our life, and that by visualizing what we truly want, we can bring those things to fruition. His powerful, motivational message of personal success and achievement was highly influential, and would be copied by self-help gurus from Norman Vincent Peale to Tony Robbins.

PESSIMISM

"I'm a pessimist because of intelligence, but an optimist because of will."

— Antonio Gramsci
Italian Philosopher, Politician
1/22/1891 – 4/27/1937

Sure, it may look difficult, even impossible, but sometimes that's because we've allowed our intellect to underestimate the power of our own determination.

Don't let doubt overrun your confidence, and never allow pessimism to get in the way of your potential. The cause is never truly lost until you stop believing.

———◇———

Antonio Francesco Gramsci was a Marxist philosopher and a founder of the Communist Party of Italy. A prolific writer and political theorist, his strategic propositions would have a profound impact on the development of Western communist parties. His "blueprint" for the overthrow of the capitalist order concluded that organizations such as churches, charities, the media, primary schools, and universities must first be invaded by socialist thinkers in order to subvert the existing social order. In this manner, societies may be changed slowly, from within, rather than by a frontal assault.

Initially, Gramsci was a socialist, but he soon embraced communism, and even lived in the Soviet Union for a few years. He returned to Italy and in 1924 was elected to the country's Chamber of Deputies. In 1926, Benito Mussolini's Fascist government instituted a series of emergency laws and outlawed the Communist Party. Gramsci was arrested and sentenced to twenty years in prison. He was released in 1934 due to poor health, and died a few years later.

INTUITION

"Intuition will tell the thinking mind where to look next."

— Jonas Salk
American Medical Researcher
10/28/1914 – 6/23/1995

There is no substitute for knowledge and wisdom, but when we venture into the unknown, we often find that our ignorance outweighs our ability, and our success is going to depend on our looking beyond what we think we know.

Why not try something a little unconventional, or even counterintuitive? Sometimes the only way around a dead-end is to make a new path.

———————◇———————

Jonas Edward Salk was a medical researcher and virologist. After attaining his medical degree from the New York University School of Medicine, he chose to do medical research instead of becoming a practicing physician. His decision would lead to the development of one of the first successful vaccines for polio, an infectious disease that attacked the nervous system, usually leading to paralysis or death.

At the time of Salk's discovery, hundreds of thousands of children were struck by the disease every year. In 1952, there were more than 57,000 cases of polio reported in the United States. Ten years later, there were fewer than 1,000.

Salk never patented the vaccine or earned any money from his discovery; he simply wanted it to be distributed as widely as possible. Hailed as a national hero, he received numerous awards, including the Congressional Gold Medal and the Presidential Medal of Freedom. In addition, the U.S. Postal service issued a postage stamp in his honor, many schools across the country were named after him, and his birthday is World Polio Day.

October 29th

WORRY

"Worry is interest paid on trouble before it comes due."

— William Ralph Inge
English Priest, Author
6/6/1860 – 2/26/1954

Would that trouble never found us; that grief never darkened our door. But that isn't life, is it? Worrisome things often make an appearance in spite of our best-laid plans. They just do, and we know that they do.

Can we mitigate worry? Sure we can: By not granting undue power to those things over which we have no control.

William Ralph "Dean" Inge was an author, an Anglican priest, a professor of divinity at Cambridge, and the Dean of St. Paul's Cathedral, in London. He was a Knight Commander of the Victorian Order (KCVO), a Fellow of the British Academy, and the recipient of Honorary Doctorates in Divinity, Law, and Literature from some of the most prestigious universities in the United Kingdom.

Inge was a prolific writer. He was the author of forty books, in addition to a prodigious number of lectures, sermons, and various articles he wrote as a long-time columnist for the *Evening Standard*, London's preeminent daily newspaper. He was nominated for the Nobel Prize in Literature three times and, in 1924, he was featured on the cover of *Time* magazine.

Inge subscribed to views that were unusual for his time. Noting the madness of mob rule, he disapproved of democracy, calling simple majority rule "an absurdity." He was known for his support of nudism, decrying local laws that insisted that beachgoers wear full bathing suits. He was also a proponent of individual spirituality, preferring what he called "autonomous faith" to the coercive authority exhibited by certain organized religions.

October 30th

MEMORY

"The past is what you remember, imagine you remember,
convince yourself you remember, or pretend you remember."

— Harold Pinter
English Playwright, Nobel Laureate
10/30/1930 – 12/24/2008

Memory is a fickle and funny thing. Why do we remember one thing, but forget another? Or remember things just a little bit differently than they actually were?

We improvise. We polish. We improve — or we erase.

We all have our own individual timeline: a register of people, places, and events. It isn't important that our memories are recalled with perfect detail — details aren't necessarily the most important things — but rather that we remember the unforgettable people with whom we chose to spend our time. And remember: They chose you, too.

Harold Pinter was a Nobel Prize-winning playwright, poet, screenwriter, actor, and director whose career spanned more than fifty years. His best-known plays include *The Birthday Party*, *The Homecoming*, and *Betrayal*, each of which were made into movies. He also wrote a number of successful motion-picture screenplays, most notably *The Last Tycoon*, *The French Lieutenant's Woman*, and *Sleuth*.

In 1966, Pinter was appointed a Commander of the British Empire. Later, when he was to be honored with a knighthood, he turned it down. He did, however, accept the 2005 Nobel Prize for Literature, as well as induction into the French Legion of Honour, in 2007.

GOODNESS

"The fragrance of flowers spreads only in the direction of the wind.
But the goodness of a person spreads in all directions."

— Chanakya
Indian Philosopher, Teacher, Royal Advisor
c. 371 BC – c. 283 BC

For good or ill, our actions impact others — whether we realize it or not.

It's the traveler who sees you pick up a piece of trash off the sidewalk.

It's the old woman who overhears you telling a child that you are proud of them.

It's the boy you give a thumbs up to, and the girl you help with her groceries.

It's the smile, the handshake, and the "Thank you."

It's all of these things, and more. So much more . . .

———————◇———————

Chanakya, also called Kautilya or Vishnugupta, was a statesman, philosopher, and professor of political science and economics. He served as Prime Minister and chief advisor to the Indian Emperor Chandragupta, the first ruler of the powerful Mauryan Empire.

Chanakya's best-known work is his book, *Arthashastra*, which translates to "The Science of Material Gain." It is essentially a handbook of practical and unsentimental advice for running an empire in the most efficient and effective manner possible. While it includes detailed information on diplomacy, war, taxation, trade, governmental administration, and the law, it also encourages spying on the citizenry and the use of assassination as a political tool. For this, Chanakya is often compared to Machiavelli.

November 1st

PUBLIC OPINION

"A wise man makes his own decisions;
an ignorant man follows the public opinion."

— Grantland Rice
American Sportswriter, Author
11/1/1880 – 7/13/1954

Whenever you see the results of so-called "opinion polls," it would be wise to consider the source of the questions as well as the questions themselves. A great many polls are conducted in order to get a particular (and predetermined) outcome. This is done through careful phrasing, and by targeting a particular audience — those whose known ideology aligns with the desired conclusion.

Anyone can nod their head and agree with the prevailing popular opinion on virtually any particular issue, but it takes a little bit more than that for any self-respecting Thinker. Be sure that you know the facts before offering — or defending — your opinion.

———◇———

Henry Grantland Rice was a sportswriter known for his elegant prose and expressive writing, which helped to elevate the sports heroes of the day to near-mythical status. He was a pivotal figure in the development of sports journalism and a multi-media star, publishing stories in newspapers all over the United States, broadcasting on the radio, and writing and producing short motion pictures that covered a variety of major sporting events.

Rice was the first play-by-play announcer to call a World Series game live, had well over two hundred writing and producing credits to his name, and famously called the University of Notre Dame's backfield "the Four Horsemen of the Apocalypse," but he is perhaps best remembered for reminding us all that "It's not whether you win or lose, it's how you play the game."

INEQUALITY

"The worst form of inequality is to try to make unequal things equal."

— Aristotle
Greek Philosopher, Scientist
c. 384 BC – c. 322 BC

We are the same, yet we are not identical. Each of us has, without exception, different strengths and different weaknesses. We face obstacles and we embrace opportunities, but our outcomes are neither predestined nor guaranteed. Nor should they be. Like most other things, we are primarily the product of our own efforts.

Aristotle is one of the greatest intellectual figures of Western history. His intellectual range was vast and varied, spanning many of the arts and most of the sciences, including biology, botany, zoology, physics, chemistry, and logic. Along with his teacher, Plato, Aristotle is often referred to as the "Father of Western Philosophy."

Aristotle studied under Plato for 20 years, and eventually opened his own academy, called the Lyceum, which attracted students from throughout the Greek world. In addition to science, his curriculum included the study of ethics, history, metaphysics, political theory, rhetoric, and of course, philosophy.

Aristotle wrote hundreds of treatises and other works encompassing virtually all areas of philosophy and science; however, none have survived in finished form. Although all that remains are clipped and abbreviated fragments that appear to be lecture notes, the Roman philosopher Cicero has been quoted as saying, "If Plato's prose was silver, Aristotle's was a flowing river of gold."

COMMON SENSE

"Common sense is the knack of seeing things as they are,
and doing things as they ought to be done."

— Josh Billings (Henry Wheeler Shaw)
American Humorist, Lecturer
4/21/1818 – 10/14/1885

We are introduced to common sense through words; we become friends with it through experience.

Do a thing because you have learned that it is right, not because some social convention says that you must. Just because everyone else is doing it doesn't necessarily mean that it is worthy of emulation.

———◇———

Josh Billings was the pen name of humorist Henry Wheeler Shaw, who gained fame as a home-spun writer and lecturer in the years following the Civil War. His folksy demeanor and droll observational humor made him wildly popular, perhaps second only to Mark Twain.

Billings wrote in an informal "down home" style, using slang and crude phonetic spelling to portray himself as a cracker-barrel philosopher, dispensing common-sense wisdom with wit and panache. He is known for *Josh Billings' Farmer's Allminax*, a parody of The Old Farmer's Almanac, but he is probably best remembered for his aphorism "The squeaky wheel gets the grease."

November 4th

JUDGMENT

"Good judgment comes from experience,
and a lot of that comes from bad judgment."

— Will Rogers
American Humorist, Actor
11/4/1879 – 8/15/1935

Sometimes it seems we are forced to pay a dear price for the difficult lessons we learn, but in hindsight we often see that it was cheap at twice the cost.

———◇———

Of Cherokee descent, William Penn Adair Rogers was a cowboy-turned-humorist from Oklahoma. He was a star of the stage and screen, a widely read newspaper columnist, and a social commentator who became so popular that he was nominated for the governorship of Oklahoma.

Rogers graduated from military school, but his first real job was cowboying in Argentina. He also made appearances in Wild West shows, showing off his skill with horse and lasso. In 1905, while visiting New York City, a wild steer broke out of a pen inside Madison Square Garden and began to scramble into the stands. Undaunted, Rogers grabbed a rope and lassoed the beast, delighting the crowd and getting himself on the front page of the newspapers. Offers came pouring in for vaudeville performances, personal appearances, and movie roles, and Rogers took full advantage of them.

America couldn't get enough of Will Rogers. His quick-witted, off-the-cuff commentaries on everyday life (and politics) led to a regular column for the *Saturday Evening Post*, best-selling books, and one of the top-rated radio programs in America, which was broadcast every Sunday evening.

In 1935, the nation was stunned when Rogers was killed in a plane crash while on his way to survey the wild Alaskan frontier.

November 5th

ORDER

"In my youth I stressed freedom, and in my old age I stress order.
I have made the great discovery that liberty is a product of order."

— Will Durant
American Writer, Historian, Philosopher
11/5/1885 – 11/7/1981

It is interesting to note how our priorities change with the passage of time, and the attainment of experience. What seems most important to us in our youth often changes as we begin to grasp the multitude of connections between our actions and the (often unintended) consequences that are attendant to those actions.

———————————•———————————

William James "Will" Durant was a historian and philosopher who first gained attention with *The Story of Philosophy*, which sold more than two million copies and was translated into several languages. He is probably best known for *The Story of Civilization*, an eleven-volume set of books that chronicle the advance of Western civilization.

As a young man, Durant was drawn to the priesthood, but he developed an interest in socialism and became a teacher and a writer, instead. He began writing a series of pamphlets to educate workers, and *The Story of Civilization* evolved from those early works. Although it was written in collaboration with his wife, Ariel Durant, she was not given formal recognition for her work until the seventh volume, *The Age of Reason Begins*, was published in 1961. Their tenth volume, *Rousseau and Revolution*, won the Pulitzer Prize for General Non-Fiction in 1968.

Husband and wife passed away, within two weeks of one another, in 1981.

November 6th

ENCOURAGEMENT

"When you encourage others, you in the process are encouraged
because you're making a commitment and difference in that person's life.
Encouragement really does make a difference."

— Zig Ziglar
American Motivational Speaker
11/6/1926 – 11/28/2012

To encourage another is to participate in one of those win-win situations:
Whether giving or receiving, you are connecting with another human being,
inspiring or being inspired to be the best possible version of your Self. Being
supportive of others contributes to that process.

Sometimes, all it takes to embolden others to achieve what we know they
can is a little bit of belief and reassurance. Always cheer for others.

———————◇———————

Hilary Hinton "Zig" Ziglar was an author, salesman, personal development guru, and a world-renowned motivational speaker. He has been called
"America's most influential and beloved encourager and believer that everyone
could be, do and have more."

In addition to speaking, Ziglar wrote or co-wrote thirty-three books. His
first, *See You At The Top*, was rejected by publishers nearly forty times before
it was finally published in 1975. It has sold over 1.5 million copies and is still
in print today.

COINCIDENCE

"Rather, trust involves the faith that there is no coincidence in the world and that every occurrence under the sun is by His proclamation."

— Chazon Ish (Avrohom Yeshaya Karelitz)
Belarusian Rabbi
11/7/1878 – 10/24/1953

Do you believe that concurrent, seemingly connected events are coincidental? Or, do you think that everything happens for a reason?

Avraham Yeshaya Karelitz was an Orthodox rabbi who came to be known by the name of his magnum opus, *Chazon Ish*, which means Vision of Man. Born in Belarus, young Karelitz was blessed with a photographic memory and the intellect of a genius. By age thirteen, he was already a qualified Talmud Sage, and during his Bar Mitzvah, he publicly promised to devote his entire life to the study of Torah. He remained true to his word during the rest of his life.

When the Chazon Ish settled in Palestine, in 1933, his modest home quickly became a magnet for thousands who sought his guidance. His reputation for knowledge and saintliness drew people from all walks of life, including David Ben-Gurion, the founder and first Prime Minister of Israel.

Although he held no official position — he was essentially an academic scholar — the Chazon Ish nevertheless became a recognized worldwide authority on all matters relating to Jewish law, religious life, and institutions. He is remembered for his devotion in the worship of God, his pursuit of clarity in Talmud study, and for encouraging loving-kindness in all relationships.

November 8th

GRUDGES

"Life appears to me too short to be spent in nursing animosity,
or registering wrongs."

— Charlotte Brontë
English Novelist, Poet
4/21/1816 – 3/31/1855

I really hope that Miss Brontë took her own advice and didn't keep score of each wound and every injustice she suffered in her short life, because she is right — life goes by too quickly.

None of us are long for this world as it is, and I cannot imagine a less noble, less worthwhile pursuit than holding a grudge or wallowing in self-pity. Okay, so it happened. Move on, and get busy with living!

———◇———

Charlotte Brontë was a novelist and poet, the eldest of the three Brontë sisters whose novels became classics of English literature. Brontë is best known for *Jane Eyre*, her gothic tale of a governess who falls in love with her employer, Mr. Rochester, who is hiding a mysterious secret from her. She also wrote two other novels, *Shirley* and *Villette*, and contributed to a book of poetry with her sisters, Emily and Anne.

The Brontë family was cursed by a spate of premature deaths. When she was five, Charlotte's mother, Maria, died of cancer, and her two older sisters died during a typhoid epidemic a few years later. Her younger sisters, Emily and Anne, would also precede her in death, aged thirty and twenty-nine, their deaths attributed to tuberculosis. Her only brother, Branwell, would also die young, his death certificate noting "chronic bronchitis." Charlotte herself died three weeks before her thirty-ninth birthday, of complications due to pregnancy. She had been married just nine months.

HARMONY

"The universe is not required to be in perfect harmony
with human ambition."

— Carl Sagan
American Astrophysicist, Author
11/9/1934 – 12/30/1996

Our plans are small in the grand scheme of things, and we really shouldn't be so surprised when they are not granted the deference we believe they should be. And yet we are.

Carl Edward Sagan was an astronomer, cosmologist, astrophysicist, astrobiologist, author, and creator of the influential PBS series *Cosmos*, which he wrote and hosted. As one of the most well-known scientists of the 1970s and 1980s, Sagan used his popularity to dissect and discuss a variety of topics he was passionate about, such as the feasibility of interstellar flight, the idea that aliens visited the earth thousands of years ago, and the possibility of terraforming Venus into a habitable world. He was also a vocal anti-nuclear activist, and in 1983 he coined the term "nuclear winter" to describe the global cooling that would occur in the wake of an intercontinental war involving the use of nuclear weapons. According to his theory, the resulting firestorms would inject particulate matter into the atmosphere, block out the sun, and kill off most of the life forms on Earth.

Sagan wrote numerous books, including *Cosmic Connection: An Extraterrestrial Perspective*, *Other Worlds*, and *The Dragons of Eden: Speculations on the Evolution of Human Intelligence*, which won the Pulitzer Prize in 1978. His 1985 novel, *Contact*, was made into a film starring Jodie Foster, in 1997.

Sagan received numerous awards and honors throughout his life and career, most notably NASA's Distinguished Public Service Medal (twice) and the National Academy of Sciences' Public Welfare Medal.

November 10th

TRANSCENDENCE

"I more fear what is within me than what comes from without."

— Martin Luther
German Theologian, Professor
11/10/1483 – 2/18/1546

Just as the mind has the power to summon inner peace and tranquility, it also has the power to disrupt and destroy — particularly our own inner peace and tranquility.

———————◇———————

Martin Luther was a professor of theology, a composer, a priest, and a monk. He is best known for nailing ninety-five theses to the door of the Castle Church in Wittenberg, Germany, which initiated one of the greatest crises in Western Christianity. The theses proposed debates on the matter of indulgences, in which the Church would accept money in exchange for absolution of sin, instead of requiring the sacrament of penance. Luther's manifesto sparked a protest among theologians throughout Europe and led to the Protestant Reformation. He is regarded as one of the most influential figures in the history of Christianity.

November 11th

PERFECTION

"Be intent upon the perfection of the present day."

— William Law
English Priest
c. 1686 – 4/9/1761

Don't pine for yesterday, or sit idly waiting for tomorrow. This day, *today*, is the perfect day for doing what needs to be done — and it's right in front of you. Grab hold of it and do something!

———————◇———————

William Law was a Church of England priest who seemingly lost everything when he was twenty-eight years old. A graduate of Cambridge, he was serving as a priest at Emmanuel College when Queen Anne died. Since she had no heir, her German cousin, George I, ascended to the throne. Law refused to swear an oath of allegiance to the new King and was summarily dismissed from his position. Forced to give up his fellowship, and effectively cut off from any official capacity within the Church or in any academic institution, Law had to recalibrate his life's direction.

For many years, Law worked as a tutor, but he began to focus on writing and soon retired to his family home in King's Cliffe. A solitary and celibate man, he honed his writing skills and devoted himself to the subject of renewing Christian values, with an emphasis on morality, holiness, and devotion. His best-known work, *A Serious Call to a Devout and Holy Life*, challenges readers to confront their apathy and charge ahead; to shake off their stupor, and embrace all that life has to offer.

November 12th

UNDERSTANDING

"To understand the things that are at our door is the best preparation
for understanding those that lie beyond."

— Hypatia

Roman Philosopher, Astronomer, Mathematician

c. 355 AD – c. 3/415

There is more similarity and synchronicity in this world than we can possibly imagine, but in order to truly comprehend the reality of others, we must first ensure that we fully understand our own.

Bigotry and animosity are twin poisons of an unexamined life. Knowledge and self-awareness are the antidotes. Never assume that your way is the best way, or worse, the only way; instead, be open to the very real possibility that there are other, equally valid ways of living life.

———◇———

Hypatia of Alexandria was a leading mathematician, astronomer, and scientist. She was also a much-sought-after teacher, a prolific writer, and a Neoplatonic philosopher who was known for engaging random strangers in thoughtful conversation about Plato and Aristotle.

Records tell us that Hypatia was both beautiful and celibate. Considered a leading intellectual, she lived in Alexandria during a period of growing religious conflict that engulfed Christians, Jews, and Pagans. A practicing Pagan, Hypatia did nothing to hide her convictions, which included the belief that everything in the universe can trace its origins to a single deity: a transcendent God who bestowed upon each of us a mind and a soul.

As the religious zealotry grew, so too did the violence, and Hypatia was targeted by the Christian majority. Accused of being an idol worshipper, she was kidnapped, dragged through the streets, tortured, and killed. Her shocking murder turned her into a martyr of the Neoplatonists, who became increasingly opposed to Christianity. During the Middle Ages, however, the Christian faith co-opted her as a symbol of Christian virtue.

TRAVEL

"The world is a book, and those who do not travel read only a page."

— Saint Augustine
Algerian Theologian, Philosopher
11/13/354 – 8/28/430

One's worldview is shaped by a great many things, perhaps none as pervasive as familial traditions, politics, and prejudices. It turns out, however, that *every* encounter we have contributes to how we view the world, and the more we experience of it, the clearer our vision becomes.

———————————◆———————————

Augustine of Hippo was an early Christian theologian and Neoplatonic philosopher. A Roman African whose writings were extremely influential in the development of Western Christianity, Augustine is generally considered the second-most significant Christian thinker, after St. Paul.

Born in Tagaste, near the Mediterranean coast in Africa, Augustine attended primary school in his hometown. He studied at the university in Madauros, and eventually landed in the Roman super-city of Carthage. At age twenty-eight, he left Africa for Milan, where he taught as a professor of rhetoric.

Augustine was in Milan for only two years before he resigned and returned home, where he was recruited to become a junior clergyman in the coastal city of Hippo. In 391 AD, he was ordained a priest.

Augustine became one of the most prolific Latin authors in history, and he was known throughout southern Europe and the Middle East in his own time. His distinctive theological style helped to shape the practice of biblical interpretation and provided a road map for Christian thought and practice. More than one hundred of his works survive, the most important being *Confessions*, *De Doctrina Christiana*, and *The City of God*.

November 14th

FREE WILL

"Life is like a game of cards. The hand you are dealt is determinism;
the way you play it is free will."

— Jawaharlal Nehru
Indian Prime Minister
11/14/1889 – 5/27/1964

In life, as in cards, it isn't the hand that matters; it's the player. Just as good cards don't guarantee a win, bad cards don't mean you are destined to lose.

———————◇———————

Pandit Jawaharlal Nehru was an independence activist and a central figure in Indian politics. The political heir of Mahatma Gandhi, Nehru was a signatory to India's first Constitution and served as India's first Prime Minister. His daughter, Indira Gandhi, and grandson, Rajiv Gandhi, would later also serve as Prime Ministers.

When Nehru took office, he faced many daunting challenges. How does one unite a vast population that contains a multitude of different religions, cultures, and languages? Nehru's approach was to institute a series of five-year plans to address the various economic, social, and educational issues facing the country. The blueprint called for massive industrialization, in order to increase agricultural production; encouraging universities to emphasize research in science and technology; providing free public education and meals for Indian children; granting women the legal right to get a divorce; and prohibiting discrimination based on caste.

Nehru's forward-looking reforms helped to unite and modernize India. His efforts earned him the respect and admiration of millions of Indians, and made him a national hero.

November 15th

ATTITUDE

"Good cheer is no hindrance to a good life."

— Aristippus
Libyan Philosopher
c. 435 BC – c. 356 BC

The Sages teach that the way a person approaches a task will influence how they will perform it. Have you noticed the truth of this statement in your own life?

Not everyone has a cheerful attitude, but there is no reason why *you* shouldn't; it just may be that last missing ingredient needed to ensure your success.

———————◇———————

Aristippus, the founder of the Cyrenaic school of hedonism, was born in Cyrene, Ancient Libya, around 435 BC. It is said that Aristippus came to Greece to attend the Olympic Games, and when he asked Ischomachus about Socrates, his description of the great man filled Aristippus with an ardent desire to meet him. He went to Athens for that very purpose, and ended up becoming one of his students.

Although he was a pupil of Socrates, Aristippus would eventually adopt a very different philosophical outlook, centered around his belief that men should dedicate their lives to the pursuit and enjoyment of pleasure. At the same time, he also taught that they should exercise good judgment and self-control in order to mitigate powerful human desires. His outlook came to be called "ethical hedonism."

Aristippus lived the values he preached, enjoying a luxurious and sensuous lifestyle; he took pride in extracting enjoyment from every quarter, under all circumstances. He financed it all by taking money for his teaching, something no other disciple of Socrates had ever done.

November 16th

THE PRESENT

"I have realized that the past and future are real illusions, that they exist in the present, which is what there is and all there is."

— Alan Watts
British Philosopher, Writer, Speaker
1/6/1915 – 11/16/1973

We look to the past and make plans for the future from the very same vantage point: Today.

Today is where the real living takes place. Be *present*.

Alan Wilson Watts was a philosopher who interpreted and popularized Eastern wisdom for a Western audience. Born in Chislehurst, England, he lived most of his life in the United States.

After receiving a master's degree in theology, Watts briefly served as an Episcopal priest before moving to New York to study Buddhism. In 1951 he moved to San Francisco, where he taught Buddhist studies. By 1956 he was hosting a popular radio program, "Way Beyond the West," which provided national exposure. With the rise of the counterculture movement in the 1960s, Watts — who described himself as a "philo-sophical entertainer" — was seen as a natural ally and was adopted as a spiritual spokesman for the cause.

Watts wrote dozens of books and articles on subjects important to both Eastern and Western religions, including one of the first best-selling books on Buddhism, *The Way of Zen*. He also wrote an autobiography, *In My Own Way*.

Watts continued to write and travel until his passing, on a mountaintop, in 1973.

SCANDAL

"Longevity conquers scandal every time."

— Shelby Foote
American Historian, Writer
11/17/1916 – 6/27/2005

Although we'd like to think that all villains are condemned forever, the general public has a very short memory. The truth is, given enough time, nearly anyone's reputation can be rehabilitated. It's not a particularly flattering reflection on society, but it's a good thing to remember the next time you think you've done something that is unforgivable.

You *will* be given a second chance. It is a certainty. Make the most of it.

———————◆———————

Shelby Dade Foote Jr. was a writer and historian best known for *The Civil War: A Narrative*, his meticulously researched, three-volume history of the American Civil War, as well as his commentary in the 1990 Ken Burns documentary, *The Civil War*. His books earned him his reputation; his participation in the documentary made him a cultural icon.

Foote was born Nov. 7, 1916, in Greenville, Mississippi. He was an avid reader, and he liked to write. As a high schooler, he edited *The Pica*, the student newspaper. At the University of North Carolina, he began contributing pieces to *Carolina Magazine*, UNC's award-winning literary journal. It was also during this time that he began to develop the outlines of his first novel.

Foote joined the National Guard, and in 1944, while serving as a captain in WWII, he was accused of being absent without leave (he was visiting an Irish girl in Belfast). He ended up being court martialed and was dismissed from the service. Undaunted, he joined the Marines — and married the girl.

EXTRAVAGANCE

"A miser grows rich by seeming poor;
an extravagant man grows poor by seeming rich."

— William Shenstone
English Poet, Landscape Artist
11/18/1714 – 2/11/1763

There is nothing wrong with being rich, but if you want to stay that way, don't live that way. Nothing good comes from ostentation; be prudent, instead. Those who live within their means see their means grow exponentially.

———————◇———————

William Shenstone was an eighteenth-century poet and "man of taste" who spurned the trend toward Neoclassical formality in English gardens in favor of greater naturalness and simplicity. He was one of the earliest practitioners of "landscape gardening" (he coined the term), installing paths and sitting areas that took advantage of the many picturesque views he cultivated on his estate, The Leasowes. Shenstone's theories and concepts are outlined in his book, *Unconnected Thoughts on Gardening.*

In 1786, long after Shenstone had died, Thomas Jefferson and John Adams toured the gardens of The Leasowes. Adams wrote of the "variety of beauties" they found there, and Jefferson noted that the sheer amount of work and money that went into the property must have ruined a man of such relatively modest means.

Today, The Leasowes is listed on the English Heritage's Register of Parks and Gardens, and is home to the Halesowen Golf Club. The garden is open to the public, and can be visited for free.

DUTY

"People tend to forget their duties but remember their rights."

— Indira Gandhi
Indian Prime Minister
11/19/1917 – 10/31/1984

No one else is obliged to make improvements to your life; that duty is yours alone. If you want a better life, then work hard, mind your business, and start making better choices. Never allow yourself to get caught up in the belief that the world owes you anything, because it owes you nothing; it never did.

Indira Priyadarshini Gandhi was a politician, stateswoman, and the first and only female Prime Minister of India. Her father, Jawaharlal Nehru, was the first prime minister of India. Her son, Rajiv, would also serve as Prime Minister.

Gandhi's leadership style could be described as authoritarian and, at times, intransigent. Once she made up her mind, there was no going back, and those who disagreed with her would often find themselves ostracized, if not imprisoned.

In 1984, amid growing pressure from Sikh separatists in Punjab, she ignited a confrontation by sending the army to their sacred Golden Temple in Amritsar. A bloody conflict ensued, with several hundred casualties reported. Later that year, on October 31st, Gandhi was assassinated by two of her bodyguards, who were Sikhs, in retaliation for the attack at the Golden Temple. She was cremated three days later in a Hindu ritual.

DISCRETION

"It is well for one to know more than he says."

— Plautus
Roman Playwright
c. 254 BC – c. 185 BC

There are many good reasons to pause and reflect before you speak, but the very best reason — the most honorable reason — is to save some-one else from embarrassment.

Always choose discretion. There is no justification for bringing shame or humiliation to another human being. Ever.

Titus Maccius Plautus is considered one of ancient Rome's greatest comic playwrights. His plays, many of which are loose adaptations of Greek plays, were noted for their racy and colloquial language, lively action, and farcical humor that often strained credulity in order to maximize comedic effect.

Plautus wrote in Latin, a language over which he had total command. Employing the coarse dialect of the ordinary Roman, Plautus was a master at choosing the perfect words and then marrying them to the action, usually in surprisingly hilarious ways.

APPRECIATION

"Appreciation is a wonderful thing: It makes what is excellent in others belong to us as well."

— Voltaire
French Writer, Philosopher, Historian
11/21/1694 – 5/30/1778

We like to think that the beauty or ability of our friends is a reflection of our own aesthetic — which is why we tend to befriend those in whom we see some measure of ourselves. Thankfully, we are also blessed with the ability to appreciate those magnificent souls who possess gifts that are very different from our own.

François-Marie Arouet, known by his nom de plume, Voltaire, was a writer, philosopher, and historian who lived during the French Enlightenment. A relentless critic of the religious and social mores of his time, Voltaire was as famous for his cutting wit as he was for his outspoken advocacy of civil liberties. In a time and place where suppression and censorship were rigorously enforced — Voltaire would spend nearly a year in the Bastille prison for implying that the French regent had an incestuous relationship with his daughter — he nonetheless led a lifelong crusade against tyranny, cruelty, and hypocrisy.

Voltaire was a prodigious writer who embraced a wide range of interests, from science and history to politics and philosophy. He is credited with over two thousand books and pamphlets, including fifty plays, dozens of technical dissertations, and numerous history books. He also maintained various correspondences with friends and contemporaries that ran to some twenty thousand letters. Voltaire's best-known works are probably his satirical novella *Candide*, and his *Lettres Philosophiques*.

SELF-IMPROVEMENT

"It is never too late to be what you might have been."

— George Eliot
English Novelist, Poet
11/22/1819 – 12/22/1880

We all should strive to do something — even the tiniest little thing — every single day, in order to help make ourselves a better version of the person we were yesterday.

Merely being conscious of a goal puts us one step closer to attaining it. Who or what do you want to be? What steps are you taking to make it happen?

George Eliot was the pen name of Mary Ann Evans, a novelist and poet who is considered to be one of the leading writers of the Victorian era. Her nom de plume paid homage to her long-time lover, the (married) philosopher and critic, George Lewes.

Eliot is best remembered as a novelist, and for writing classic books like *Middlemarch* and *Silas Marner*. A 2015 BBC poll of book critics from around the world cited *Middlemarch* as the greatest British novel of all time. She also wrote a collection of short stories, *Scenes of Clerical Life*, and published two volumes of poetry. In her best-known poem, "O May I Join the Choir Invisible," Eliot argues that the dead live on through their generous deeds, which gives them lasting permanence, and immortality.

November 23rd

REMORSE

"There is no refuge from memory and remorse in this world.
The spirits of our foolish deeds haunt us, with or without remorse."

— Gilbert Parker
Canadian Novelist, Politician
11/23/1862 – 9/6/1932

We do ourselves a great disservice when we are determined to discount or disregard all of the good we have done in our lives, and focus instead only on the very worst that we have said or done.

Regret and remorse do have their place, however: while they remind us of the terrible things we are capable of, they also help us to learn from our mistakes so we do not repeat them. This is the treasure among the ruins.

———————◇———————

Sir Horatio Gilbert George Parker was a Canadian novelist and British politician. Born in Addington, Ontario, he moved to England in 1889. Settling in London, Parker quickly gained fame with historical novels that both dramatized and romanticized French-Canadian life. He would later do the same for England and the British Empire. A noted poet and short story writer as well, he was knighted Sir Gilbert Parker in 1902, by King Edward, for his service to Canadian literature.

A strong supporter of the crown, Parker was elected to Parliament in 1900 as a Conservative member for Gravesend, in northwest Kent. He would serve a total of eighteen years in the House of Commons, winning reelection in 1906 and 1910.

Parker died of a heart attack, in London, in 1932. He was buried in his beloved Ontario.

November 24th

THE PAST

"If you want the present to be different from the past, study the past."

— Baruch Spinoza
Dutch Philosopher
11/24/1632 – 2/21/1677

Too often, it seems that we are destined to do the same dumb things over and over. It isn't as if we have no records of the past, no examples to look to, no eyewitness accounts or first-hand experiences to learn from, because we do: we have all of these things. So why do we stubbornly cling to the same bad habits and the same foolish ideas?

———————◆———————

Baruch Spinoza was a leading philosophical figure of the Dutch Golden Age. Along with René Descartes, he is considered a seminal figure of the Enlightenment. His masterwork, the five-volume treatise *Ethics*, was published posthumously, the year he died.

Born to Jewish parents, Spinoza's worldview evolved into that of a moral relativist. Although he believed in one God, he also believed that God and Nature were two sides of the same coin; essentially two names that represent the same underlying reality. For publicly stating this concept of God, and for straying from Jewish orthodoxy, he was excommunicated.

As a Rationalist, Spinoza understood the importance of intellect and reason in our attempts to govern our passionate natures, but at the same time, he also recognized that desire, too, plays a significant role in our decision-making process. It is, in fact, this ongoing and eternal battle between intellect and emotion that fuels the conflict between doing what is right — what we know is right, what has been proven to be right — and simply doing what we want to do.

COMPROMISE

"I shall argue that strong men, conversely, know when to compromise and that all principles can be compromised to serve a greater principle."

— Andrew Carnegie
American Industrialist, Philanthropist
11/25/1835 – 8/11/1919

One of the surest indications of an intelligent mind is the ability to compromise as additional information becomes available. Devotion to truth must always supersede dedication to Principle.

———————◇———————

Andrew Carnegie was an industrialist who led the expansion of the American steel industry in the late nineteenth century. Rising from humble beginnings, he became one of the richest Americans in history, and a leading philanthropist in the United States and the British Empire.

Carnegie learned the value of investing as a young man, while working for the railroad, and by the time he was in his early thirties he had made his first fortune. He entered the steel business in the 1870s, and soon revolutionized the industry by consolidating the various resources needed to make the manufacturing process more efficient. By owning the raw materials and the various transportation systems needed to deliver them to the plants he built around the country, he was able to achieve economies of scale and attain dominance within the industry.

In 1901, Carnegie sold the Carnegie Steel Company to banker John Pierpont Morgan for $480 million, and then then devoted himself to philanthropy. He would eventually give away more than $350 million to various causes and institutions, most notably for the construction of over 2,500 libraries around the world.

November 26th

SELF-RELIANCE

"You cannot help people permanently by doing for them,
what they could and should do for themselves."

— Abraham Lincoln
American President
2/12/1809 – 4/15/1865

What do we teach when we deny others the opportunity to do things for themselves? That they are powerless? That they have no purpose? Or that one person's sense of charity is more important than another person's sense of pride?

Abraham Lincoln was a lawyer and statesman, and the sixteenth president of the United States. He led the nation through the Civil War, but was shot and killed by a Confederate sympathizer on April 14th, 1865, five days after the war had ended.

Born in a one-room log cabin, Lincoln's formal education was restricted by the need for him to work in order to help support his family. He was determined to learn, however, and read everything he could get his hands on, usually by candlelight, at night, when he should have been sleeping.

Lincoln eventually settled in New Salem, Illinois, where he worked as a shopkeeper and a postmaster. He ran for office and was elected to the state legislature in 1834. After moving to Springfield, the new state capitol, Lincoln passed the state bar examination, and by 1836 he was earning a living as an attorney. He quickly gained a reputation as "Honest Abe."

Lincoln entered national politics during the debate over the practice of slavery. He strongly denounced it, declaring slavery a violation of the most basic tenets of the Declaration of Independence, in particular that "all men are created equal." In 1863, Lincoln would harken back to these sentiments in his most famous speech, the Gettysburg Address, which has become one of the most widely quoted speeches in history.

LONELINESS

"Man's loneliness is but his fear of life."

— Eugene O'Neill
American Playwright, Nobel Laureate
10/16/1888 – 11/27/1953

Perhaps the underlying cause of loneliness is that too many of us spend far too much time inside our own heads — and not enough time outside our so-called "comfort zones" — to make real and lasting connections with others. Have you ever considered that the same person who defines these "zones" is also the same person who decides what constitutes "comfort"?

Loneliness is often a prison we build around ourselves. The good news is, you have the key.

Eugene Gladstone O'Neill was a playwright, and is widely considered America's foremost dramatist, often mentioned in the same breath as William Shakespeare and George Bernard Shaw. He wrote dozens of plays. His best-known works include *The Iceman Cometh*, *Long Day's Journey into Night*, and its sequel, *A Moon for the Misbegotten*. A four-time Pulitzer Prize winner, O'Neill is the only American playwright ever to receive the Nobel Prize for Literature.

November 28th

WRATH

"I was angry with my friend: I told my wrath, my wrath did end.
I was angry with my foe: I told it not, my wrath did grow."

— William Blake
English Poet, Painter
11/28/1757 – 8/12/1827

Left unchecked, a minor irritation or petty resentment can begin to simmer. Speak up! Let some of that steam escape before it boils over and makes a mess of everything.

William Blake was an English poet, painter, and printmaker. He developed a relief-printing process that was reminiscent of the illuminated manuscripts of yore, eked out a meager living as an engraver, and is known for providing illustrations for several famous books, including *Paradise Lost*, *The Book of Job*, *The Pilgrim's Progress*, and *The Divine Comedy*.

Of his own work, Blake is probably best remembered for his illustrated collection of poetry, *Songs of Innocence and of Experience*, and for his epic poem, *Milton*, in which he undertakes a mystical journey with *Paradise Lost* author John Milton, who has returned from Heaven. Otherwise, his writing often expressed a disdain for the monarchy, and for the political, social, and theological tyranny prevalent in eighteenth-century England.

Blake was a nonconformist who associated with some of the leading militant thinkers of his day, such as Thomas Paine, Mary Wollstonecraft, and Joseph Priestly. Although largely neglected (if not ignored) during his lifetime, Blake is now considered one of the leading lights of English poetry and a lasting figure of the Romantic Age. In a 2002 BBC poll ranking the 100 Greatest Britons, Blake came in at number 38.

November 29th

INSPIRATION

"Inspiration usually comes during work, rather than before it."

— Madeleine L'Engle
American Writer
11/29/1918 – 9/6/2007

Inspiration is one-half insight and one-half motivation. Maybe you know a little (or a lot) about what you want to do, and maybe you have some idea how to go about it, but you keep finding ways to tell yourself it can't be done. Why not? Have you tried? Have you tried a different way?

Here's the thing: Inspiration is often found in the details. Don't sit around waiting for it; meet it halfway. Get started, dig in, and it will come.

Madeleine L'Engle Camp was a writer of fiction, non-fiction, and poetry. She wrote more than sixty books, across multiple genres, often infusing her work with science, religion, or both. She is best known as the Newbery Award-winning author of *A Wrinkle in Time*, and its four sequels.

L'Engle finished writing *A Wrinkle in Time* in 1960, but it was rejected dozens of times before it was finally published, in 1962. Booksellers didn't know how to classify it, or market it, and there was also the matter of the spirituality it exuded. As it turned out, none of that mattered. *A Wrinkle in Time* was a hit: it went on to sell over sixteen million copies and was translated into more than thirty languages.

L'Engle become one of America's most beloved authors. In addition to the Newbery Medal, she won a National Book Award, was awarded seventeen honorary doctorates, and was honored with the National Humanities Medal in 2004.

November 30th

PERSEVERANCE

"Success is not final, failure is not fatal.
It is the courage to continue that counts."

— Winston Churchill
British Prime Minister, Writer
11/30/1874 – 1/24/1965

There is something disheartening about watching someone give up, or give in, because we all struggle, and we all fight, and while we don't always win our battles, we take pride in fighting them; we take pride in trying like hell. And we take pride in seeing others try like hell, as well.

There are fighters, and there are quitters. Be a fighter, to your very last breath.

———————◇———————

Sir Winston Leonard Spencer-Churchill was an army officer, a writer, and a politician who is widely regarded as the greatest statesman of the twentieth century. As Prime Minister of the United Kingdom (1940-1945), he led Britain to victory in the Second World War. A masterful orator, his patriotic speeches ("We shall fight on the Beaches," "Blood, toil, tears, and sweat," "This was their finest hour") helped to maintain the morale of British soldiers and civilians alike.

When the Nazis took power in Germany, Churchill began sounding the alarm about the growing threat of German nationalism. He was largely ignored, until Germany invaded Poland and the fire of World War II was lit. Churchill was named Prime Minister in 1940. He readied the country for war, rallied his country to victory — and was ousted by British voters in 1945, just months after Germany's surrender.

In 1953, Churchill won the Nobel Prize for Literature, for his six-volume memoirs of World War II. He was serving his second stint as Prime Minister at the time (1951-1955).

December 1st

FAME

"Worldly fame is but a breath of wind that blows now this way,
and now that, and changes name as it changes direction."

— Dante Alighieri
Italian Poet
c. 1265 – c. 9/1321

In today's over-connected world, fame is often bestowed upon the most minor of talents, and it goes just as quickly as it comes. What does this tell us about the value of celebrity?

It is the doing, the *achieving*, that really matters. Let that be your lasting legacy.

———————◇———————

Durante di Alighiero degli Alighieri, commonly known as Dante Alighieri, or simply as Dante, is considered the greatest Italian poet of all time. He is famous for his epic poem, *The Divine Comedy*, which follows a man as he journeys to Hell, Purgatory, and Heaven. Written in the Italian vernacular, instead of the traditional Latin, *The Divine Comedy* would highlight Italian culture and lead to Italian becoming the dominant literary language in Western Europe for the next three hundred years.

The protagonist of Alighieri's poem is generally thought to be Alighieri himself, and the tale an allegory about his own experience of exile from his hometown, the city-state of Florence. In 1302, while serving as a city judge, or *priore*, Alighieri was banished as a result of his political activities — he had deported numerous rivals from the city, and now he was to be exiled, under the threat of death. As he and his family wandered from town to town, seeking protection, he began to work on his masterpiece, *The Divine Comedy*. Dante would never return to Florence.

EXISTENCE

"To be and to have meaning are the same."

— Parmenides

Greek Philosopher

c. 501 BC – c. 470 BC

No one is put on this earth without purpose or meaning. A few of us may have a sense of our purpose, and many of us will spend a lifetime trying to figure it out, but know this: We may not always have understanding, but we will always have meaning, and always have purpose.

We are here for a reason.

————◇————

Parmenides of Elea was a pre-Socratic Greek philosopher. He is considered the Father of Metaphysics, or ontology, which is essentially the study of existence and reality. The Eleatic School of philosophy taught a strict Monistic view of reality, in which everything is comprised of a single, unchanging, indestructible substance, and that existence itself is timeless.

Parmenides insisted that many things in life are quite different than how we believe them to be, and that our senses can never be trusted to reveal the truth. He taught that there is a way of fact (or truth), and a way of opinion. His rejection of relativism (subjective opinion) would have a profound effect on Plato, Aristotle, and the whole of Western Philosophy.

December 3rd

POTENTIAL

"To be what we are, and to become what we are capable of becoming, is the only end in life."

— Robert Louis Stevenson
Scottish Novelist, Poet, Musician
11/13/1850 – 12/3/1894

In some way, in some manner, each one of us possesses the potential for greatness. For some, greatness is found only when we have reached our full potential; for most, our greatness exists in our striving for greatness.

We can't all be Da Vinci, or Catherine the Great, or Albert Einstein, but we can all be the best version of the person we are. Ponder your potential.

———————◇———————

Robert Louis Stevenson was an essayist, poet, and author of travel books and novels, most notably *Treasure Island, Strange Case of Dr. Jekyll and Mr. Hyde,* and *Kidnapped.* It was the publication of *Treasure Island* that initially launched his celebrity, and when *Jekyll and Hyde* and *Kidnapped* were both released in 1886, his reputation as a literary force was cemented.

Stevenson traveled frequently, usually for health reasons. He endured chronic respiratory problems for much of his life, and it is assumed that he suffered from tuberculosis. His travels undoubtedly fed many of his literary adventures.

In 1890, Stevenson purchased four hundred acres in Upolu, an island in Samoa. The climate suited him, and he found his new home to be very conducive to writing. He became something of a luminary among the locals, who consulted him for advice at his estate in the village of Vailima. When he died suddenly, of a cerebral hemorrhage, the Samoans carried his body to the top of Mount Vaea, where he was buried, overlooking the sea.

HEALTH

"He who has health, has hope; and he who has hope has everything."

— Thomas Carlyle
Scottish Philosopher, Historian, Essayist
12/4/1795 – 2/5/1881

As long as you are alive, you can make a difference — in someone else's life, if not your own. Anything is possible. Take care of yourself; if not for you, for those who love you.

Thomas Carlyle was a man of many interests; he was a writer, historian, teacher, translator, mathematician, philosopher, and an essayist who is regarded as one of the most important social commentators of his time. He is best known for *The French Revolution: A History*, which was the inspiration behind Charles Dickens' 1859 novel, *A Tale of Two Cities*. He is also known for *On Heroes, Hero-Worship, and the Heroic in History*, in which he asserts that history is but a biography of great people and their deeds.

Although he taught mathematics, Carlyle was drawn to the drama of history. While working on his book about the French Revolution, Carlyle asked his learned friend, John Stuart Mill, to critique his manuscript. One night, a servant in the Mill household accidently incinerated the manuscript. When Mill told him what had happened, Carlyle remained eerily calm, and instead of being angry, he simply set about rewriting the manuscript. It took him over a year to finish it, but in the end, *The French Revolution* was a hit, winning not only critical and popular success, but also leading to numerous invitations to lecture.

Owing to his stature, Carlyle was given the opportunity to be interred in Westminster Abbey, but the offer was declined. Per his wishes, he was buried next to his parents, in southern Scotland.

COMPETITION

"I have been up against tough competition all my life.
I wouldn't know how to get along without it."

— Walt Disney
American Animator, Entrepreneur
12/5/1901 – 12/15/1966

Competition and rivalries are good for us: They not only hone our edges and sharpen our skills, they motivate us to innovate, and to do what has never been done before.

———————◇———————

Walter Elias Disney was an animator, entrepreneur, film producer, and voice actor. He was a pioneer of the American animation industry, and the most successful animator of all time.

Disney tried to serve in World War I, but by the time he got to France, the war was over. Back at home, he won a scholarship to the Kansas City Art Institute. He soon found work as a commercial illustrator, but his dream was to do original animation.

In 1928, Disney produced three animated cartoons starring a new character: Mickey Mouse. When the first two didn't sell, he added sound, and *Steamboat Willie* was an instant success. A host of new characters were quickly introduced, including Minnie Mouse, Donald Duck, Goofy, and Pluto.

By 1934, Disney was making full-length animated feature films. His first, *Snow White and the Seven Dwarfs*, was a critical and commercial sensation, and over the next five years, Disney released hit after hit, including *Dumbo*, *Pinocchio*, and *Bambi*.

The public loved Disney, and so did the movie industry: As a film producer, he was nominated for fifty-nine Academy Awards, and he won twenty-two Oscars. Both are records.

SPITE

"Don't take the wrong side of an argument just because your opponent
has taken the right side."

— Baltasar Gracián
Spanish Writer, Philosopher
1/8/1601 – 12/6/1658

It's okay to be a little bit jealous of someone whose abilities you admire;
to relish the chance to compete against them or to argue with them because
it seems like they are always right, and they always win. This is an illusion, of
course, but do you know what makes it seem like things always go their way?
They are practiced in the art of making good decisions; they have learned how
to make good choices.

Acting smart helps to make you smart. Instead of trying to get the best
of someone, try to better yourself by putting aside your ego and trying to
learn from them.

Spite is a hindrance to personal growth, and it never ever helps those
who employ it.

Baltasar Gracián y Morales was a Jesuit philosopher and writer. A proponent of *conceptismo*, or conceptism, Gracian addressed serious ideas and
issues through the use of witticisms. He is best known for *The Hero, The
Compleat Gentleman, Subtlety and the Art of Genius,* and in particular, *The Art
of Worldly Wisdom: A Pocket Oracle,* which contains three hundred maxims; it
is full of commentary designed to educate people in the morals and principles
of worldly life.

December 7th

OPTIMISM

"Optimism is the foundation of courage."

— Nicholas M. Butler

American Philosopher, Diplomat, Educator, Nobel Laureate

4/2/1862 – 12/7/1947

It is no great secret that if you believe a thing can be done, you are much more likely to give 100 percent of your effort toward attaining it. This is because Optimism sees what Pessimism does not: Success.

———————◇———————

Nicholas Murray Butler was an educator, philosopher, and diplomat. At forty-three years, his was the longest tenure as president in the history of Columbia University. Under his leadership, the campus doubled in size and the student body grew from four thousand to thirty-four thousand. He is also remembered for his work on the College Entrance Examination Board, which helped to establish a standardized exam for entrance to the nation's colleges and universities.

Butler also served as president of the Carnegie Endowment for International Peace. He proposed the Kellogg-Briand Pact, an inter-national treaty that renounced war as an acceptable means of implementing national policy. The Pact of Paris, as it became known, was signed on August 27th, 1928. Eventually, there would be sixty-two signatories to the treaty. In recognition of his tireless efforts as an advocate of peace, he was awarded the Nobel Peace Prize in 1931.

Over the course of his life, Butler received thirty-seven honorary degrees and numerous decorations and accolades from around the world. He was considered so influential and well-respected that his annual Christmas greeting to the nation was printed in *The New York Times*.

December 8th

ADVERSITY

"Adversity reveals genius, prosperity conceals it."

— Horace
Roman Poet
12/8/65 BC – 11/27/8 BC

We rarely learn as much from the good times as we do from the bad. The easy life passes by, unremarked and hardly noticed, while adversity and privation forces us to think, to plan, to do, so that we might truly *live*.

I wish for you plenty of hardships. They are the grain that we store for winter, and the bread that we eat in the spring.

Quintus Horatius Flaccus was a leading poet, satirist, and critic during the time of Augustus.

Although he wrote in many different meters, genres, and themes, Horace is best known for his *Odes*, which often express seemingly ordinary thoughts about commonplace events and everyday concerns. His talent, however, lies in how he uses these universal sentiments to pull the individual reader into his inner circle, as if he is sharing his innermost secrets with his dearest of friends.

Along with Virgil, Horace is regarded as one of the most celebrated of the so-called Augustan poets. He continued to influence writers and poets well into the twentieth century, most notably Ben Jonson, Alexander Pope, Alfred Lord Tennyson, W.H. Auden, and Robert Frost.

December 9th

HELL

"The mind is its own place, and in itself can make a Heaven of Hell,
a Hell of Heaven."

— John Milton
English Poet, Polemicist
12/9/1608 – 11/8/1674

Things aren't always going to work out the way you'd like them to. You will have your share of good days, but you will also *most assuredly* have bad days. The trick is: Don't make the bad days worse than they really are by focusing on what didn't go your way; focus instead on how truly fortunate you have been — and will be again.

Counting your blessings is the surest way to keep negativity at bay.

John Milton was a poet and intellectual who is best known for *Paradise Lost*. Written in blank verse, with over ten thousand lines, *Paradise Lost* tells the story of Satan's rebellion and Adam and Eve's disobedience and redemption. It is considered by many to be the greatest epic poem in the English language. Milton also published a sequel, *Paradise Regained*, which is an account of Satan's temptation of Christ.

Milton was a Puritan who believed in the authority of the Bible, but politically he advocated against the Church of England and the tyranny of a monarchy that supported a state-sponsored religion. In Milton's view, one's religion was a personal matter of conscience, and the freedom to worship, or not to worship, was to be tolerated if not respected.

Milton died on November 8th, 1674 and was buried inside St. Giles Cripplegate Church in London. There is a monument dedicated to him in Poet's Corner in Westminster Abbey.

ECSTASY

"Find ecstasy in life; the mere sense of living is joy enough."

— Emily Dickinson
American Poet
12/10/1830 – 5/15/1886

There is so much to take delight in, and so many things to be truly grateful for.

The ordinary experience of being alive, in this moment, for this instant, is actually an extraordinarily precious gift. Never take it for granted.

———————◇———————

Emily Elizabeth Dickinson is widely considered to be one of the leading poets of nineteenth-century America. Born in Amherst, Massachusetts, Dickinson was an exceptional student. She attended the Amherst Academy (now Amherst College) for seven years, and Mount Holyoke Female Seminary (now Mount Holyoke College), but left after one year.

Throughout her life, with the exception of her school years, Dickinson seldom left home and had little face-to-face contact with people outside of her family. She was very close with her brother, Austin, who became an attorney, and her younger sister, Lavinia, who also lived at home for her entire life. Dickinson's siblings would be her primary intellectual confidants, although she also maintained numerous long-term correspondences.

Dickinson loved to read poetry, and she was especially fond of Ralph Waldo Emerson and Elizabeth Barrett Browning. Her own poetry had a certain poignancy — no doubt a reflection of the solitary life she led — and she often wrote of unrequited love.

While Dickinson was a very prolific writer, credited with over 1,800 original works, she went largely unacknowledged during her lifetime. The first volume of her poetry would not be published until 1890, four years after she had died, at home, in Amherst.

TALENT

"Talent is always conscious of its own abundance,
and does not object to sharing."

— Aleksandr Solzhenitsyn
Russian Novelist, Historian
12/11/1918 – 8/3/2008

Few things in life are more rewarding than using our talents and abilities to help others. It isn't merely that we are being charitable, or kind; it isn't that we take pride in feeling competent and capable. No, we help others when we can, because it's what we do. It's what we were born to do.

———————————◇———————————

Aleksandr Isayevich Solzhenitsyn was a novelist, short story writer, historian, mathematician, and a life-long critic of Communism. His best-known works, *The Gulag Archipelago* and *One Day in the Life of Ivan Denisovich*, were based on his experiences as a prisoner in the Soviet Union's forced-labor camp system.

Born near Moscow, Solzhenitsyn wanted to be a writer but he was educated in mathematics. He fought in WWII, but near the end of the war he was arrested for criticizing Soviet dictator Joseph Stalin. He spent the next eight years in prisons and labor camps, and when he was released, he took a job as a math teacher — and began to write.

Solzhenitsyn's books helped to raise global awareness of the brutality of the Gulag system, and the success of his novels made him a celebrity — and a target of Soviet authorities. When he won the Nobel Prize in 1970, Solzhenitsyn refused to go to Stockholm to receive it, fearing that he would not be allowed to return if he left the country. In February of 1974, he was exiled from the Soviet Union; in December, he took possession of his Nobel Prize.

MASTERY

"One can be the master of what one does, but never of what one feels."

— Gustave Flaubert
French Novelist
12/12/1821 – 5/8/1880

We can master a great many things, but our emotions are not among them. In certain times, in certain situations, even the most practiced and stoic among us are doomed to be conquered by sentiment.

———◇———

Gustave Flaubert was a highly influential novelist and is considered the leading proponent of literary realism in French literature. He published ten books but is known primarily for his debut novel, *Madame Bovary*, a tragic tale of lies, misunderstandings, and adultery. A French tribunal brought Flaubert and his publisher to trial, claiming the book promoted immorality, but they were narrowly acquitted.

Flaubert was not as productive as his contemporaries; not from a lack of effort, but because he was a perfectionist who wrote with an exactitude that bordered on obsession. His goal was to instill rhythm and cadence in his prose, invisibly, by carefully choosing words and constructing phrases with as much attention paid to their precise meaning as to the harmony of their syllables. In this way, Flaubert hoped to appeal not only to the reader's intellect but, much like a musical score, also to the subconscious mind.

A cynic and a pessimist, Flaubert claimed that one must be stupid in order to be happy. He died suddenly of a stroke in 1880, and is buried in the family vault, in Rouen, France.

OBJECTIVITY

"You must accept the truth from whatever source it comes."

— Maimonides
Jewish Torah Scholar, Philosopher
c. 1135 – 12/13/1204

There is and always will be an inclination to hear what we want to hear, to see what we want to see, and to believe what we want to believe. It is a part of our nature, after all, to ignore certain unpleasant truths; to abandon fact, logic, and reason when they confront and confound our preferred reality — even when we know it is folly to do so.

———————◇———————

Moses ben Maimon was commonly known as Maimonides and is often referred to by the acronym Rambam. Born in Spain, he spent most of his life in Egypt, where he was a preeminent physician, astronomer, and philosopher.

Maimonides was one of the most prolific and influential Torah scholars of all time. Among his best-known works are his commentaries on the *Mishna*, the first written collection of Jewish law and traditions, also known as the Oral Torah; the *Mishneh Torah*, which systematically codifies all Jewish law and doctrine; and *The Guide for the Perplexed*, a major philosophical work in which he attempts to reconcile Jewish thought under the auspices of science, philosophy, and religion.

Maimonides was the foremost intellectual figure of medieval Judaism, and he is considered a pillar of traditional Jewish faith. His copious work remains a cornerstone of Jewish scholarship and tradition, and his *Thirteen Articles of Faith*, a summary of the teachings of Judaism found in his *Mishna* commentaries, would eventually become an essential part of the orthodox liturgy.

DENIAL

"Denial helps us to pace our feelings of grief. There is a grace in denial.
It is nature's way of letting in only as much as we can handle."

— Elisabeth Kubler-Ross
Swiss-American Psychiatrist, Author
7/8/1926 – 8/24/2004

Denial is a mechanism we use to protect ourselves from psychological harm. It can be helpful, up to a point, but be advised: Use it sparingly, because denial is how small problems become big problems.

Elisabeth Kubler-Ross was a psychiatrist, a pioneer in near-death studies, and the author of over twenty books on death-related subjects, including *To Live Until We Say Goodbye*, *Living with Death and Dying*, and *The Tunnel and the Light*. She is best known for her groundbreaking book, *On Death and Dying*, in which she first presented her "five stages of grief" theory, noting that most terminally ill patients will experience denial, anger, bargaining, depression, and acceptance. Her theory became known as the "Kubler-Ross model."

Kubler-Ross described death as the "greatest mystery in science," and through her teaching, writing, and research, she was able to help revolutionize the approach that medical professionals took in caring for terminally ill patients. In 1995, she suffered a series of strokes, leaving her partially paralyzed and confined to a wheelchair. She found waiting for death to be an unbearable existence, and wished that she could decide her own time of death, declaring in 2002 that she was ready for it. She died in 2004.

THE COSMOS

"To the dumb question, 'Why me?' the Cosmos barely bothers
to return the reply, 'Why not?'"

— Christopher Hitchens
English-American Author, Essayist, Critic
4/13/1949 – 12/15/2011

We are infinitesimally small, critically flawed, and here but for the blink
of an eye. But does that mean that no One is paying any attention to us?

Christopher Eric Hitchens was an author, columnist, essayist, journalist,
orator, social critic, and an often controversial polemicist. He famously got
involved in public debates with those with whom he disagreed, and wrote
numerous books and essays that skewered cultural sacred cows. His dictum,
"What can be asserted without evidence can be dismissed without evidence",
is known as Hitchens' Razor.

Hitchens wrote or edited dozens of books on culture, politics, religion,
and literature, and his quick wit and seemingly endless philosophical knowledge led to over seventy film and television appearances. An avowed atheist, he
believed that organized religions, specifically Christianity, Judaism and Islam,
were responsible for all of the hatred in the world. He even wrote a book called
God Is Not Great: How Religion Poisons Everything.

In 2010, Hitchens discovered he had esophageal cancer, the same illness
that had killed his father. He continued debating and writing articles until
his death in 2011. Before he died, ever true to his character, Hitchens made a
point of issuing a public statement that he was resolute in his belief that God
did not exist, and that he would not become a stereotypical deathbed convert
to any religion.

December 16th

SELFISHNESS

"Selfishness must always be forgiven you know,
because there is no hope of a cure."

— Jane Austen
English Novelist
12/16/1775 – 7/18/1817

Selfishness may be a default position, but it is easy enough to overcome. Right or wrong, fair or not, sometimes it is abundantly clear that someone desperately needs a break. Why not be the one to give it to them?

Jane Austen was a novelist who wrote just six novels, but her ability to capture, critique, and comment on eighteenth-century British society gained an international following and a devoted fan base that have remained loyal to her, and to her timeless classics, for over two hundred years.

Austen was a master at conjuring up a time and place, and circumstances, which resonated in the hearts of the hopelessly romantic. Her two best-known works, and perennial fan favorites, are *Pride and Prejudice* and *Sense and Sensibility*, both of which have been made into numerous films, TV movies, and mini-series.

Due to societal pressures at the time, Austen's books were published anonymously, although it was apparent that they were written by a woman, as her pen name was "A Lady." Her works received good reviews and were very popular. It is said that the prince regent (who would later become King George IV) enjoyed her novels so much that he had them installed in each of the royal residences.

Austen's identity was announced to the world only posthumously, when her brother Henry published the last two of her novels, *Persuasion* and *Northanger Abbey*, in 1818. Her works have been in print, continuously, since then.

POSSIBILITIES

"Optimism doesn't wait on facts. It deals with prospects."

— Norman Cousins
American Journalist, Author, Professor
6/24/1915 – 11/30/1990

When something excites us, *really* excites us, we don't let facts get in the way, and we don't wait for a better opportunity; we bend and shape the possibilities around us, and we take action.

Norman Cousins was a political journalist who became the executive editor of the Saturday Review in 1940, a position he would hold for over thirty years. He is perhaps best known, however, for his work as an author and professor, specifically for his interest in the biochemistry of human emotions — a matter he was intimately familiar with due to personal experience.

In the mid-1960s, Cousins was struck by a connective tissue disease and his doctors told him that he had a 1-in-500 chance of recovering. Ignoring the odds, he began looking at alternative medicine and unconventional approaches, and soon developed his own regimen for addressing his disease. In addition to massive doses of Vitamin C, Cousins made a conscious effort to laugh; he watched funny TV shows and comic films that induced peals of laughter. To his amazement, he quickly discovered that humor and laughter brought intervals of relief from his pain.

Cousins' interest in the connection between attitude and health led to a book, *Anatomy of an Illness as Perceived by the Patient*, which explored the ability of the human mind to heal physical ailments. He would continue to research the role of optimism, positivity, and laughter in the treatment of disease for the rest of his life, convinced that they were crucial components to overcoming illness.

December 18th

PRIVILEGE

"When you arise in the morning think of what a privilege it is
to be alive, to think, to enjoy, to love..."

— Marcus Aurelius
Roman Emperor
4/26/121 – 3/17/180

Every morning we awaken to the gift of a brand new day. How do you receive this gift? Are you grateful, or grumpy? Receptive, or resentful? Are you looking forward to the possibilities, or do you just want to pull the covers over your head?

Get up! Get going! Get ready to take advantage of this day, for it won't always be this way; one of these mornings you won't have the opportunity to appreciate what has been given to you.

———◇———

Caesar Marcus Aurelius Antoninus Augustus was the emperor of Rome from 161 to 180, the last ruler of the Pax Romana, a Golden Age of relative peace and stability for the Roman Empire. He instituted a number of reforms, primarily in Law, in order to mitigate the undue harshness and injustices that plagued the lower classes. He is considered the last of the Five Good Emperors, a Philosopher King who served not for his own aggrandizement but to help his people.

Aurelius embraced Stoicism, a philosophy that emphasizes reason and denies self-pity. He is best known for his *Meditations*, in which he reflects on how to live the best life possible. It has been suggested that he wrote down his day-to-day thoughts in order to steel himself against the daunting responsibilities of being emperor. For remaining true to his principles, no matter what, historians and biographers often refer to Aurelius as, simply, "The Philosopher."

PRAYER

"If the only prayer you ever say in your entire life is thank you,
it will be enough."

— Meister Eckhart
German Philosopher, Theologian
c. 1260 – c. 1328

Just waking up in the morning is reason enough to be thankful, and many different religious, spiritual, and mystical traditions include waking prayers. In the Jewish faith, for example, it is proper to recite the *Modeh Ani* — giving thanks to God for faithfully restoring your soul — before you even get out of bed!

There are undoubtedly far worse ways to start your day than through prayerful contemplation, or a mindful expression of gratitude. Try it. Make thankfulness an everyday occurrence.

———◆———

Eckhart von Hochheim, commonly known as Meister Eckhart, was a medieval Dominican theologian, philosopher, and mystic. He is best known for his treatise on the distinction between Being and Intellect, and for his description of the union between the human soul and God.

Eckhart's deeply metaphysical approach to divinity and the search for God, while original, does bear signs of Greek, Neoplatonic, Arabic, and academic influence. Although it is often difficult to unwind many of his philosophical writings — he created many new and somewhat abstract terms — one does get the distinct sense that Eckhart's overriding goal was to expand ecumenical understanding, in order to help people to develop a deeper spirituality. If we may derive a central theme from his writing, it is that one must desire, above all else, to do some good.

December 20th

HUMOR

"A sense of humor is a major defense against minor troubles."

— Mignon McLaughlin
American Journalist, Author
6/6/1913 – 12/20/1983

They say that life is equal parts comedy and tragedy, but you can change that ratio, substantially, by applying a little perspective: As long as you are alive and kicking, all of your so-called 'troubles' are relatively minor.

Life is a series of hills and valleys. Humor helps us to appreciate the view, no matter where we are.

Mignon McLaughlin was born in Baltimore, Maryland, and grew up in New York City. She attended Smith College in Northampton, Massachusetts, and when she graduated in 1933, she returned to New York and soon found work as a journalist. McLaughlin gained a reputation for her poignant and compelling short stories, which ran in *Redbook*, *Cosmopolitan*, *Vogue*, and other magazines. She would eventually become the Managing Editor of *Glamour* magazine.

In the late '40s, she and her husband, Robert McLaughlin — also an editor, at *Time* magazine — co-wrote a play, *Gayden*, which ran on Broadway.

McLaughlin is best known for her sharp wit and pithy aphorisms. Her clever observations on love, life, marriage, careers, and all of the everyday ups and downs in between, were published in three books: *The Neurotic's Notebook*, *The Second Neurotic's Notebook*, and *The Complete Neurotic's Notebook*.

The McLaughlin's eventually retired to Coral Gables, Florida. Bob died in 1973, and Mignon passed in 1983.

MANNERS

"Circumstances are beyond human control,
but our conduct is in our own power."

— Benjamin Disraeli
British Prime Minister
12/21/1804 – 4/19/1881

Manners are not merely saying "please" and "thank you." Perhaps more important is how we make others feel when they are around us.

Strive to consistently be of good temper, because it is your behavior toward others that will always be remembered.

Benjamin Disraeli, 1st Earl of Beaconsfield, was a statesman and novelist who twice served as Prime Minister of the United Kingdom. He played a central role in the creation of the modern Conservative Party, which he associated with patriotism and the expansion of the British Empire.

Disraeli wrote all his life, publishing fifteen novels, a book of poetry, and numerous works of non-fiction. None were particularly good, however, and so he turned to business, which also turned out poorly. Deep in debt, he decided to run for political office. This, too, would prove a challenge: he lost his first four elections. When he finally did win, in 1837, he was shouted down during his first speech in the House of Commons. Before he relinquished his time, he told his fellow MPs, "I will sit down now, but the time will come when you will hear me."

In spite of his rocky start, Disraeli rose among the ranks: he served as the Chancellor of the Exchequer three times, and as Prime Minister twice. As PM, Disraeli is perhaps best known for purchasing the shares that secured the Suez Canal for British trade, and for pushing through the legislation that named Queen Victoria "Empress of India."

December 22nd

SECRETS

"There are no secrets that time does not reveal."

— Jean Racine
French Playwright
12/22/1639 – 4/21/1699

Would that we could avoid our regretful actions in the first place, and have no need for secrets; but it seems the best we can do is to make a habit of acting with integrity — even when it hurts. After all, secrets may have an expiration date, but your reputation is eternal.

Along with Molière and Corneille, Jean-Baptiste Racine is considered one of the three great playwrights of seventeenth-century France. He primarily wrote tragedies, and is widely regarded as the foremost practitioner of tragedy in French history. Among his best-known works are *Andromaque, Athalie, Bérénice, Britannicus,* and *Phèdre.*

Racine's first two plays were staged by Molière's troupe, at the Palais-Royal Theatre in Paris. However, when Racine seduced Molière's leading actress and convinced her to join a rival troupe at the Hôtel de Bourgogne, his friendship with Molière was irrevocably broken. Nonetheless, Racine achieved one remarkable success after another and became the first French author who could live principally on the income provided by his writing.

Racine withdrew from the stage at the height of his popularity to accept the coveted post of royal historiographer to the court of King Louis XIV. His work chronicling Louis's military campaigns further elevated his status and substantially increased his fortune.

In 1699, while composing his last work, *Short History of Port-Royal,* Racine died of liver cancer. He was buried in Port-Royal, where he had been raised by his grandmother.

December 23rd

SELF-RESPECT

"Self-respect is the fruit of discipline; the sense of dignity grows
with the ability to say no to oneself."

— Abraham Joshua Heschel
Polish-American Rabbi, Philosopher
1/11/1907 – 12/23/1972

A funny thing happens when you make a conscious decision to *not* do a thing simply because you know it to be hurtful, petty, or wrong: that's when you realize that you have respect for the person you are trying to become. This is a very good thing, because you will be living with this person for the rest of your life.

———◇———

Abraham Joshua Heschel was a Polish-born rabbi and one of the leading Jewish theologians and philosophers of the twentieth century. Deported from Nazi Germany in 1938, he settled in New York City, where he took residence as a professor of Jewish ethics and mysticism at the Jewish Theological Seminary of America, a post he held until his death in 1972. A prolific writer, his best-known works are *Man Is Not Alone: A Philosophy of Religion*; *God in Search of Man: A Philosophy of Judaism*; and *Prophetic Inspiration After the Prophets: Maimonides and Others*.

Heschel was captivated more by the mystical and prophetic aspects of Judaism than the strictly critical study of scripture. He also believed that actions were imperative to achieving social change, and that to be silent was to be an accessory to injustice. A man dedicated to his principles, Heschel lived what he preached: he attended several anti-Vietnam War protests in the nation's capital, and marched with the Reverend Dr. Martin Luther King, Jr., in Selma, Alabama.

December 24th

NATURE

"The clearest way into the Universe is through a forest wilderness."

— John Muir
Scottish-American Naturalist, Author
4/21/1838 – 12/24/1914

When you want to contemplate life, God, or the world and your place in it, there is no better place to do it than the great outdoors. Make it a point, every so often, to get away from all the noise and strife; to moon at the moon, pine at the pines, and stare at the stars. Whether it's a national park or a corner of your own back yard, just get out there. You'll be happy you did.

John Muir was a naturalist, author, environmental philosopher, and an early advocate for the preservation of wilderness in the United States of America. He was a founder of the Sierra Club and is widely regarded as the "Father of the National Parks."

Muir first visited Yosemite in 1868, and he took jobs as a ranch hand and as a shepherd, occupations that gave him the opportunity to study the land's flora and fauna. He began to sketch and write about the area's natural beauty, and soon earned a reputation as an authority on Yosemite. His articles on preservation and the proper use of America's natural resources would eventually lead the U.S. Congress to establish Yosemite National Park, in 1890, and would be instrumental in the creation of the Grand Canyon and Sequoia national parks.

Muir served as president of the Sierra Club from its creation in 1892 until his death, on Christmas Eve, in 1914.

CULTURE

"There can be hope only for a society which acts as one big family,
not as many separate ones."

— Anwar Sadat
Egyptian President
12/25/1918 – 10/6/1981

As human beings, we share many of the same values. If peace on earth is our goal, let us focus on where our cultural similarities overlap, instead of where they do not.

———————◇———————

Muhammad Anwar el-Sadat was the third President of Egypt. He had been one of the high-ranking participants in the coup that overthrew King Farouk in the Egyptian Revolution of 1952, and then served in several high-level government positions. In 1970, he succeeded the coup's leader, Gamal Abdel Nasser, as President of Egypt.

Sadat is best known for his efforts to achieve peace in the Middle East, in particular for his unprecedented negotiations with Israel. In spite of strong opposition from most of the Arab world, Sadat and Israeli Prime Minister Menachem Begin reached a preliminary agreement in 1978, for which they received the Nobel Prize for Peace. The following year they signed a peace treaty between their countries — the first of its kind between Israel and any Arab country.

On October 6th, 1981, Sadat was assassinated by Muslim army officers while viewing a military parade commemorating the Yom Kippur War of 1973. In addition to Sadat, eleven others were killed, including the Cuban ambassador, an Omani general, a Chinese engineer, a Coptic Orthodox bishop, and four military liaison officers from the United States.

December 26th

DEVOTION

"True strength lies in submission, which permits one to dedicate his life, through devotion, to something beyond himself."

— Henry Miller
American Writer
12/26/1891 – 6/7/1980

The true measure of our lives is that we commit ourselves to many but devote ourselves to few. Such is the difference between what we plan, and what we do; those whom we respect, and those whom we truly adore.

Consider for a moment who or what you value above yourself, because it is important to love someone or something more than yourself.

———————◇———————

Henry Valentine Miller was an American writer who gained an international audience by disregarding all of the literary rules. His uncensored, first person, semi-autobiographical novels were written in a groundbreaking stream-of-consciousness style that blended the mystical with the profane, the explicit with the avant-garde. He was beloved by friends and fans alike for his quirky take on life, in particular for his willingness to admit to thoughts and feelings that others would tend to conceal out of embarrassment.

Miller is best known for two novels, *Tropic of Cancer* and *Tropic of Capricorn*, both of which were written in Paris during the 1930s. Loaded with candid descriptions of sex, the books were banned in Great Britain and denied publication in the United States for nearly thirty years due to long-standing obscenity laws. In 1964, however, the U.S. Supreme Court rejected state court findings that the books were obscene, declaring them works of literature.

December 27th

APPROVAL

"I much prefer the sharpest criticism of a single intelligent man
to the thoughtless approval of the masses."

— Johannes Kepler
German Mathematician, Astronomer
12/27/1571 – 11/15/1630

There is something very comforting about consensus, and a certain harmony in accord. We like our opinions to be acknowledged, accepted, and even parroted, and whether they are factually correct is often of little consequence. The thing about groupthink, however, is its unreliability. History is replete with catastrophic follies that were based on false assumptions, and foolishness that could have been avoided had someone simply asked, "Is it true?"

Surround yourself with those who know the truth, and aren't afraid to tell you when you are mistaken.

———————◆———————

Johannes Kepler was an astronomer, a mathematician, and an astrologer, and a key figure in the seventeenth-century scientific revolution. Well-versed in Copernican theory and a contemporary of Galileo, it was Kepler's laws of planetary motion which formed the basis for Isaac Newton's theory of universal gravitation. Kepler, a former theology student, did not regard them as "laws," per se, but rather as celestial harmonies; a divine symphony in which each planet's elliptical orbit plays a part.

Kepler is also known for his contributions to the field of optics: he invented an improved version of the refracting telescope, and developed a new (and correct) theory of how vision is processed. He was also a noted astrologist, tasked with making regional weather forecasts, as well as individual horoscopes, for the Holy Roman Emperor Rudolf II.

December 28th

DRAMA

"The drama of life begins with a wail and ends with a sigh."

— Minna Antrim

American Writer

10/13/1861— 1950

We enter this world scared, confused, and annoyed. Unsurprisingly, we often leave it in much the same manner.

It isn't the beginning or the end that matters; it's what we do in between.

Minna Thomas Antrim was a writer. Born in Philadelphia, she was the daughter of William Preston Thomas and Lauretta Robbins. She was educated at St. Mary's Hall in Burlington, New Jersey, and in 1878 she married Mr. W. H. Antrim (an editor) in Philadelphia.

Although she lived to be almost ninety, Antrim's entire writing career took place over the span of six years, while she was in her forties. She published ten books, most notably *Naked Truth and Veiled Allusions*, *The Wisdom of the Foolish & the Folly of the Wise*, *Sweethearts and Beaux*, and *Don'ts for Bachelors and Old Maids*. She was also well known for her collection of toasts.

ALTRUISM

"What we have done for ourselves alone dies with us;
what we have done for others and the world remains and is immortal."

— Albert Pike
American Attorney, Writer
12/29/1809 – 4/2/1891

We earn our labels, and they live on, long after we are gone — in the recollections of our friends, our families, and all of those we either helped or hobbled along the way.

———————————◦———————————

Albert Pike was an author, journalist, lawyer, frontiersman, soldier, and humanitarian, and a prominent member of the Freemasons. A 33rd degree Mason, he was named Grand Commander of North American Freemasonry in 1859, and retained that position until his death in 1891.

Born on December 29, 1809 in Boston, Pike was the oldest of six children. He passed the entrance exams for Harvard, but the costs were prohibitive so he embarked on a program of self-education instead. After a stint as a schoolteacher, he headed west. In Arkansas, he became the first reporter for the state's Supreme Court, and immersed himself in the study of law. He was admitted to the bar in 1837, and was soon specializing in claims on behalf of Native Americans against the federal government.

When the Civil War came, Pike served as a Brigadier-General in the Confederate Army. He was given a command in the Indian Territory, where he trained regiments of Indian cavalry. Later, when some of his Native American troops were accused of scalping soldiers in the field, Pike resigned his commission. He is the only Confederate general with a statue on federal property in Washington, DC.

December 30th

RESOLUTIONS

"Making noble resolutions is not as important as keeping
the resolutions you have made already."

— Seneca

Spanish-Roman Stoic Philosopher, Statesman

c. 4 BC – c. 65 CE

Nothing is easier than saying you are going to do a thing; the difficulty lies in actually doing it. Therefore, think carefully about the promises you make, because when you honor your commitments, you honor yourself.

———◇———

Seneca the Younger, Lucius Annaeus Seneca, known simply as Seneca, was a statesman, orator, dramatist, and Stoic philosopher. In his time, he was Rome's leading intellectual figure and wielded significant influence during the reign of Emperor Nero. Denounced by his enemies as having played a part in a conspiracy to kill Nero, Seneca was ordered to commit suicide, in 65 CE. He did so promptly, with grace and composure.

There is a belief that Seneca knew St. Paul, and it is known that he was studied by St. Jerome and St. Augustine. Dante, Chaucer, and Petrarch were also familiar with his works, which were a part of the wider Latin culture during the Middle Ages. The first complete English translation of Seneca's moral treatises appeared in 1614, edited by the great scholar Erasmus, who is known as the first editor of the New Testament.

Seneca's best written and most compelling work is his *Moral Letters to Lucilius*, a series of 124 essays (letters) which focus on a variety of ethical quandaries. Although the letters are ostensibly addressed to Lucilius, it is clear that Seneca anticipated a much wider audience.

ENDINGS

"A poem begins in delight and ends in wisdom."

— Robert Frost
American Poet
3/16/1874 – 1/29/1963

The first thing we notice about a poem is the words, and while we read them, our (subconscious) mind begins to seek a pattern. There it is! And, as we venture forward, taking in the ever-so-clever manner in which these turns of phrase are constructed, we anticipate: How will the poet reconcile this puzzle, again and again, and again? How? And yet, in the end, we find that not only did everything come together — beautifully, memorably —somehow we also managed to learn something; usually about ourselves.

Robert Lee Frost was perhaps the most widely admired American poet of the twentieth century. Although he was a relatively late bloomer — he did not publish a single book of poetry until he was almost forty, and his first would be published in England before it was published in the U.S. — Frost would become a four-time Pulitzer Prize winner and America's Poet Laureate. He famously recited his poem, "The Gift Outright," at the inauguration of President John F. Kennedy, in 1961.

Frost was renowned for his use of American colloquial speech in his portrayals of ordinary people going about their day-to-day lives. He was initially pigeon-holed as a "Northeastern" poet, for his many depictions of life in rural New England, but people everywhere connected with the universal nature of his themes.

Frost has often been referred to as "America's Poet." His most famous poems include "Stopping by Woods on a Snowy Evening," "The Road Not Taken," "Birches," and "Nothing Gold Can Stay."

AFTERWORD

You've just read the worldly wisdom of some of the brightest people who have ever drawn a breath. What did you think?

I'll tell you what I think. I think if there is one thing to take away from this collection of thoughtful insights, it is this: Strive to do good. Always. That includes in word, in deed, and in attitude (be positive!).

I also think we need to share more of ourselves with our friends and family. By that I mean we need to talk about the spiritual stuff, and the existential stuff; the stuff that we all think about, deep in our psyches, but don't always share with others. I think life is too short to hold anything back. We all have these private inner lives. Why not talk about them? Share your thoughts. You might be surprised to learn that others are thinking many of the same things that you are.

I do have a few suggestions for additional reading. As previously mentioned, there's Seneca's *Letters to Lucilius*. It's a joy to read, and you can find a copy online if you don't want to buy a printed version or an eBook. As for daily readers, I really enjoyed *The Daily Stoic*, by Ryan Holiday and Stephen Hanselman. On the spiritual side, there are good daily bibles out there, like *God Sightings: The One Year Bible*, and I really enjoy reading the Chumash, which isn't formatted in daily reader form, but I read three or four pages a day and that translates to about one year. There's also the weekend (Saturday) edition of *The Wall Street Journal*; specifically, the Review section. It has lots of detailed book reviews, quotes, and eclectic articles.

I would like to acknowledge some of the many different places that I used to find or verify the quotes and biographical information for this book. In no particular order, I'd like to say thank you to azquotes, brainyquote, goodreads, britannica, biography, and history.com; Stanford.edu; IMDB; and the ever-present Wikipedia. There were also countless other one-off places where I found information as well as inspiration, and I tip my hat to those who put in the hard work that helps to enlighten us all. Kudos also to my editor, Dylan Garity, whose proficiency (and patience) made this book possible.

Let me close with a question, my friend, for I am curious: Amongst all of this material, did you happen to notice that this book was formatted so that most of the Thinkers' quotes were placed on the day they were born, or the day that they died? It was part of that "thread" thing I mentioned at the start, and just one more way to help tie things together. I hope it helped.

Thank you for reading *The Daily Dose*. Good luck, and good life.

"Keep me away from the wisdom which does not cry, the philosophy which does not laugh and the greatness which does not bow before children."

— Khalil Gibran

A

Abstinence · 32

Absurdity · 76

Accountability · 98

Achievement · 78

Action · 183

Adams · 49, 273

Addiction · 74

Adler · 40

Admiration · 3

Adventure · 200

Adversity · 345

Advice · 8

Aeschylus · 12

Aesop · 37

Affection · 202

Akenaton · 156

Alcuin · 88

Alighieri · 338

Allende · 217

Allston · 193

Altruism · 366

Ambition · 81

Amiel · 85

Amis · 167

Amundsen · 200

Ancestry · 181

Anderson · 151

Anger · 236

Animosity · 132

Anselm · 94

Antrim · 365

Anxiety · 272

Apologies · 146

Appetite · 104

Appreciation · 328

Approval · 364

Aquinas · 69

Aristippus · 322

Aristophanes · 293

Aristotle · 309

Arrogance · 154

Art · 68

Aspiration · 79

Assumptions · 37

Atticus · 56

Attitude · 322

Auerbach · 122

Austen · 353

Authority · 108

Avicenna · 237

B

Bacon · 24

Baldrige · 42

Balfour · 209

Ballou · 123

Bandura · 177

Barclay · 26

Baudelaire · 102

Beecher · 178

Behavior · 216

Belief · 94

Bellow · 164

Benson · 219

Betrayal · 295

Bias · 197

Bierce · 146

Billings · 310

Blake · 335

Blame · 96

Bonaparte · 230

Boredom · 203

Brande · 14

Brontë · 315

Brzezinski · 149

Buck · 180

Buckley · 201

Buddha · 153

Burr · 260

Burroughs · 96

Buscaglia · 1665

Butler · 344

Byron · 159

C

Caesar · 197

Calvin · 194

Camus · 6

Carlin · 75

Carlyle · 341

Carnegie · 332

Carver · 15

Catherine the Great · 125

Caution · 144

Censorship · 113

Chanakya · 307

Change · 255

Channing · 100

Chaos · 49

Character · 18

Charity · 50

Charlemagne · 95

Chaucer · 301

Chazon Ish · 314

Chesterton · 168

Chief Seattle · 206

Choice · 20

Churchill · 337

Cicero · 5

Circumstance · 176

Clarity · 221

Clark · 90

Clay · 105

Cocteau · 189

Cohorts · 164

Coincidence · 314

Colette · 30

Columbus · 241

Commitment · 149

Common Sense · 310

Communication · 165

Compassion · 190

Competition · 342

Composure · 71

Compromise · 332

Condemnation · 137

Confidence · 291

Confidentially · 6

Conflict · 100

Confucius · 274

Conscience · 280

Consensus · 35

Consent · 224

Consequence · 88

Contemplation · 24

Contempt · 86

Contentment · 143

Coolidge · 188

Cosmos, The · 352

Courage · 29

Courtesy · 105

Cousins · 354

Covetousness · 266

Covey · 300

Cowardice · 109

Crane · 135

Creativity · 251

Criticism · 125

Cruelty · 61

Culture · 362

Curiosity · 121

Cynicism · 75

D

da Vinci · 108

Dalai Lama · 190

Dali · 81

Darwin · 112

de Bono · 142

de Cervantes · 275

de Clapiers · 221

de Gaulle · 198

de Montaigne · 138

de Saint-Exupery · 183

de Sales · 236

de Talleyrand · 140

de Tocqueville · 213

de Valera · 64

de Vries · 233

Death · 231

Debate · 182

Dedication · 38

Deeds · 13

Defiance · 174

Delight · 62

Democritus · 277

Denial · 351

Deprivation · 178

Derrida · 199

Descartes · 93

Desire · 302

Desperation · 220

Destiny · 192

Determination · 57

Devotion · 363

Dewey · 296

Dickens · 104

Dickinson · 347

Dignity · 120

Diogenes · 269

Disappointment · 189

Discipline · 275

Discretion · 327

Disney · 342

Disraeli · 358

Distractions · 241

Divinity · 228

Dodds · 118

Doubt · 19

Douglass · 53

Drama · 365

Dreams · 226

Dumas · 208

Durant · 312

Duty · 326

Dyer · 133

E

Eban · 35

Ebner-Eschenbach · 259

Eckhart · 356

Eco · 7

Ecstasy · 347

Edison · 44

Education · 134

Effort · 247

Ego · 268

Einstein · 76

Eisenhower · 290

Elections · 47

Eliot · 272, 329

Elizabeth II · 114

Ellison · 63

Embarrassment · 172

Emerson · 148

Emotions · 111

Empathy · 45

Encouragement · 313

Endings · 368

Endurance · 26

Enthusiasm · 209

Envy · 238

Epictetus · 72

Epicurus · 265

Equality · 69

Erikson · 169

Eriugena · 73

Esteem · 54

Ethics · 256

Euripides · 145

Evil · 17

Excuses · 80

Existence · 339

Expectation · 91

Experience · 225

Extravagance · 325

Extremism · 52

F

Failure · 150

Fairness · 292

Faith · 227

Fame · 338

Family · 283

Fanaticism · 161

Fate · 9

Fear · 215

Feelings · 273

Fellowship · 219

Fidelity · 147

Flaubert · 349

Foote · 324

Forbidden · 301

Ford · 214

Forgiveness · 279

Forster · 3

Fortitude · 271

Fortune · 145

Foucault · 179

Francis of Assisi · 279

Franklin · 19

Fraternity · 233

Free Will · 321

Freedom · 212

Freud · 129

Friendship · 22

Frost · 368

Frugality · 277

Frustration · 14

Future, The · 141

G

Galileo · 48

Galsworthy · 229

Gandhi, I. · 326

Gandhi, M. · 278

Gawain · 276

Generalizations · 208

Generosity · 11

Gibran · 8

Glory · 140

Goals · 274

God · 73

Goldman · 137

Goldsmith · 97

Goldwater · 52

Goodness · 307

Gossip · 163

Grace · 59

Gracián · 343

Gramsci · 303

Gratification · 218

Gratitude · 168

Greatness · 242

Greed · 265

Grief · 114

Grudges · 315

Guilt · 284

H

Habit · 127

Hamilton · 157

Happiness · 12

Harmony · 316

Havel · 281

Hawking · 10

Hayes · 280

Hazlitt · 103

Healing · 33

Health · 341

Heaven · 299

Hebbel · 80

Hegel · 242

Hell · 346

Helps · 202

Hemans · 271

Hemingway · 205

Heraclitus · 18

Heritage · 64

Heroditus · 235

Heroism · 210

Heschel · 360

Hill · 302

Hippocrates · 33

History · 213

Hitchens · 352

Hobbes · 253

Holland · 284

Holmes, E. · 23

Holmes, Sr. · 244

Homer · 77

Honesty · 138

Honor · 188

Honor Code · 186

Hope · 152, 240

Horace · 345

Horizons · 237

Horton · 211

Howe · 107

Hugo · 59

Hume · 282

Humility · 5

Humor · 357

Huxley · 225

Hypatia · 319

Hypocrisy · 103

I

Idealism · 201

Ignorance · 156

Ikeda · 4

Indecision · 289

Indifference · 107

Indignation · 267

Inequality · 309

Influence · 269

Inge · 305

Inspiration · 336

Instinct · 112

Insult · 129

Integrity · 187

Intellect · 253

Intelligence · 42

Intentions · 133

Intrigue · 122

Introspection · 285

Intuition · 304

Irving · 249

J

Jackson · 246

James · 13

Jealousy · 249

Jean Paul · 83

Jefferson · 106

Jesus · 84

John Paul II · 141

Johnson · 264

Joy · 194

Judgment · 311

Jung · 74

Justice · 258

Justification · 245

K

Kafka · 187

Kant · 115

Keller · 181

Kepler · 364

Kettering · 91

Kierkegaard · 128

Kindness · 264

King, Jr. · 17

Knowledge · 263

Koestler · 251

Krishnamurti · 134

Kubler-Ross · 351

L

la Bruyere · 231

La Fontaine · 192

La Rochefoucauld · 261

Lactantius · 215

Language · 95

Lao Tzu · 150

Laughter · 152

Law · 199

Law, W. · 318

Lawrence · 257

le Carré · 295

Leadership · 300

Learning · 48

Lec · 58

Legacy · 230

Leibniz · 124

L'Engle · 336

Letting Go · 65

Lewis · 29

Liability · 288

Liberty · 179

Lies · 281

Life · 128

Lincoln · 333

Livy · 220

Locke · 67

Lodge · 184

Loneliness · 334

Longevity · 58

Longfellow · 60

Longinus · 247

Lovasik · 163

Love · 166

Lowy · 298

Luck · 90

Luther · 317

M

MacArthur · 174

MacDonald · 62

Machiavelli · 126

MacLeish · 113

Macmillan · 43

Madame de Stael · 252

Maimonides · 350

Malice · 232

Mann, H. · 127

Mann, T. · 160

Manners · 358

Marcus Aurelius · 355

Marley · 248

Mastery · 349

Maturity · 259

Maugham · 88

Maurois · 285

McCourt · 203

McLaughlin · 357

McLuhan · 216

Meir · 78

Memory · 306

Menander · 51

Mencius · 136

Mencken · 258

Mentality · 36

Metaphysics · 153

Michelangelo · 68

Mill · 143

Miller · 363

Milton · 346

Mind, The · 193

Mindfulness · 110

Misery · 16

Moderation · 162

Modesty · 97

Moliere · 50

Mood · 180

Morality · 282

Motivation · 89

Muir · 361

N

Nathan · 47

Nature · 361

Nehru · 321

Niebuhr · 175

Nietzsche · 22

Nimitz · 57

Nobility · 21

Normalcy · 40

O

Objectivity · 350

Obligations · 196

Obstacles · 214

O'Neill · 334

Opinions · 67

Opportunity · 99

Optimism · 344

Order · 312

Origen · 20

Ovid · 82

P

Pain · 286

Paine · 162

Palmer · 147

Parker, G. · 330

Parker, T. · 239

Parmenides · 339

Pascal · 173

Passion · 70

Past, The · 331

Patience · 246

Patriotism · 198

Pauling · 121

Paulos · 101

Perception · 142

Perfection · 318

Pericles · 117

Perseverance · 337

Perspective · 92

Pessimism · 303

Petrarch · 204

Phelps · 66

Philosophy · 41

Pike · 366

Pinter · 306

Pity · 229

Planning · 290

Plato · 139

Plautus · 327

Pleasure · 260

Pliny the Elder · 240

Plutarch · 9

Poetry · 7

Politics · 126

Pope · 144

Popper · 263

Possibilities · 354

Potential · 340

Poverty · 117

Power · 139

Prayer · 356

Predestination · 10

Prejudice · 195

Preparation · 278

Present, The · 323

Pride · 261

Priestley · 86

Principles · 155

Privacy · 217

Privilege · 355

Procrastination · 102

Productivity · 298

Prosperity · 276

Proverb, Arabian · 154

Proverb, Danish · 32

Proverb, French · 245

Proverb, Zen · 65

Prudence · 222

Public Opinion · 308

Punctuality · 119

Purpose · 34

Pythagoras · 294

Q

Quintilian · 87

Quitting · 235

R

Racine · 359

Rand · 99

Reaction · 72

Reading · 93

Reality · 51

Reason · 207

Rebellion · 53

Reddy · 34

Reflection · 39

Regret · 257

Relationships · 248

Religion · 115

Remorse · 330

Reputation · 55

Resilience · 177

Resistance · 148

Resolutions · 367

Respect · 85

Responsibility · 287

Revelation · 83

Revenge · 211

Reverence · 4

Reward · 124

Rice · 308

Ridicule · 106

Righteousness · 46

Rights · 191

Rilke · 224

Riqueti · 71

Robespierre · 212

Rogers · 311

Roosevelt, E. · 287

Rousseau · 182

Rules · 244

Russell · 111

S

Saadi · 11

Sacks · 70

Sacrifice · 239

Sadat · 362

Sadness · 151

Sagan, C. · 316

Sagan, F. · 250

Sages, The · 46

Saint Augustine · 320

Saint Ignatius · 299

Salk · 304

Sallust · 238

Sand · 185

Santayana · 161

Saraswati · 45

Sartre · 288

Scandal · 324

Schadenfreude · 250

Schopenhauer · 158

Schweitzer · 16

Scorn · 116

Secrets · 359

Security · 118

Self · 169

Self-Assurance · 157

Self-Control · 186

Self-Improvement · 329

Selfishness · 353

Self-Reliance · 333

Self-Respect · 360

Self-Restraint · 27

Selye · 28

Seneca · 367

Serenity · 175

Sex · 167

Shakespeare · 119

Shame · 173

Shaw · 210

Shenstone · 325

Simmons · 232

Simms · 110

Sin · 84

Sincerity · 136

Skepticism · 296

Sloth · 87

Smith · 170

Socrates · 266

Solitude · 25

Solomon · 61

Solon · 21

Solzhenitsyn · 348

Sophocles · 207

Sorrow · 60

Soul · 294

Spinoza · 331

Spirituality · 23

Spite · 343

Stanhope · 268

Stein, B. · 227

Stein, G. · 36

Stendhal · 25

Stevenson, A. · 38

Stevenson, R.L. · 340

Stewart · 256

Strength · 56

Stress · 28

Struggle · 159

Stubbornness · 158

Study · 160

Success · 44

Suffering · 131

Superiority · 205

Superstition · 223

Suspicion · 204

Suzman · 172

Swift · 54

Szasz · 254

T

Tacitus · 171

Tagore · 130

Talent · 348

Talib · 79

Taylor · 228

Teaching · 243

Temperance · 31

Temptation · 30

Tertullian · 286

Thatcher · 289

Thich Nhat Hanh · 297

Thinking · 254

Thoreau · 196

Thucydides · 41

Time · 130

Timing · 82

Tolstoy · 255

Tradition · 43

Tragedy · 270

Transcendence · 317

Travel · 320

Trepidation · 297

Truffaut · 39

Truman · 131

Trust · 135

Truth · 234

Tutu · 283

Twain · 262

U

Uncertainty · 101

Understanding · 319

Unity · 206

Ustinov · 109

V

Values · 63

Vanity · 185

Virgil · 291

Virtue · 170

Vision · 15

Voltaire · 328

von Clausewitz · 155

von Goethe · 243

von Humboldt · 176

W

Walpole · 270

Ward · 92

Washington, B.T. · 98

Washington, G. · 55

Watts · 323

Waugh · 218

Wealth · 171

Welfare · 184

Wells · 267

Whichcote · 223

White · 195

Wilde · 292

Will · 191

Willard · 31

Willpower · 77

Wisdom - 293

Wit - 252

Wittgenstein · 222

Wollstonecraft · 120

Wonder · 66

Woolf · 27

Wordsworth · 116

Work · 262

Worry · 305

Wrath · 335

Wright · 234

X

Xun Kuang · 132

Z

Zeal · 123

Zeno of Citium · 165

Zhuangzi · 226

Ziglar · 313